Sex Cultures

Cultural Sociology series

Wayne H. Brekhus, *Culture and Cognition: Patterns in the Social Construction of Reality*
Amin Ghaziani, *Sex Cultures*
James M. Jasper, *Protest: A Cultural Introduction to Social Movements*
Paul McLean, *Culture in Networks*
Frederick F. Wherry, *The Culture of Markets*

Sex Cultures

Amin Ghaziani

polity

Copyright © Amin Ghaziani 2017

The right of Amin Ghaziani to be identified as Author of this Work has been asserted in accordance with the UK Copyright, Designs and Patents Act 1988.

First published in 2017 by Polity Press

Polity Press
65 Bridge Street
Cambridge CB2 1UR, UK

Polity Press
350 Main Street
Malden, MA 02148, USA

All rights reserved. Except for the quotation of short passages for the purpose of criticism and review, no part of this publication may be reproduced, stored in a retrieval system or transmitted, in any form or by any means, electronic, mechanical, photocopying, recording or otherwise, without the prior permission of the publisher.

ISBN-13: 978-0-7456-7039-3
ISBN-13: 978-0-7456-7040-9 (pb)

A catalogue record for this book is available from the British Library.

Library of Congress Cataloging-in-Publication Data
Names: Ghaziani, Amin, author.
Title: Sex cultures / Amin Ghaziani.
Description: Cambridge, UK ; Malden, MA : Polity Press, [2017] | Includes bibliographical references and index.
Identifiers: LCCN 2016038603 (print) | LCCN 2017004430 (ebook) | ISBN 9780745670393 (hardback) | ISBN 9780745670409 (pbk.) | ISBN 9781509518579 (Mobi) | ISBN 9781509518586 (Epub)
Subjects: LCSH: Sex.
Classification: LCC HQ21 .G465 2017 (print) | LCC HQ21 (ebook) | DDC 306.7--dc23
LC record available at https://lccn.loc.gov/2016038603

Typeset in 11 on 13 pt Sabon by Servis Filmsetting Ltd, Stockport, Cheshire
Printed and bound in the United Kingdom by Clays Ltd, St Ives PLC

The publisher has used its best endeavours to ensure that the URLs for external websites referred to in this book are correct and active at the time of going to press. However, the publisher has no responsibility for the websites and can make no guarantee that a site will remain live or that the content is or will remain appropriate.

Every effort has been made to trace all copyright holders, but if any have been inadvertently overlooked the publisher will be pleased to include any necessary credits in any subsequent reprint or edition.

For further information on Polity, visit our website: politybooks.com

Chapter 1 draws on material previously published in: Ghaziani, Amin (2015) "The Queer Metropolis," pp. 305–330 in *Handbook of the Sociology of Sexualities*, ed. J. DeLamater and R. F. Plante. New York: Springer. Reprinted with permission.
Chapter 2 draws on material previously published in: Ghaziani, Amin, Verta Taylor, and Amy Stone (2016) "Cycles of Sameness and Difference in LGBT Social Movements," *Annual Review of Sociology* 42: 165–83. Reprinted with permission from the *Annual Review of Sociology*, Volume 42 © 2016 by Annual Reviews, http://www.annualreviews.org.

Contents

Introduction: Feeling Flustered?   1

1   The City   22
2   Politics and Protest   57
3   Heterosexualities   86
4   Studying Sexuality   128

Conclusion: Culture Wars?   171

Notes   *187*
References   *195*
Index   *209*

Introduction:
Feeling Flustered?

Case Study: Toemaggedon

In April 2011, the global retailer J. Crew published a photo spread in its catalogue that showed the company's president and creative director, Jenna Lyons, laughing with her five-year-old son Beckett, holding his tiny feet in her hand. The caption reads: "Lucky for me, I ended up with a boy whose favorite color is pink. Toenail painting is way more fun in neon" (see figure i.1). The ad incited public fury about the meaning of gender and sexuality. The *Los Angeles Times* reported, "To some the photo depicts a sweet moment between a stylish mom and her equally stylish son. To others, however, it reads as a questionable endorsement of parental support of transgendered or gender-neutral children."

The journalist interviewed experts who represented competing points of view. Speaking for one side, the psychiatrist Keith Ablow observed, "This is a dramatic example of the way that our culture is being encouraged to abandon all trappings of gender identity – homogenizing males and females when the outcome of such 'psychological sterilization' . . . is not known." In a separate interview with Fox News, Dr Ablow insisted that the ad "crossed a line" by violating socially important gender and

Introduction: Feeling Flustered?

sexual distinctions. It was an "attack on masculinity," he said, and it threatened the foundations of heterosexuality. Parenting expert Dr Susan Bartell disagreed. Liking the color pink is unrelated to gender or sexuality, she argued. "[A kid's] gender is going to emerge naturally as part of who they are and has nothing to do with whether we put pink nail polish on them."

The screaming spread from a fashion catalog to the print media and eventually found its way onto television, where *The Daily Show* apocalyptically declared the coming of "Toemaggedon." Jon Stewart presented a satiric interview with a self-described "senior gender analyst" and sexuality expert who asserted, "You've got to teach your kids appropriate gender-specific behavior from the get-go. You have to model. I want my boy to be straight."

J. Crew did not comment, saying that they did not want to add fuel to what they considered a "nonstory."[1]

❖ Which perspective do you agree with?
❖ Are there any other positions that you can identify?
❖ What does this episode tell you about the assumptions people make related to sex, gender, and sexuality?

Figure i.1 Saturday with Jenna

Introduction: Feeling Flustered?

Let's Talk about Sex

People are obsessed with sex – or, I should clarify, we are obsessed with talking about it, even if it sometimes leaves us feeling flustered. From Internet memes to college classrooms and everything in between, it seems like sex shows up all the time in our conversations. But just because we use the word a lot doesn't mean that we agree on what it signifies. Hardly. To muddy the matter, we often say "sex" when we really should say "gender" or "sexuality" – and our discussions get inflamed fast, as they did about one little ad from J. Crew. Why's it so complicated? The snag, I think, comes from some deep-rooted assumptions that we make about sex, without even realizing it, which then blind us to a bigger picture. Three stand out to me as the most common culprits: sex is natural, private, and timeless. Let's take at quick look at each one so that we don't make the same mistakes over and over again.

Assumption 1: Sexual Essentialism

Sex is natural. It is "a basic biological mandate," Arlene Stein (1989:1) explains. Our genitals, libidos, chromosomes, and hormones exist in its service, and we express it in physical acts that have reproduction as the end goal. Sex "is a natural force that exists prior to social life," Gayle Rubin remarks when she discusses how people think about bodies, biology and nature – "a natural libido yearning to break free of social constraint" (Rubin 1993: 9–10). Notice that Rubin repeats the word "natural." She is drawing our attention to an idea that scholars call "sexual essentialism": we confuse the relationship between "sex" and "society." Sex allegedly comes first. It is *sui generis*. Then society is what we humans develop over time in our institutions – the family, churches, governments, and the media, among others. While sex and society are ideas that are important in their own right, separating them conceals the profound ways that we express our libidinal urges based on the communities we create and in

Introduction: Feeling Flustered?

which we participate. The word "sexuality" better captures the interactions between sex and society.

Think about the J. Crew controversy. Dr Susan Bartell told a reporter from the *Los Angeles Times* that Beckett's gender and sexual orientation will emerge "naturally," and that it has "nothing to do with whether we put pink nail polish on them." Painting a boy's toenails is harmless, a form of play that will not affect his natural essence. Bartell assumes that our gender and sexual orientation are genetically hardwired. They are biological characteristics that are beyond the purview of society, politics, or culture. Her logic finds wide support, echoed by people as different as former Harvard University president Lawrence H. Summers and former Olympic champion Caitlyn Jenner. Both conveyed that men and women have innate genetic differences and different brains.[2]

Reflect as well on an interview that Domenico Dolce and Stefano Gabbana, the former power couple and business partners behind the fashion label Dolce & Gabbana, gave to an Italian magazine in 2015. In an effort to learn about their #DGfamily twitter campaign, the reporter asked, "What is a family for Dolce & Gabbana?" Dolce replied, "I am gay, I cannot have a child. Life has a natural course, some things cannot be changed. One is the family." Later in the conversation, he condemned IVF for producing "synthetic children" by offering "wombs for rent, seeds selected from a catalog."[3] We falsely naturalize sex in many ways. Dolce's identity as a gay man doesn't determine the type of sex that he can have or wants to have, nor does it constrain his family life (many heterosexuals also rely on IVF). If who we are is a function entirely of biology, if we are all "born this way," as Lady Gaga likes to say, then we would erroneously conclude that sex must be asocial – that it has no social basis – or presocial – that sex precedes our social relationships. More troubling, this essentialist vision leads us down a dangerously slippery slope: monogamous, married, procreative heterosexual couples are "natural," whereas others are "unnatural," especially those in same-sex relationships, who provide a foil against the straight gold standard. This is life's "natural course," Dolce said in the interview, and it "cannot be changed."

Introduction: Feeling Flustered?

Our belief in the natural is entrenched in the way we think. Its origins are in sexology, a so-called science of human sexuality that focuses on what we like and what we do. The German psychiatrist Richard Freiherr von Krafft-Ebing is credited with establishing sexology with the publication in 1886 of his book *Psychopathia Sexualis*, and the American zoologist Alfred Kinsey popularized it after World War II with *Sexual Behavior in the Human Male* (1948). Drawing on empirical evidence and using the scientific method, sexologists identify what they claim is the "truth" of sex, or the "laws" that govern it. These include the presumption that sex is part of the biological makeup of all people, that our sex drive is as important to our survival as eating or sleeping, and that sex is a heterosexual instinct based on a natural attraction between men and women. The companion belief in gender differences – "men are from Mars, women are from Venus" – explains why it's diffcult to talk about sex without also saying something about gender, as in the J. Crew example. Like sexual essentialism, "biological determinism" is another phrase that scholars use to describe our misguided emphasis on bodies that somehow are extracted from the social worlds they inhabit (Weeks 2010: 47). Ideas such as sexual essentialism and biological determinism are useful because they help us to distinguish "sex" from "sexuality." Do a quick search in Google images for the word "sexuality." What do you notice?

Assumption 2: Privacy and Individuality

The expression of sex, gender, and sexuality is a personal matter, you might think. Jenna Lyons' decision to paint her son's toenails pink was no one else's business. All the attention that it received was invasive, and it intruded on her private life. According to this view, sex is at the center of our sense of self. Just as sexology shaped our thinking about the status of bodies and biology, the discipline of psychology has heavily influenced this second assumption. Sigmund Freud, who was among the most influential thinkers about sex in Western civilization, agreed that it has a biological basis, but he disagreed with sexologists that our instincts are always reproductive and heterosexual. For Freud,

Introduction: Feeling Flustered?

they were also oriented toward personal pleasure and individuality. According to his universal theory of sexual development, our desire to pursue erotic pleasure can be dangerous if we do not balance it against social norms of respectability and self-control (Freud 1905). Thus, our chief challenge in life is to manage the sex drive. If we don't do it adequately, then we will feel psychologically and socially unstable. If we repress our sex drive too much, however, then we risk psychosexual frustrations that lead us down a path of personal unhappiness. We manage this struggle privately as we try to align our carnal instincts with our self-concept.

The assumption of privacy has a wide range of applications – from Freud's psychoanalytic theories to a legal concept in American jurisprudence. James Joseph Dean (2014: 10–11) describes three US Supreme Court rulings from the 1960s to the 2000s that protected reproductive rights and sexual intimacy as matters related to "the sexual autonomy of the individual," "the right to privacy," and "the right 'to be let alone.'" In *Griswold v. Connecticut* (1965), the Court struck down state laws that criminalized contraception and ruled that married couples have a right to privacy when it comes to reproduction. It extended this protection to unmarried couples in 1972 in *Eisenstadt v. Baird*. The next year, the Court decided *Roe v. Wade*, a famous case that protected abortion as a woman's right to privacy over the choices she makes about her body. Finally, in 2003, the Supreme Court overturned its own 1986 *Bowers v. Hardwick* ruling in which it had upheld state sodomy laws as constitutional. *Lawrence v. Texas* extended privacy rights to gay and lesbian couples. Notice a pattern? The highest court in the United States has consistently defended sexual autonomy, and the country's federal laws define intimacy as a private matter.

Assumption 3: Fixity

Sex is "eternally unchanging," to borrow again from Rubin (1993: 9). We assume that the sex drive is a natural biological force that we acquire at birth. It is intimately connected with who we are yet difficult to control or change, in part because we think that our libido is independent of social structures (society

Introduction: Feeling Flustered?

changes; libidos don't). These assumptions explain why many of us experience our sexual identity, especially the gay or straight binary, as "fixed and stable" (Valocchi 2005: 754). We believe that categories such as heterosexual and homosexual, along with the identities they represent, are "ahistorical" (they have no history), "transhistorical" (they have remained stable across time), and "culturally invariant" (they do not differ across societies). The notion of the "fixity of our sexualities" misleads us into concluding that they are resilient against our or others' efforts to change them (Weeks 2010: 59).

We heard hints of this assumption in the case study when Dr Ablow attacked the J. Crew ad for crossing a line. He thinks that gender and sexuality, especially masculinity and heterosexuality, are as old as time itself. Dr Ablow fears that there will be grave consequences for trying to change something so timeless. Jonathan Ned Katz, who has devoted his career to examining heterosexual history, elaborates on this "common sense conjecture" by invoking the imagery of Adam and Eve: "Heterosexuality is as old as procreation, ancient as the lust of Eve and Adam," he remarks. "That first lady and gentleman, we assume, perceived themselves, behaved, and felt just like today's heterosexuals. We suppose that heterosexuality is unchanging, universal, essential: ahistorical" (Katz 1990: 7). We can hear echoes of Katz's biblical narrative two decades later in Pope Benedict's protest against the legalization of same-sex marriage in Europe and other parts of the developed world. The union of one man and woman "is not a simple social convention," he defended in a 2012 address to diplomats from 180 countries, "but rather the fundamental cell of every society." The pope affirmed that "pride of place goes to the family," which he defined singularly as "the marriage of a man and a woman." For him, efforts to modify definitions of marriage and the family were fatal: "Policies which undermine the family threaten human dignity and the future of humanity itself."[4] As a fundamental cell rather than a social convention, the pope sees heterosexuality as fixed, eternal, and immutable. The only reason why the future of humanity could possibly be at risk is if we tampered with something that has always been, and should always remain, timeless.

Introduction: Feeling Flustered?

Table i.1 Assumptions about sex

Assumption	Explanation	Example
Essentialism	Sex is a natural force and a basic biological fact.	Dolce & Gabbana's Twitter campaign
Privacy	Sex is a personal matter and at the core of our sense of self.	Supreme Court rulings on reproductive rights and sexual intimacy
Fixity	Sex is eternally unchanging.	The pope's protest against same-sex marriage

Fashion icons Dolce & Gabbana, the Supreme Court of the United States, and the Catholic pope have something in common: they've each made assumptions about sex (see table i.1). This shouldn't surprise us. It is the nature of assumptions, after all, even if there is some truth to them. Assumptions simplify a world that is complex and anxiety-inducing, and they create a calmer state of mind for us and a common ground with others. But just because you believe that something is true doesn't (necessarily) make it so. Unquestioned or unqualified beliefs about biology, privacy, and fixity obscure the messy but life-affirming ways in which we struggle to make sense of our sexuality. Even scholarship sometimes "fails to be sensitive" to the "hidden assumptions it harbors" about sexuality (Stein and Plummer 1994: 184). Such sensitivity will not escape us in this book! We're going to unmuzzle the social, the political, and, especially, the cultural study of sexuality.

Sex + Culture = Sexuality

We cannot deny the "biological facticity" of the body, to borrow a percussive phrase from Judith Butler (1990: 273). This pertains to "sex," a word we use to mean two different things. The first employs sex as a noun, a reference to being male or female. We call this "biological sex" – our chromosomes, genitalia, and reproductive functions, primary sex characteristics, and post-puberty features such as facial hair, breasts, and the tonality of our voice.

Introduction: Feeling Flustered?

We also use the word sex when we want to talk about physical acts of intercourse and intimacy – as in "to have sex" or "sex acts." Sex as a verb draws attention to our pursuit of pleasure, love, relationships, and children. Unlike the first instance of bodily categories, the second view allows sex to inform our identities by hinting at the visceral attraction that we can feel for another person.

The use of sex as a noun and as a verb compels David Halperin to assert that "sex has no history." It is "a natural fact," he explains, "grounded in the functioning of the body, and, as such, it lies outside of history and culture" (Halperin 1993: 416). The notion of sex existing independent of history and culture, as some kind of free-floating reality, is a beguiling one. The genitals we are born with are biological facts, sure; yet what our bodies mean and how we experience them in the world is culturally produced. (And as our awareness of intersex and transgender individuals grows, so too does our understanding of the mutability of biology. Our bodies are more changeable and saturated with meanings than our grandparents ever thought possible. So, even sex has a history.)

That meaning-making becomes even greater when we talk not just about sex, but about sexuality. The word "sexuality" describes how morality, politics, and ideologies drape themselves over our bodies and present them as cultural expressions. "Sexuality is not a somatic fact; it is a cultural effect," Halperin (1993: 416) adds, as he compares the meaning of the two words. Halperin was inspired by the writings of Michel Foucault, who rejected the claim that sexuality is "a natural given." Instead, it is "a historical construct" that specifies the meanings we give to our bodies, how we use them, the pleasures they bring to us, how institutional agents compel us to talk about those pleasures, and the way all this generates "special knowledges" (Foucault 1978: 105–6) and regulatory regimes, ranging from politics to protest to city planning).

Sex plus culture equals sexuality. This is the principal formula of the book. As it suggests, the word "sexuality" draws our attention to how the materiality of the body comes to bear cultural meanings as it encounters other bodies, social customs, and institutions (Butler 1990). Biology is not irrelevant, but sexuality is not biologically ordained either. Rubin offers a helpful metaphor: "The

Introduction: Feeling Flustered?

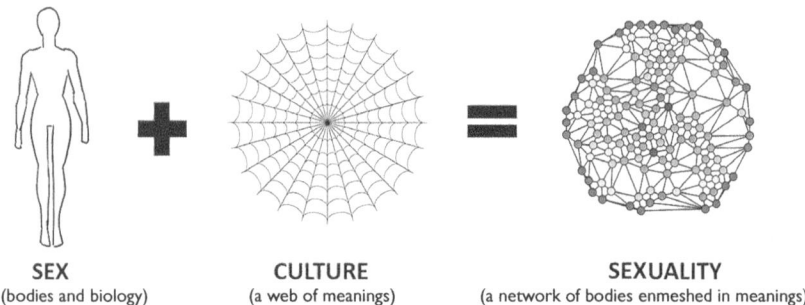

SEX
(bodies and biology)

CULTURE
(a web of meanings)

SEXUALITY
(a network of bodies enmeshed in meanings)

Figure i.2 Sexuality

belly's hunger gives no clues as to the complexities of cuisine. The body, the brain, the genitalia, and the capacity for language are all necessary for human sexuality. But they do not determine its content, its experiences, or its institutional forms. Moreover, we never encounter the body unmediated by the meanings that cultures give to it" (Rubin 1993: 10). Culture – that behemoth of meaning that surrounds us and the other bodies we interact with every day – shapes sex into sexuality (see figure i.2).

Recall the Toemaggedon episode from the case study and the expert Jon Stewart interviewed. "You've got to teach your kids appropriate gender-specific behavior from the get-go," he said. "You have to model. I want my boy to be straight." The commentator is comedic but incisive. Gender and sexuality are not natural, private, or timeless in some irreducible sense, he tells us. They are part of a sphere of cultural meanings that have evolved over time and have become embodied in symbols, such as nail polish, which we use to think about our bodies. Institutional agents, from your parents to the media to your friends, influence the decisions you make every day about how to express yourself. Gender and sexuality are interactive accomplishments (West and Zimmerman 1987) and particular ways in which we stylize our bodies (Butler 1990). Labeling someone a boy or a girl, or gay or straight, is a cultural decision that is motivated by our beliefs about gender and sexuality (Fausto-Sterling 2000). These beliefs come from societal scripts that teach us and tell us how to act (Gagnon and Simon 1973),

Introduction: Feeling Flustered?

the many roles we fill (McIntosh 1968), the labels we use when we talk to and about each other (Plummer 1975), and the more abstract "fields" in which we negotiate our worth as sexual beings (Green 2008).

These "essentialist-constructionist debates" have been raging in social sciences since at least the 1960s, when Peter Berger and Thomas Luckmann published their book *The Social Construction of Reality* (1966). Applying the insights of constructionism to sexuality, Joshua Gamson (2010: 96) argues, "Sexuality is not just a phenomenon of nature, and not just 'personal,' but a phenomenon of society, and political." Although biology matters, we need culture to "fashion a biological reality into 'sexuality,'" Steve Seidman (2011: 3) says. In fact, and returning again to Gamson (2013: 802), "whatever 'sexuality' nature provides does not tell us a whole lot about the shapes and meanings it takes on." There is no essential, predetermined, natural, or true way of being. Your sexuality is fluid and contingent – "always in process," according to Stuart Hall. It does not develop in "a straight, unbroken line, from some fixed origin" (Hall 1990: 222, 226). The meanings and material expressions of sexuality emerge in specific historical moments, they reflect cultural viewpoints, and they are socially shared with other people. We are different from animals such as salmon, who are genetically wired to swim upstream to spawn at just the right time and place, in that nature determines only a small part of our sexuality. This is why we need culture. The sex organs that we have and the sex acts that we perform wouldn't have much meaning without the cultures we have created and in which we participate.

All this buzz about sexuality and culture is finally drawing the attention that I think it deserves. For instance, it pleases me to say that the president of the American Sociological Association (ASA) selected "Sexualities in the Social World" as the theme for the 2015 professional conference. This was the first time since the founding of my professional organization in 1905 that it elevated sexuality as a central node for intellectual inquiry and exchange. I admired the call for the annual meeting: "Sex usually occurs in private and is seen as deeply personal, yet it is also profoundly social," declared the president of the ASA (sound familiar?).

Introduction: Feeling Flustered?

"Cultural norms and social institutions such as religion, education, mass media, law, and the military all affect what we do sexually with whom. These social forces also affect what is seen as beyond the bounds of legitimacy" (England 2013: 5).

The intuition of the ASA is right, but the trouble is that the idea of sexuality is so elaborate that it's difficult for us to talk about it with clarity or precision. To grapple with its complexities, we will rely on insights from different disciplines. Unfortunately, existing frameworks aren't always helpful (and academics like me can make matters worse!). The concepts of sexuality that emerge from the humanities are often highly abstract. Muse for a moment on queer theory's dense prose, the soporific sentences of post-structuralism, or the jargon of psychoanalytic feminism. The social sciences, meanwhile, slip into the axiomatic. Think about the well-rehearsed debates about nature versus nurture and the social construction of everything. This book will provide you with a cultural introduction to the study of sexuality. Together, we will find a way beyond the obfuscation and a way around all the simplistic assumptions that bedevil our thinking about sexuality. We are going to uncover a more useful means of understanding it: through the union of sex and culture. But, to understand what I mean, we must first understand culture.

Your Cultural Imagination

"Culture" is one of the most complicated words in the English language (Williams 1976: 87). It is also a controversial idea among academics; indeed, a lot of sociologists are skeptical about whether we should rely on the word at all. After all, they say, culture can mean nearly *everything* – from the hot new song you just downloaded to the violent debates between ISIS and al-Queda over whose version of Islam is correct. Thus, does "culture" really mean *anything*? I believe it does. And I also believe that we must acknowledge the messiness of the word in order to appreciate the equally messy ways we think about our bodies and our identities as sexual beings.

Introduction: Feeling Flustered?

An analogy might help. A half century ago, C. Wright Mills introduced the concept of the "sociological imagination" (Mills 1959). This is a mindset, a way of seeing and thinking about the world around us. It is tempting to assume that the choices you make each day, or the worries that bubble up inside you as you fall asleep at night, have nothing to do with the rest of us. But that's false. The sociological imagination teaches us that neither the life of the individual nor the history of a society can be understood apart from the other. There is a close interplay between you and society – of "biography and history," Mills would say, of self and world. Our personal troubles are expressions of public issues and public concerns. When you can situate the ebbs and flows of your own life in a larger societal context, you have acquired a sociological imagination.

Just as Mills encouraged us to connect our personal troubles with the public issues of society, here we will reckon with our "cultural imagination." We can think about the notion, this entwining of sexuality with the wider world, as a "web of meanings" that we pass among ourselves over time and which we embody in symbols (Geertz 1973). It is within this web that sexuality grows. Just as "biography and history" are inextricably linked, so too are sex and culture. Growing up, we learn a great many ideas about sex and sexuality from our parents, from advertisements, from books and university courses, from our friends, and from Internet porn. As you travel along the path of discovery, it's easy to assume that your sexuality is just your own, that you make your own choices apart from the rest of the world. After all, you decide whether to flirt or not with the person sitting next to you, right? And you decide whether to join the gay–straight student alliance, right? And you decide whether to have sex after the first date, right? And you decide whether to sign off your text message with x's and o's, right?

Wrong. Of course, on one level, you *are* making these choices for yourself; you are the one who says yes or no. But you are never acting entirely by yourself. Your decisions are all impacted by the people and places and the information and ideas that surround you every minute of every day – the web of meanings. When we

Introduction: Feeling Flustered?

recognize that our sexuality is absolutely public and social, we have acquired a cultural imagination.

It's okay if you don't believe me – just yet. It can be frustrating to come to terms with how much our lives are shaped by the busy world outside our own skin. Many of us resist the notion that the "we" might be more powerful than the "me." Meditating on the symbols that we use in our life might help. To think about culture as a web of meanings highlights the importance of these symbols, what Wendy Griswold (2008: 22) refers to as "shared significance," or the ability of an object to suggest something else. The color red on a stop light or stop sign "means" that you should stop driving, or a flag lowered to half-mast on a pole "means" that a country is in mourning. Meanings matter for us because we are not genetically programmed like the salmon we encountered earlier. "We all know that living beings grow and act according to instructions encoded in their genes," Griswold (ibid.: 23–4) comments about biology in a separate piece. "[A] hare instinctively knows to run from the scent of a fox but not from the scent of a chipmunk. Most of what animals do and know is genetically given – hardwired, so to speak." The same is not true for us human beings. "A kitten, once weaned, could survive in the woods without other members of its species to show it what to do, but a one-year-old child could not. Humans must learn to live." This is why culture matters. "[L]earning in humans is a social process of interaction and socialization whereby culture is transmitted." Culture compensates for our genetic insufficiencies. It provides the tracks along which our actions, attitudes, beliefs, and worldviews unfold. Embodied in symbols, the meanings we make as we travel along the way acquire a significance that surpasses the materiality of its respective object. Stopping at a red light is not optional. Its power to determine our behavior far exceeds the glass that makes up signal lights, the steel poles, and the electric controller that prompts the light to turn from green to yellow to red.

Sexuality, as we know from our own experiences, has many meanings and many symbols. Some of these collide against others – think of the difference between what Jenna Lyons saw in her son's pink toes compared to what Dr. Ablow saw in those

Introduction: Feeling Flustered?

same tiny toes. Struggles over sexuality (and gender) are inherently cultural. They highlight "webs of significance [that man] himself has spun" (Geertz 1973: 5). Concrete things such as nail polish, a lowered flag, or a red light symbolize something that can be totally removed from their material reality: gender bending, mourning, and the need to stop. Sometimes, our public struggles over sex and sexuality blow up into outright "culture wars," or society-wide fights about what something means (Gitlin 1995; Hunter 1991). For instance, do you say "Merry Christmas" or "Happy Holidays?" Why do you think people get so hot and bothered about the question? These debates will be useful for us to explore in this book. Usually, our ideas about sexuality are surprisingly hidden – they are assumptions that are so deeply instilled within us that they can be hard to see, let alone to articulate. These moments of conflict are like a cauldron in which meanings and assumptions bubble up to the surface for us to analyze. To recognize this is yet another way to awaken your cultural imagination.

It is my hope that you will arouse your cultural imagination as you read this book. Little by little, you'll start to see that immense web of meanings about sexuality you are a part of, both influenced by and influencing in return. Each of us has the ability to tap into our cultural imagination, although most of us, most of the time, are probably not all that aware of it. As you become accustomed to this innovative way of thinking and of seeing the world, you'll recognize your cultural imagination for the powerful tool that it is. My objective is to inspire you to use that tool and to see what you can do with it.

Sex Cultures

This book is about how culture shapes sex into sexuality. Both "culture" and "sexuality" are elegant yet complicated words, and our goal is to figure out how they come together in various aspects of our lives – settings that range from the metropolis to movements for social justice. We will challenge the conventional assumptions that pit sex against society by gleefully embracing the

Introduction: Feeling Flustered?

notion of their inseparability. Thus, rather than focusing on sex acts, we will think about sex cultures.

So what exactly is a sex culture anyway? The term, I hope, has caught your eye. By "sex culture," I don't mean what the religious right or worried parents fear: that we are living in a culture that is obsessed with sex (that may be true, but it's not my point). Instead, I'm thinking about something that is perhaps a bit more elusive, yet I believe much more important and accurate: our biological sex and acts of sex are meaningful only because of the communities in which we experience them, because of the institutions that try to regulate them, and because of the traditions that celebrate them. Sex cultures refer to the diverse contexts and customs that give meaning to our bodies and the ways we use them in our pursuit of pleasure. We are immersed in sex cultures every day. There are many of them that are operating at any given moment, around the world and across history, and they rub against each other all the time. As we'll see later, we can identify the sex cultures of gay liberationists in 1970s New York City to those of straight men and women today. The frat boys and sorority girls at your school are a part of sex cultures too. Each of us travels in several sex cultures at the same time, from the celibate nun to the lingerie model, from the school teacher to the drag queen, and everyone in between (myself included). The more we use our cultural imagination, the more we can see that these exquisite sex cultures are all around us.

By the time you finish this book, it's my hope that you will have gained three major insights. First, learning about culture and sexuality will make you rethink the significance of sex, a word that denotes anatomy and physiology, hormones and chromosomes, and primary and secondary sex characteristics. All these things matter, but the story is bigger than just bodies and biology. Rubin reminds us with another metaphor about hunger: "The needs of sexuality and procreation must be satisfied as much as the need to eat, and ... these needs are hardly ever satisfied in any 'natural' form, any more than are the needs for food." Enter culture. "Hunger is hunger, but what counts as food is culturally determined and obtained." The same goes for sex, a point that Rubin is careful

Introduction: Feeling Flustered?

to make. "Sex is sex, but what counts as sex is equally culturally determined and obtained" (Rubin 1975: 165). Bodies and biology mean something greater than the sum of their parts.

Second, learning about culture and sexuality will expand your view away from the private toward the public. We can't reduce sexuality to a personal or a psychological phenomenon; it is "profoundly social," as the ASA president declared. As we will see again and again, what sex means emerges in our interactions with others, how we use language and our bodies to perform our sexual sense of self in social context.

Finally, learning about culture and sexuality will help you see that the meaning of sex is a product of a particular time and place. Halperin (1993) identified in ancient Greece a society populated by "molles," or effeminate men, and "tribades," or masculine women. In early twentieth-century New York, a man could have sex with another man without anyone questioning his heterosexuality. George Chauncey (1994) describes a world of diverse masculine men called "trade," "husbands," and "wolves" who existed in a gender-segregated bachelor subculture alongside the more feminine "fairies," "third-sexers," and "punks." All these categories smash apart our modern binary of straight or gay, as well as the gendered expressions of masculinity or femininity. A cultural view will compel you to see that sexuality is, "in a word, constructed" (Epstein 1994: 188) – and it varies considerably across countries. In some Latin cultures, sexual identity is not always linked with the gender of your partner but instead is based "on the scripted sexual role (active/passive, masculine/feminine) that one plays in the sexual act" (Valocchi 2005: 754). Tomás Almaguer (1993) elaborates, "Chicano men who embrace a 'gay' identity (based on the European-American sexual system) must reconcile this sexual identity with their primary socialization into a Latino culture that does not recognize such a construction: there is no cultural equivalent to the modern 'gay man' in the Mexican/Latin American sexual system." Our cultural approach to the study of sexuality will investigate these types of meanings that people assign to sex and desire as they emerge in face-to-face interactions, on our bodies, in time and space, and across institutional settings.

Introduction: Feeling Flustered?

The Journey Ahead

This book will showcase several ways in which sex mingles with culture to form sexuality. We will review current research on the topic, especially those studies which have been highly influential and which offer interdisciplinary ways of knowing. In our discussion, we will use case studies to illuminate the hotly contested terrain of sexuality. The cases that you will encounter, like the one from the opening pages of this chapter, are the first distinguishing aspect of the book. What is a "case" anyway, and how do "case studies" work? Case studies allow you to explore how complex ideas unfolded in real-life settings. I have crafted them around the central touchstone of this book: sex + culture = sexuality. Cases will provide some but certainly not all of the information that you need to understand a situation; they will challenge you to fill in the blanks as needed. Cases never present all the facets that transpired, and not everything you read will be relevant (necessarily). Thus, case studies harness the power of ambiguity; that is deliberate to the design and their appeal. Case studies will teach you ways of thinking and analyzing that you can't just memorize. They are powerful because they distill "critical thinking" skills, that pervasive and prized buzzword that we hear so often from the classroom to the boardroom. Cases will challenge you to figure out how to define a problem, isolate what's most relevant about it, and how to analyze that problem by linking it to the ideas that we have been discussing in a chapter. Cases will train you how to execute such sophisticated analytical tasks by frequent and varied application to the real world. That's why they are so compelling, even if these qualities also make them quite challenging.

Each substantive chapter has an opening and closing case study. The logic for the opening is to introduce a topic through the central theme of the book, while the closing case will encourage you to apply what you have learned. I have designed both to stimulate conversations that you can have in class or a coffee shop and to teach you how to breathe life into academic ideas by applying them. I have crafted the cases around a series of debates that

Introduction: Feeling Flustered?

have arisen in countries around the world. My international focus and debate-driven approach are the second and third distinguishing aspects of this book. Debates are an effective tool for learning because they allow unspoken assumptions to rise to the surface, and learning about events that happened in other countries helps us to see how we are all connected. I hope the unique case study, debate-driven, and international design of the book will energize your cultural imagination and instruct you on how to use it to gain a better understanding of sexuality.

I have been teaching in universities for more than a decade. Over the years, my students have given me some great advice that has found its way into these pages. They tell me that they appreciate opportunities to apply the theories we learn in class to events that happen in their daily lives. My students also say that they like to think about sexuality in specific settings rather than in abstract, highly theoretical, and jargon-heavy ways. I believe that their counsel is important; it helps us appreciate why what we are reading is pertinent. The guidance to be specific and concrete also stands on guard against the temptation to dismiss an idea as just "academic" (read: irrelevant). Heeding the wisdom of my students, I have organized this book around four themes that offer opportunities to learn about different kinds of sex cultures: urban planning, political protest, the ongoing invention of heterosexuality, and the science of sexuality. We'll begin with topics that are specific and then blossom into a set of broader explorations.

For a topic as knotty as sexuality, knowing what we will *not* do is just as valuable as knowing what we will do. This book is unlike any other introduction that you have encountered. It's pretty short, first off, which means that we can't cover everything there is to say about sexuality (not even close). I have not included a standalone chapter on "theoretical frameworks," so often the first in books like this – one that would review a range of perspectives from sexology to psychoanalysis, from economics to feminism. Others have done a terrific job of this (for one brilliant example, see Seidman 2011). Nor am I including a chapter that details the relationship between sexuality and gender or that goes into depth about transgender issues. Sexuality acquires its meanings

Introduction: Feeling Flustered?

in the context of a highly gendered, raced, and classed world, and scholars like Patricia Hill Collins have detailed these intersections with great urgency and clarity (Collins 2000). In this matter, I side with Jeffrey Weeks. "We cannot derive sexual subjectivities from gender," he argues. Even to try would give these other categories "an *a priori* significance that would deny the intricacies of the social organization of sexuality" (Weeks 2010: 41). I expect that our briefer explorations of these intersections within the four settings that I enumerated earlier will entice you to seek out more materials about the areas that interest you.

I tackle the field of sexuality through a distinctively cultural lens. My approach, which is the fourth and final distinguishing feature of this book, will help you make connections between big ideas such as "sexuality" and "culture" that too often remain vague abstractions. Using the common thread of culture to weave together different topics will allow me to present clearly an extraordinary amount of information on everything from changes in the urban landscape and the rise of the LGBT movement to the hetero–homo binary, fraternity hazing rituals, bro-jobs, and gay vague.

As we prepare to move forward, it's time to release the all-too-typical questions that dominate our thinking about sexuality: "Are we born gay, or do people choose it?" or "Isn't sexuality natural?" or "Why is this anyone else's business but my own?" These are tiresome inquiries. It's time to let go of our entrenched beliefs and embrace a more creative perspective that comes from acknowledging how culture shapes sex into sexuality. Let's ask new questions: What does sexuality mean – and for whom? How do those meanings change over time? What forms does sexuality take in different social, political, and urban contexts? How well (or poorly) do your sexual experiences align with our existing categories and frameworks? What can we learn about the significance of sexuality from those moments when your behaviors and the cultural schemas that our categories represent do not neatly match up? What role do conflicts and controversies play as we try to make sense of our sexuality?

After you have finished reading this book, you will be poised to analyze the cultural aspects of sexuality as you actively encounter

Introduction: Feeling Flustered?

them in your life. What's the point of learning something, after all, if the ideas you encounter in a book stay behind to collect dust once you close its pages? So brace yourself. It's time to dive into the tidal allures of sexuality.

Questions to Consider

1 What are the differences between "sex," "gender," and "sexuality?"
2 What assumptions dominate our thinking about sexuality?
3 What are the advantages of a cultural approach to the study of sexuality?
4 Revisit the case study, and compare a cultural approach to the study of sexuality with the conventional assumptions we often make about sex. What does each perspective bring to light? What does each conceal?
5 What is the value in focusing on sexual conflicts as they arise in specific cases? What do those cases and the conflicts that they embody reveal about the relationship between sex, culture, and sexuality?

1

The City

Case Study: There Goes the Gayborhood

"Gay enclaves face prospect of being passé." This alarmist front-page headline in the *New York Times* predicted the demise of San Francisco's Castro district – arguably the most famous gay neighborhood in the world. The journalist Patricia Leigh Brown lamented, "These are wrenching times for San Francisco's historic gay village, with population shifts, booming development, and a waning sense of belonging that is also being felt in gay enclaves across the nation, from Key West, Fla., to West Hollywood, as they struggle to maintain cultural relevance." The story describes how these local shifts mirror broader trends "where you are seeing same-sex couples becoming less urban, even as the population becomes slightly more urban." One indicator is "the influx of baby strollers – some being pushed by straight parents, some by gay parents." For residents of gayborhoods like the Castro, strollers symbolize that the area "has gone from a gay-ghetto mentality to a family mentality."

The meanings of sexuality are upending from what they were just a generation ago when gay neighborhoods first formed. "Cities not widely considered gay meccas have seen a sharp

The City

increase in same-sex couples. Among them: Fort Worth; El Paso; Albuquerque; Louisville, KY; and Virginia Beach." The demographer Gary Gates told Brown, "Twenty years ago, if you were gay and lived in rural Kansas, you went to San Francisco or New York. Now you can just go to Kansas City."[1] These changes are contentious. "We often clamored for equality where gay and straight could co-exist," said gay Mayor John Duran of West Hollywood to Brown. "But we weren't prepared to give up our subculture to negotiate that exchange." Many residents agree. Amy Sueyoshi, a dean at San Francisco State University, describes her typical hangout spots in the Castro: "I've noticed more straight people making out at these places where I go deliberately to NOT feel like I am oppressed by heterosexuality. Really, straight people, do you HAVE to make out in the Castro as well? Good Lord."[2]

In response to the conflicts, the Gay, Lesbian, Bisexual, and Transgender Historical Society of Northern California hosted a roundtable session that urgently asked, "Are Gay Neighborhoods Worth Saving?" According to a press release for the event, the session reflected "an upsurge of dialogue about the potentially imperiled future" of gayborhoods across the country. Board member Don Romesburg cautioned that the meanings of a neighborhood arise within specific circumstances: "We tend to assume that[,] once created, queer neighborhoods will be self-sustaining. That's not true ... [O]ur neighborhoods get built within particular economic, political, and cultural circumstances. When those change, so do our neighborhoods."[3]

What we see in the United States represents an international trend of reinventing urban sex cultures. In Toronto, the Gay Village used to be "the centre of the universe," says a journalist writing for the *National Post*. Gay couples are still visible on the streets, but so are straight men and women. "Some are pushing baby carriages – a lot more than a decade ago." Micah Toub, a journalist with the *Globe & Mail*, interviewed a real estate agent who noted, "I guess more people just feel like, 'I don't care if it's a gay village, or any village – I want to be downtown.'"[4]

The City

The noticeable numbers of straight bodies in the gay village of Montreal motivated Alexander Dunphy, the city's official tourism blogger, to write a piece entitled "A Straight Friendly Guide to Montreal's Gay Village." Dunphy asks a poignant question that's on a lot of people's minds: "The Gay Village is rich in history, culture and concentrated fun. But is it only for us gays?"[5] Residents of Vancouver's Davie Village have noticed the same thing. In contrast to Dunphy's perspective, many Vancouverites feel that the presence of straight people in their gayborhood forces them to "straighten up."[6] American and Canadian restlessness draws our attention to the disquieting question of whether we need gayborhoods anymore, especially to create and preserve queer cultures.

Across the pond, a story published in *The Independent* screamed at the straight people who were socializing in gay bars in London, Manchester, and Edinburgh: "Please keep out of gay bars and clubs. It's uncomfortable to start snogging [kissing] on a dance floor and surface to find a hen [bachelorette] party staring in amazement."[7] Writing for *The Guardian,* Feargus O'Sullivan took his readers on a quick jaunt: "The waning of gay-identified neighbourhoods . . . is happening in Paris' Marais, Berlin's Prenzlauer Berg and Munich's Glockenbachviertel." The gay and lesbian residents of these districts have not always welcomed their new straight neighbors with open arms. "Many locals have mobilized to protect their communities' meeting points, but amid the fightbacks and general hand-wringing there's also a sense of confusion."[8]

Urban sex cultures are changing in Canada, France, Germany, the United Kingdom, the United States, and elsewhere as more straight people move into gay neighborhoods while gays and lesbians fan out to other parts of the city. The cultural meanings of these migrations are fiercely debated. Consider an article called "The Party's Over" which *The Advocate* published in 2016. The story focuses on twenty-six "dead (or dying) gay bars" in New York City, Los Angeles, and San Francisco. "Cities around the country, and globe, have seen many of their most beloved gay and lesbian watering holes close down – often after the area's queer population diffuses or the owner simply gets priced out . . . [These bars] served as de facto community centers, offering a kind of glue that kept our disparate minority together."[9]

❖ *Why do you think more straight people are moving into gayborhoods while gays and lesbians are leaving them?*
❖ *What do you think gayborhoods teach us about how the meanings of sexuality are changing?*
❖ *How does culture shape sex into sexuality in an urban environment?*

Albuquerque, Berlin, El Paso, Kansas City, Key West, London, Los Angeles, Louisville, Manchester, Montreal, Munich, New York, Paris, San Francisco, Toronto, Vancouver, and West Hollywood: these are all culturally distinct places, yet they have something important in common. They show us that cities have become "a catalyst for homosexual activity" (Aldrich 2004: 1731). Scholars first took an interest in urban sex cultures during the early twentieth century. "The city was as much a sexual laboratory as a social one," Heap (2003: 458) remarked in his review of scholarship produced by the esteemed Chicago School of Urban Sociology (see Park and Burgess 1925). In fact, "by 1938, Chicago sociologists' association of homosexuality with particular urban spaces was so complete that Professor Burgess could expect students . . . to provide an affirmative answer to the true–false exam question, 'In large cities, homosexual individuals tend to congregate rather than remain separate from each other'" (Heap 2003: 467).

So sweeping is the reach of sexuality in our lives that our discussion of the nexus of sex and culture could begin anywhere. I have chosen to start our conversation in the city, an important part of human history and our lives today. We have witnessed a staggering increase in urbanization over time. In 1800, only 3 percent of the entire world's population resided in cities. By 1900 that number had jumped to 14 percent, and fifty years later 30 percent of the world's population was living in an urban area. The World Health

The City

Organization reports that the urban population in 2014 made up 54 percent of the total global population. By 2045, the World Bank adds, the number of people who will live in cities will soar 1.5 times, to a stunning 6 billion – 2 billion more than the present day. The trend of urban population growth shows no signs of stopping anytime soon, and cities will become more central to our lives with each passing year.[10]

Cities are home to many neighborhoods, but here we will focus on the gayborhood. It is a topic of great personal interest, as I have been living in and writing about these districts for the better part of the past decade. More importantly for us, the gayborhood offers a concrete manifestation of those elements of our story that are not always so obvious. It is home to many urban sex cultures – an alchemy of bodies (especially those that desire other bodies of the same sex), customs (those that challenge heteronormativity and traditional ideas about sex and the family), commemorations (pride parades and street festivals), symbols (ranging from the rainbow flags that adorn the streets to strollers), institutions (bars, nonprofit organizations, gay-friendly churches), and histories (from the role of the Castro in helping to elect the first openly gay person to public office in California to Chicago becoming the first city in the world where the municipality used tax-funded dollars to mark its gay district). The gayborhood allows us to examine how these and other elements come together in one place – which often is just a few blocks long! – to create the abundance of cultural meanings that we call sexuality. Gay districts are clearly shaped by sex – imagine the pronounced presence of gay and lesbian bodies on the streets – and they embody ways of life, or cultures – from the bars that flourish there to the fights that break out over who is moving in and out. From that mixture, we can learn a great deal about sexuality.

Studying how sex and culture form sexuality in the city has the added advantage of allowing us to see how much things have changed over time. If culture evolves, as we know it does, so too must sexuality. This chapter will show that sex cultures are "a historical construct," as Foucault (1978: 105–6) told us in the Introduction. Sex cultures animate the meanings we assign to our bodies, how we use them, the pleasures they bring to us, and the

The City

conflicts they cause – all in specific places and at specific moments in time. Focusing on the transformation of urban sex cultures will show us how an academic insight about the tides of history works on the ground in the city. To put all these ideas into play, we'll review sex cultures in North American cities across three time periods: the closet era (1870 to World War II), the coming out era (World War II to 1997), and the post-gay era (1998 to the present). Ask yourself as you read these pages: In an urban environment, how does culture shape sex into sexuality?

Scattered Gay Places

The homosexual as a species was born in 1870. Michel Foucault, one of the most influential thinkers about sexuality, explains what he means by this provocative distinction between sex and sexuality: "As defined by the ancient civil or canonical codes, sodomy was a category of forbidden acts; their perpetrator was nothing more than the juridical subject of them" (Foucault 1978: 43). In the nineteenth century, the "homosexual became a personage," as medical practitioners reimagined the cultural significance of sex from a set of acts to an expression of identity. "Homosexuality appeared as one of the forms of sexuality when it was transposed from the practice of sodomy onto a kind of interior androgyny, a hermaphrodism of the soul. The sodomite had been a temporary aberration; the homosexual was now a species." Foucault's finding teaches us that gays as people are a product of history.

Capitalism assisted in the cultural transition from sex to sexuality. Seventeenth-century colonial white families were self-sufficient, and their households contained all production-related activities that they needed to farm the land. Sex at this time furthered the goals of procreation and, while homosexual behavior existed, gay identity did not. You could have sex with someone of your own sex, or love that person, but those were just acts (aberrant ones, mind you), not a way of life or a means of proudly defining yourself. The economic necessity of procreation began to decline in the mid-1800s as the development of wage labor altered social norms of sex away "from the 'imperative' to procreate" (D'Emilio 1993: 470). The industrial revolution separated our homes from work and created "gendered spheres of production, reproduction, and male–female experiences" (Knopp 1992: 663). Wage labor allowed people to carve out a personal space within which they could not merely have sex but also define their identity around it. That increasingly common carving led some people to create an entire life around their erotic and emotional attractions to others of the same sex, although they still experienced a profound tension between their new erotic self-awareness and persisting public pressures to conform and to marry someone of the opposite sex.

Industrial capitalism contained contradictions that allowed homosexuals to manage this strain in gender-specific ways. Men relied on "underground networks" to build bars, clubs, and baths in which they pursued same-sex eroticism in "commodity form," while women turned to the domestic sphere, but also some places in school and at work, to nurture more personal interactions. Some of these spaces had staying power and provided long-term resources to build "alternative communities and identities" (Knopp 1992: 664). Lawrence Knopp argues that urban sex cultures had a spatial component: they emerged through "sexual relations in space, sexual representations of space, and sexual symbols in space" (ibid.: 660). Although the experience of being gay varied by gender, crucial for both men and women was the construction in space of "otherness." The development of their "place-based identities" thus became "the material basis of social and political struggles" (ibid.: 661).

Take New York as an example. A gay male world emerged between 1890 and the start of World War II as several bohemian rebellions inspired men to develop their own commercial establishments. George Chauncey (1994: 23) characterizes the sex cultures of the city at this time as a "topography of gay meeting places" – or, to borrow another visual image from Ann Forsyth (2001: 343), "scattered 'gay places.'" Such phrases communicate the unique form of urban sex cultures at this time. The bars, cabarets, theaters, restrooms, public parks, and other cruising areas that attracted those who desired others of the same sex were located in

The City

progressive parts of the city, such as Greenwich Village for white gay men or Harlem for blacks, which had reputations for "flouting bourgeois convention" (Chauncey 1994: 227). Even those men who were considered "normal" were permitted to have sex with other men, especially the effeminate "fairies," as they were called, provided that the normal man acted in a masculine manner and "played (or claimed to play) only the 'masculine,' or insertive, role in the sexual encounter" – meaning that they were not sexually penetrated. If they met these gendered conditions, then "neither they, the fairies, nor the working-class public considered *them* [the normal men] to be queer" (ibid.: 66). Fairies were the ones who were stigmatized, although even they were tolerated as "woman-like men" (Dean 2014: 60). None of these individuals "set the tone" of the neighborhood (Chauncey 1994: 228), however, which is why it would be a mistake to say that the scattered gay places of the closet era were basically gay neighborhoods.

Urban histories of so-called romantic friendships between women (Rupp 2001) are harder to find. Literacy rates for women lagged behind those for men, and thus we have fewer written records of women's intimacies with other women (Faderman 1999b: 56). Women had restricted access in the nineteenth century to paying jobs and public spaces, which limited opportunities for them to form subcultures like those of gay men. Even existing records are not always easy to decipher. It's difficult to distinguish friendship and affection between women from their erotic sexual relationships, since romantic friendships included both types of expressions (Dean 2014). This is why it is a historically daunting task to align sexual labels with behaviors and identities. That said, scholars agree that nineteenth-century romantic friendships were integral to the lesbian identities and subcultures that flourished in later years. Terms like "fiery man-eaters" (Friedan 1963: 80), "the lesbian" and "menacing female monster" (Katz 1990: 18), and "the mannish lesbian/congenital invert" (Newton 1993: 291) were all circulating by the 1920s, and they hinted at an alternative to heterosexuality and traditional gender roles for women. Some reappropriated these labels to create self-consciously lesbian spaces, thereby laying the groundwork for lesbian sex cultures.

The City

Kennedy and Davis (1993) document one such working-class and racially diverse community that thrived in Buffalo, New York. Here, women cultivated social networks in private house parties and some bars which became hotbeds of lesbian life. Many women used these social gatherings to craft "cultures of resistance" (ibid.: 2) and find relief from the well of loneliness that burdened their lives. The results were often transformative. "I wasn't concentrating on my school work, 'cause I was so enthused and so happy, I don't know, it's like you're in a cocoon," one woman recalled about living in Buffalo in the 1940s. Another added:

> We wound up at this bar. Now, previous to this I had never been to a gay bar. I didn't even know they existed. It was a Friday night and that was the big night . . . And we walked in and I thought, my God, this is really something. I couldn't believe it . . . I don't think there were any straight people in that bar that night . . . There were an awful lot of lesbians. (Ibid.: 45)

That evening, she met a woman who became her partner for the next eight years.

As these quotes make clear, the imagery of the closet doesn't mean an absence of queer life in the pre-war years. Chauncey (1994) identifies three popular myths that explain why we mistakenly believe that queer cultures and communities didn't exist during these early years: the myth of isolation (anti-gay bigotry compelled gay people to live solitary lives); the myth of invisibility (even if a queer world existed, it was impossible for anyone to find it); and the myth of internalization (gay people accepted pernicious societal views of homosexuality as a sickness and sin). Let's not misinterpret these myths as suggesting that society celebrated sexual diversity either; it didn't. Sex between men and sex between women was considered an offense and a punishable crime. There were few organized challenges to such repressive views about homosexuality. As a result, sex and culture came together in specific urban expressions as some men and women appropriated public and private spaces "to construct a gay city in the midst of (and often invisible to) the normative city" (ibid.: 23). Sexuality in

The City

these small worlds was associated with gender inversion because a distinct gay identity did not yet exist.

Sex and sexuality manifest in every historical epoch, but our ability to make sense of them requires that we understand the culture of the time. That is why it is hard to talk with certainty about sex cultures during the closet era: the historical evidence is small. Just as important, gay men and women were so "scattered" that many were not aware that there were others like them all over the world; there was not yet any sense that they belonged to distinct sex cultures that were regional or national. Although the scales were small, they were certain, and even the straight world started to notice. In 1931, a New York-based newspaper featured a public exposé on queer meeting places. One year later, the movie *Call Her Savage* showcased Greenwich's burgeoning queer scene. By this time, "the Village became noted as the home of 'pansies' and 'lesbians'" (Chauncey 1994: 235), and in 1936 a medical journal published the "Degenerates of Greenwich Village," an article which announced that the Village had become "the Mecca for ... perverts" (ibid.: 234). Amid these and other sensational headlines, a world-altering event unfolded that, in its wake, would revolutionize sex cultures in the city.

Gayborhoods Arrive on the Urban Scene

World War II changed the course of human history. That much is clear. Less discussed though no less important was that it changed the course of human identity as well. The war was "a nationwide 'coming out' experience" that ushered in a new sexual era (D'Emilio and Freedman 1997: 289) as it deposited young men and women into cities with major military bases – places like Chicago, Washington, DC, Seattle, San Francisco, San Diego, Philadelphia, New York, Miami, and New Orleans. The military's restrictions forbade homosexuals from service. Thus, during the war years, these areas swelled with servicemen and women who were discharged for their real or perceived homosexuality. The war and its discharges "led directly to a dawning realization by homosexuals of their numbers,

The City

which in turn led to the formation of the post-war self-conception of gays as a quasi-ethnic minority" (Wright 1999: 173).

The concentration of young gay men and lesbians in urban centers altered their cultural imagination. Bars that catered to them opened in larger numbers, and, over time, the first formal gay neighborhoods, or gayborhoods as we now call them, emerged (Ghaziani 2014b). The men and women who engineered this "society within a society" did so deliberately. "Not only did they have a sexual network to preserve, they had also to win their right to exist as citizens, they had to engage in political battles, change laws, fight the police, and influence government," wrote Manuel Castells (1983: 157). If culture shaped sex into the particular understandings of sexuality that we saw in the closet era, then men and women accomplished the task of changing the meaning of sexuality in the coming out era by re-engineering those existing cultural frameworks. This was not an easy task. To succeed, they first had to plant a flag in the ground, so to speak, which enabled them to use their marginalized position in society as the basis for political power. Thus, the emergence of the Castro gayborhood, like so many others, occurred alongside the development of social movements, a topic we'll study in the next chapter.

Before the war, it was against the law in many states for gays and lesbians to gather in public places, even in those bars that they called their own. However, a landmark California Supreme Court decision in 1951 ruled that it was illegal to shut down an establishment just because gay people were its primary patrons. "The first right to a public space had been won" (Castells 1983: 141). The California case, known as *Stoumen v. Reilly*, catapulted a national movement to safeguard gay spaces, and it politicized the bars in particular. Activists founded the Tavern Guild in 1962 to protect themselves from police raids and organize voter registration drives in and around the bars. The Guild proved pivotal for the formation of stable gayborhoods across the country which, in the same spirit as the politicized bar culture, attracted mostly gay men who sought to locate their new sex cultures in a specific part of the city.

Winning the legal right to gather in public places and forming the Tavern Guild did not provide full immunity from police

The City

harassment in San Francisco or anywhere else in the United States. On June 28, 1969, New York City police raided the Stonewall Inn, a gay bar located at 53 Christopher Street in Greenwich Village. Compliance during these raids was usually as routine as the raids themselves, but this time the bar goers and a growing crowd outside fought back, resulting in five days of rioting that forever changed the cultural imagination of gay people, and the meanings of sexuality more broadly, across the globe. Bar owners and patrons had defended themselves at other raids in New York and elsewhere, but activists and academics remember Stonewall singularly as having "sparked the beginning of the gay liberation movement" (Bérubé 1990: 271). Many scholars consider it "*the* emblematic event in modern lesbian and gay history" and as "that moment in time when gays and lesbians recognized all at once their mistreatment and their solidarity" (Duberman 1993: xvii). To this day, groups across the world use "Stonewall" in their organizational names. It is the title of the largest LGBT rights organization in Europe, for example, which has offices in the UK in both London and Edinburgh.[11] In the United States and Canada, Stonewall inspired gay people to come out of the closet in large numbers and to relocate to cities where they hoped to find others like them. This national demographic movement was called the "great gay migration" (Weston 1995: 255), and it occurred in the 1970s and into the early 1980s. San Francisco was the emblem of this migration, but the ripple effects stretched to other areas, including Cherry Grove, a small resort on Fire Island; Northampton, Massachusetts; Buffalo, New York; Columbia, South Carolina; and Des Moines, Iowa.

Why did so many gays and lesbians move to certain cities during the great gay migration? And, once they arrived, why did many live in the exact same neighborhood? Existing research identifies five triggers, each of which contributes to our understanding of how culture shapes sex into urban sex cultures (table 1.1). As gays and lesbians selected specific areas in which to live, their emergent clusters gestated a national cultural imagination; men and women began to see themselves as comprising a people and a tribe, culturally distinct from heterosexuals.

The City

Table 1.1 The gayborhood in the coming out era

Trigger	Effect on individuals	Effect on urban sex cultures
History	Gays respond to ongoing historical conditions and contingencies	Gayborhoods form as "historical accidents"
Community	Gays seek solidarity and fellowship with others who are like them, and they want access to specific institutions	Gayborhoods form as more institutions concentrate in an area
Sex and love	Gays seek opportunities for the pursuit of pleasure	Gayborhoods form to facilitate sex and relationships
Economics	Gays revitalize the city as they seek economic opportunities, affordable housing, and amenities	Gayborhoods form through capital circulation and investments
Politics	Gays are moral refugees who seek shelter from bigotry and bias	Gayborhoods form as safe spaces

History

Our external environment influences how our lives and collective experiences unfold. These "historical accidents" (Collins 2004: 1792) trigger the formation of new gayborhoods. World War II and the Stonewall riots are examples from the United States, while the decriminalization of homosexuality in the UK in 1967 helped gayborhoods to form in London, Brighton, Manchester, and Newcastle. Scholars who work in this area focus on how specific events and contingencies shape the qualities of places at precise moments in time. Their work teaches us that history has the power to define and redefine the cultural meanings of sex (D'Emilio 1989; Meeker 2006).

Community

Gayborhoods form when more businesses and non-profits that cater primarily to LGBT people open up in the same area and nurture the "institutional elaboration of a quasi-ethnic community" (Murray 1979: 165). Both gays and straights rely on institutions to identify cultural communities – even more than residential clusters (Murray 1992: 109). The identity of an area as a gayborhood, therefore, emerges more apparently when it houses gay-owned and gay-friendly bookstores, hair salons, churches, travel agencies, realtors, medical facilities, retail stores, periodicals, non-profit organizations, and political groups. These facilities shape the cultural imagination of sexual minorities as well as heterosexuals. They incubate a view of homosexuality as a public identity around which people form a minority consciousness. Participating in ritual events such as pride parades, dyke marches, and street festivals that are based in gayborhoods inspires solidarity among those who gather for it. In one study of fifty gay white men between the ages of twenty-three and forty-eight who lived in DuPont Circle in Washington, DC, more than 80 percent expressed "a desire to be among other gay men" as their reason for living in the gayborhood (Myslik 1996: 166). We hear the cultural imagination at work among residents and visitors alike when they talk to us about the district. They will call it a "gay mecca," "gay capital," and "gay village." The point may seem obvious but is still worth stating: gays migrate to an urban homeland as a path to membership in a community they can call their own.

Sex and Love

Some activists in the 1950s and 1960s thought that social change would come from building separate spaces to help gays in their "pursuit of pleasure" (Armstrong 2002: 185). Because homosexuality is not visible on the body, gays and lesbians encounter a special challenge in identifying each other and thus in seeking that pleasure. Gayborhoods offer a practical solution to the problem of invisibility. Other scholars agree that "sexual desire can be a driving force in neighborhood formation" (Doan and Higgins 2011: 15). Even if a gay bar closes, gay people will still visit certain urban districts to "go the gym, get a drink, buy a book or magazine, and well, for sex" (ibid.). The density of gays in specific parts of the city helps them find each other, whether for a night or a lifetime.

The City

Economics

The biggest debate among scholars is between our final two triggers – whether economic drivers or freedom from discrimination provides a more compelling explanation for why gayborhoods formed – and so we will spend a little more time on each one. Those who favor the former offer three economic influences on urban sex cultures: amenities, population size, and investment potential. For example, research shows strong correlations between the location of same-sex households and an abundance of amenities in cities such as Austin, Atlanta, Fort Lauderdale, Los Angeles, New York, Oakland, San Francisco, San Diego, Seattle, and Washington (Black et al. 2002). If we assume that some of these places emerged as magnets during the great migration (which we must to approximate the past, since we don't have census data on same-sex households for the coming out era), then one lesson we learn is that urban comforts matter as gays and lesbians decide where to live. There are additional correlations between the number of same-sex residences in a neighborhood and its housing stock, especially that which is older and higher in value (Anacker and Morrow-Jones 2005).

Why do gay and lesbian households settle in areas with greater offerings and desirable housing? Scholars say that this happens because of children – or, rather, the lack thereof. "Gay households face constraints that make having or adopting children more costly than for otherwise similar heterosexuals" (Black et al. 2002: 55). This frees up resources that they can allocate elsewhere, such as moving to a city with a beautiful natural environment or a mild climate, a neighborhood with well-kept Victorians, diverse restaurants, and a vibrant arts and entertainment scene. Those who emphasize the importance of amenities do not view gays or their preferences as special. Other households with high incomes and without significant demands on that income (namely, children) will make similar choices.

A second economic factor, called critical gay population size (Collins 2004: 1791), explains why gay districts emerge in areas

The City

that *lack* the amenities that we just talked about – cities that do not have a remarkable climate or neighborhoods that are deficient in appreciable aesthetic qualities. We might predict that a gayborhood will not form in such areas. Yet this is exactly what happened with the Birmingham Gay Village in England. Once a minimum number of gay people settled in the area, that density provided a "virtuous circle" which motivated more gays to migrate to the same area. Gay people define a critical population of others like themselves as itself an amenity that some cities and neighborhoods offer.

Gentrification is the third economic factor, and it is the most common explanation that many of us hear for why gayborhoods formed. Across the United States over the last forty to fifty years, federal interventions have fueled multiple waves of urban renewal efforts and private market investments that have converted socially and economically marginal areas of the city for middle-class use. Gay people – along with artists, students, and designers – were among the first to invest in "islands of renewal in seas of decay" (Berry 1985). In doing so, they helped to revitalize the very idea of the city – and birthed the gayborhood.

Politics

On the other side of the economic debate are scholars who argue that gay people are motivated more by freedom of self-expression and protection from discrimination, and they select areas to live that have a "reputation for tolerating non-conformity" (Chauncey 1994: 229). During the coming out era, gays and lesbians invested in certain urban districts "at a financial and social cost that only 'moral refugees' are ready to pay" (Castells 1983: 161). One activist shared his reverie at the Berkeley gay liberation conference in 1969: "I have a recurring daydream. I imagine a place where gay people can be free. A place where there is no job discrimination, police harassment or prejudice ... A place where a gay government can build the base for a flourishing gay counter-culture and city ... It would mean gay territory" (Armstrong 2002: 89).

Gayborhoods flourished following the Stonewall riots of 1969 as more gays and lesbians from across the country moved to them and romanticized the possibilities for freedom that they embodied. Books and magazines, television and movies, and word of mouth spread the news about these budding places. "Every friend who sends a letter back from San Francisco filled with tales of city streets covered with queers builds the city's reputation as a safe harbor for 'gay people'" (Weston 1995: 262). This buzz generated exciting sex cultures in the city, as gayborhoods shone as "a beacon of tolerance" (ibid.) in a sea of heterosexual hostility.

From a political perspective, gayborhoods operate as a "safe space" or a "free space." A widely cited passage defines these as places where people "learn a new self-respect, a deeper and more assertive group identity, public skills, and values of cooperation and civic virtue" (Evans and Boyte 1986: 17). Invoking the image to explain the emergence of the Castro gayborhood, Castells (1983: 139, 168) explained that it provided a "liberated zone" and a "free village," where gays and lesbians could "be safe together." In his study of West Hollywood, Forest (1995) also remarked on the emancipatory and empowering potential of gayborhoods. "Public spaces created by gays provide for relative safety, for the perpetuation of gay subcultures," he said. They "provide symbols around which gay identity is centered," and they enable gays "to resist [heterosexual] domination" (ibid.: 137). During the coming out era, simple personal acts like sharing a "stroll hand-in-hand or kiss in the street without embarrassment or risk of harassment" (Sibalis 2004: 1748) became deeply political. In fact, grassroots activism in defense of safe spaces has been "one means by which neighborhoods have been claimed" by gay activists in the coming out era (Hanhardt 2008: 63). The idea of gayborhoods as safe spaces from straights is a recurring one, and it suggests, importantly, that they are "a spatial response to a historically specific form of oppression" (Lauria and Knopp 1985: 152).

Gay social thinkers beyond the academy have also articulated this argument. In 1969, Carl Wittman drafted *A Gay Manifesto*, in which he described his San Francisco home as a "refugee camp for homosexuals." Gays "formed a ghetto, out of self-protection," he said, since "straight cops patrol us, straight legislators govern

The City

us, straight employers keep us in line, straight money exploits us." This is why so many gay moral refugees invested in the Castro. "We want to make ourselves clear: our first job is to free ourselves; that means clearing our heads of the garbage that's been poured into them" by straight society (Wittman 1970: 67–8).

Historical accidents such as World War II, the institutional elaboration of gay communities via organizations and businesses, the search for a one-night stand or the love of your life, capital flows into the city, and the quest to create safe spaces all triggered major changes in urban sex cultures. Men and women who yearned for others of the same sex became much more visible after the war, and they boldly challenged a repressive political system with actions such as the *Stoumen v. Reilly* court case in California, the Tavern Guild in 1962, and the Stonewall riots in New York in 1969, all of which we have talked about, along with additional activist efforts that we haven't even had a chance to cover, including the decision to commemorate the Stonewall riots with an annual parade (see Armstrong 2002) and the success that activists achieved in convincing psychiatrists to declassify homosexuality as a mental illness in 1973 (see Stoller et al. 1973), among other efforts at social change (we'll look at some of these in the next chapter). The new visibility of gays and lesbians changed cultural perceptions of homosexuality from being an act that was illegal and a diagnosis of disorder (based on classifications in the *Diagnostic and Statistical Manual* of the American Psychiatric Association) to a quasi-ethnic public identity. Those who embraced it encouraged others to do the same: smash open the doors of the closet, be proud of your sexuality, and celebrate your differences from the straight majority. As the nature of oppression against gay people changed, so too did their spatial response. Thus, the cultural dynamics of the coming out era reconfigured the scattered gay places of the closet era into a new urban form: the gayborhood.

Time never stands still. Gays and lesbians who fought for their right simply to exist as people in the post-war years could never have imagined that their new-found visibility would become a juggernaut of sorts, one so powerful in its neoliberal tones that it threatened to overwhelm and undermine the sexual, cultural, and

The City

urban distinctions that many activists fought so hard to create in the first place.

Gayborhoods Straighten

A lot of people these days wonder if gayborhoods are disappearing. Unique commercial spaces such as bars and bookstores are closing, more straight people are moving in, and gays and lesbians are choosing to live in other parts of the city. Demographers such as Amy Spring (2013) have analyzed the US census and have confirmed that zip codes associated with traditional gay neighborhoods are thinning out; fewer same-sex households lived in them in 2010 than they did in the year 2000. Same-sex partner households now reside in 93 percent of all counties in the country (Gates and Cooke 2011), and, more often than not, gay life "blends with other aspects of the city" (Aldrich 2004: 1732).

Many gay people today live their lives "beyond the closet," despite the persistence of heteronormative biases in the state, societal institutions, and popular culture (Seidman 2002: 6). While the coming out era was typified by being open and out about one's sexuality and having almost exclusively gay social networks, many people call our own era "post-gay" and see it as characterized not by a proud sense of difference but by a rapid assimilation of gay people into the mainstream. Coined by the British journalist Paul Burston in 1994, the term found a North American audience four years later when *Out* magazine editor James Collard (1998b) used it in the *New York Times* to argue: "We should no longer define ourselves solely in terms of our sexuality – even if our opponents do. Post-gay isn't 'un-gay.' It's about taking a critical look at gay life and no longer thinking solely in terms of struggle. It's going to a gay bar and wishing there were girls there to talk to." Collard clarified the urban implications of this ambiguous idea two months later in a *Newsweek* feature:

> First for protection and later with understandable pride, gays have come to colonize whole neighborhoods, like West Hollywood in L.A.

The City

and Chelsea in New York City. It seems to me that the new Jerusalem gay people have been striving for all these years won't be found in a gay-only ghetto, but in a world where we are free, equal and safe to live our lives. (Collard 1998a)

Our current moment has been given many names – "beyond the closet" (Seidman 2002), "new gay" (Aguirre-Livingston 2011; Savin-Williams 2005), "post-closeted cultural context" (Dean 2014), a "post-marriage equality world" (NeJaime 2015), or just "post-gay" (Ghaziani 2011, 2014a, 2014b). The one name we choose matters less than our efforts to grapple with the reality of the present day – and with the seismic shifts in the cultural imagination of sexuality that we all are experiencing.

Opinion polls show a dramatic shift in public attitudes about homosexuality, especially in how Americans think about the moral acceptability of gay and lesbian relations. According to Gallup, four in ten Americans found gay and lesbian relations morally acceptable in 2001. By 2014, that number was up to 63 percent. This is a stunning shift in attitudes (23 percentage points) in a short period of time (thirteen years). Using a nationally representative sample of 1,197 self-identified LGBT adults aged eighteen and older, a 2013 Pew Research Center survey found that an overwhelming proportion (92 percent) say that society has become more accepting of them in the past decade – and an equal number expect even more acceptance in the next decade.[12] This change in opinions is the first of four indicators that suggest a radical reinvention of our cultural imagination in a post-gay era.

The legal landscape is another piece of evidence for an ongoing post-gay shift. The 2012 elections were historic in this regard. A majority of voters in three states – 51.5 percent in Maine, 52.4 percent in Maryland, and 53.7 percent in Washington – supported legalizing same-sex marriage in ballot initiatives. "These electoral outcomes represent the first examples of popular majorities voting to endorse same-sex marriage in statewide initiatives" (Flores and Barclay 2013). Three years later, on June 26, 2015, the Supreme Court decided *Obergefell v. Hodges*, a case that legalized same-sex marriage across the United States. Justice Anthony Kennedy wrote the 5–4 majority opinion using riveting prose that emphasized the cultural sameness of gays and straights (we'll pick up this theme of sameness in the next chapter). "They ask for equal dignity in the eyes of the law," Kennedy said, speaking of the gay plaintiffs. "The Constitution grants them that right." In his address to the nation, President Obama hailed the arrival of a new era of equality. "This decision affirms what millions of Americans already believe in their hearts. When all Americans are treated as equal, we are all more free. Today we can say, in no uncertain terms, that we have made our union a little more perfect."[13] The landmark decision made the United States the twenty-first country to legalize same-sex marriage. The Netherlands was the first to do so in 2001, followed by Belgium in 2003, Spain and Canada in 2005, South Africa in 2006, Norway and Sweden in 2009, Portugal, Iceland, and Argentina in 2010, Denmark in 2012, Brazil, France, Uruguay, England, Wales, and Scotland in 2013, Luxembourg and Finland in 2014, and Ireland and the United States in 2015. These legal shifts have been prompted by and have pushed the post-gay era further.

A third indicator that our cultural imagination is changing in the current sexual era comes from the composition of our social networks. A 2014 survey by the Public Religion Research Institute (PRRI) of 4,509 randomly sampled adults from across the United States found that "the number of Americans who have a close friend or family member who is gay or lesbian has increased by a factor of three over the last two decades, from 22 percent in 1993 to 65 percent today." Another 2014 survey, by McClatchy-Marist, of 1,035 randomly sampled adults across the United States found that, "by 71–27 percent, American adults say they know someone who's gay. That's a dramatic change from a generation ago, when a 1999 Pew poll found that Americans said by 60–39 percent that they didn't know anyone who was gay." These changes in the composition of social networks have inspired the development of a straight allies movement of "politically gay" heterosexuals, as some scholars call them (Meyers 2008).[14]

The City

The fourth and final indicator comes from the onset of same-sex attractions and coming out of the closet. One US study found that, in 2000, "The average age that gay and bisexual boys had their first same-sex attractions was just before 8, while for girls it was 9, and in many cases the same-sex attractions started several years earlier." Lesbian, gay, and bisexual people are coming out earlier than ever before. The same study also noted, "The average coming out age has declined from 20-something in the 1980s to somewhere around 16 today." According to research conducted in Britain, the average age of coming out has fallen by more than twenty years. "The poll, which had 1,536 respondents, found that lesbian, gay and bisexual people aged 60 and over came out at 37 on average. People aged 18 and under are coming out at 15 on average."[15]

It is in this potent context that the term "post-gay" acquires its many meanings. It can express a style of self-identification, describe the tone of a specific space or an entire neighborhood, and capture the zeitgeist of a historical moment. Individuals who see themselves as post-gay subscribe to a worldview that subordinates the centrality of their sexual orientation – "I'm more than just gay," they might say. They disentangle their sexuality from a sense of militancy and struggle, feel free from persecution, and prefer sexually integrated company – hence Collard's lament for more straight girls in gay bars. Gay social networks today are more mixed, include more straight people, and are driven by common aesthetic tastes and interests (we both like red wine, for example) rather than a sense that gay people share an oppressed, minority group status with only one another (Brown-Saracino 2011). Scholars have found that some people actively resist using labels such as "gay," "lesbian," and "bisexual" (Russell et al. 2009: 888). In addition, a post-gay space like a bar is one in which "the need to clearly define and delineate our sexualities is largely deemed unnecessary"; similarly, gayborhoods no longer demand "the assertion of one identity or another. Most times they contain a majority of heterosexuals." This is possible because "'gay' identities have outlived their usefulness (Brown 2006: 136, 140). Think of it this way: during the coming out era, gay villages

The City

were "akin to what Rome is for Catholics: a lot of us live there and many more make the pilgrimage." In a post-gay era, however, they are "more akin to what Jerusalem is for Jews: most of us live somewhere else, fewer of us make the pilgrimage than in the past, [and] our political power has moved elsewhere" (Myslik 1996: 167–8).

With public acceptance of homosexuality and same-sex relationships at an all-time high, it is easier for some gays and lesbians to move into the mainstream in a way that makes them feel as if they are no different than heterosexuals. Nate Silver is a great example. Silver rose to fame for predicting the outcome of the 2008 presidential election with stunning precision. In 2009, *Time* magazine named him as among "The World's 100 Most Influential People," while in 2012 *Out* magazine selected him as their "Person of the Year." In his interview with the editor of *Out*, Silver said something that stuck with me and many other people: "I'm kind of sexually gay, but ethnically straight" (Ghaziani 2014b: 14). Silver's story has haunting implications. The shouty "We're here! We're queer! Get used to it!" from the coming out era is being replaced by the whispery post-gay apologia "I may be gay, but I'm ethnically straight." This has consequences for the decisions we make about where to live. "Maybe Dorothy doesn't need Oz anymore," Sally Hunt (2014) quipped.

Gay neighborhoods historically provided a safe space for gays and lesbians in an often unsafe world. But now the world itself is becoming safer and, as we have just seen, several indicators suggest that a profound shift is happening to our cultural imagination. Indeed, as culture touches sex in historically unprecedented ways, the meaning of sexuality changes as well. In what follows, we'll revisit the same five triggers that accounted for why gayborhoods first formed to take a closer look at how they are changing today (see table 1.2). I'm deliberately using the same triggers, holding them constant if you will, to show you how the central touchstone of this book – "sex + culture = sexuality" – is not a static formula, nor does it apply exclusively to LGBT people. Culture changes over time and, as far as we're concerned in this

The City

Table 1.2 The gayborhood in a post-gay era

Trigger	Effect on urban sex cultures
History	Gayborhoods will change by way of historical accidents
Community	Gayborhoods will change as existing institutions close or if new ones open in other parts of the city
	Gayborhoods will change as new generations come of age and as personal preferences steer people toward sexually mixed social networks
Sex and love	Gayborhoods will change if residents no longer need them for their sexual and romantic pursuits
Economics	Gayborhoods will change as a result of resurgent gentrification and municipal promotion campaigns that attract tourists
Politics	Gayborhoods will change if safety is less of a concern

chapter, it explains why gayborhoods are de-gaying (gays and lesbians are leaving them) and straightening (heterosexuals are moving in).

History

The nascence of the post-gay era makes it hard to think about history as a trigger, but I suspect that the decline of manufacturing and industrial jobs and the corresponding rise of a global service-sector economy is impacting urban sex cultures — just as they influenced how race is organized in the city (Wilson 1987) and the emergence of a new class geography (Sassen 2001). What effects can we anticipate for sexuality? To compete with a small number of powerful global cities, especially as manufacturing declined, secondary cities such as Chicago, Miami, Manchester (UK), Vancouver, Seattle, and Sydney rebranded themselves as hotbeds of culture by showing off their stock of ethnic spaces. Lately, city officials have been using gayborhoods in the same way as they do Chinatowns — as "a marker of cosmopolitanism, tolerance, and diversity for the urban tourist" (Rushbrook 2002: 188). We'll pick up this point later in our discussion of municipal promotion campaigns and tourism revenues (my reference to it here should show you that these triggers interact).

The City

Community

Gay businesses and organizations "anchor" certain neighborhoods in the minds of residents, and they can bestow a stable identity, despite residential fluctuations (Ghaziani 2014a). Earlier, we learned that people rely on distinct institutions even more than residential density when they assess urban sex cultures (Murray 1992). To make concrete why this matters in a post-gay era, consider that there were sixteen gay bars in Boston and Cambridge, Massachusetts, between 1993 and 1994, but by 2007 fewer than half remained. Bar closings have a domino effect. If enough of them shut down, so too will bookstores, restaurants, and other spaces that catered to the community. As gay businesses leave, they "sever ties that link residents to an integrated sense of neighborhood" (Usher and Morrison 2010: 277).

Generational shifts also trigger changes in urban sex cultures. Post-gays are twentysomethings that are part of a new generation of young people who prefer sexually mixed company. The journalist Paul Aguirre-Livingston says that they are skeptical about whether the "new Jerusalem" exists in a "gay-only ghetto," and so they reject them. Younger gays and lesbians feel that their sexual orientation is secondary to their place in life which, "in most ways, is not about being gay at all," he adds. They say that they "do not have that much in common with gay culture." If life for the next generation is not about being gay, then the gayborhood will not resonate for them as a site of a common community.[16]

Sex and Love

Once upon a time, people needed the gayborhood to find each other for sex and love, but has the Internet rendered that function old-fashioned and obsolete? "People still meet romantic partners in [the traditional forums of family, the workplace, and neighborhoods], but it seems to be less common," is Michael Rosenfeld's answer.[17] "The Internet is displacing those classic venues." It is now easy to find online resources about being gay, which disenfranchises the gayborhood for younger individuals or for those who come out later in life. The Internet also allows closeted gays and lesbians to find electronically mediated friendships and sex partners either for "virtual pleasure" or for "real-world fun" (Usher and Morrison 2010: 279).

The Internet has exerted a dominant influence in how same-sex couples have met since the year 2000 – over 60 percent of couples first met in this way, prompting researchers to conclude that "the Internet seems to be displacing all other ways of meeting for same-sex couples" (Rosenfeld and Thomas 2012: 532). One study of seventeen international cities asked if gay communities were "dying or just in transition" (Rosser et al. 2008: 588). The researchers found that, in every one of them, "the virtual gay community was larger than the offline physical community" (ibid.). In fact, some people condemn the Internet for creating a "diaspora of gays from traditional urban enclaves."[18]

Economics

Once again, economics and politics are the two most common explanations for why urban sex cultures are changing. Let's look at each one separately. Urban redevelopment in the United States proceeded in two waves. Federal renewal efforts fueled the first, as we saw earlier, in response to the white flight of the 1960s. Gentrification saw a resurgence in the late 1990s in a second wave that corresponded with rising home prices. Changes in the financing system of mortgages, increased privatization, and the demolition of public housing caused this second wave. Ironically, while gays and lesbians used the first wave to build many of their urban districts, the "super-gentrifiers" (Doan and Higgins 2011: 7) of the second wave have been mostly straights who have transformed gayborhoods into "visible niche markets for retail commerce and realty speculation" (Hanhardt 2008: 65). This process is called "resurgent gentrification" (Doan and Higgins 2011: 6). Some gays and lesbians perceive the sexual integration that results from it as "the pillaging of gay culture" by economically motivated straights who have no commitments to their community (ibid.: 15). In fact, as more straights move in, gay people and their businesses report *lower* levels of tolerance. Financers and straight newcomers also prefer large chain stores, which threaten "the cultural icons of queer neighborhoods" (ibid.: 16). Although this frays the fabric of sex cultures, the desire for belonging to a gay community persists, and many former residents say that they would still rather live in the area – if only they could afford it.

Municipal promotion campaigns, including mayoral efforts to boost local economic growth and tourism plans, are a second economic trigger, and they resemble the arguments about history that we saw earlier. In the late 1990s, a group of demographers and economists created a so-called Gay Index that ranks regions in the United States based on their concentration of same-sex households. Richard Florida (2002) has publicly championed it, and city agencies use it because it allegedly predicts economic competitiveness in a globalizing world. Defining gayborhoods as entertainment districts signals a shift in how the state perceives these areas – from a "regulatory problem" that required repression and containment in the 1970s and 1980s to a "marketing asset" in recent years (Rushbrook, 2002: 193). Cities such as Chicago, Philadelphia, and Manchester (UK) have a municipally marked gayborhood that they use to attract tourists, which also makes the area "the chic social and cultural centres of the city – the place to be seen, . . . regardless of one's sexual preferences" (Collins 2004: 1793, 1798). For heterosexuals, branding gayborhoods as chic allows them "to overcome their discomfort with being 'out of place' in gay space" (Brown 2006: 133).

Politics

Gentrification provides only a partial explanation for why gayborhoods are transforming; lower levels of discrimination also matter. The same increase in tolerance that allows gays and lesbians to feel comfortable beyond the borders of gay districts also contributes to straight residents feeling more at ease living and socializing in them. Gayborhoods now are safe spaces for straight women, a place where they can "escape the heterosexual male gaze" (Casey 2004: 454). Straight men are mostly on board, too. Charles Blow

The City

captured their cool in the title of an essay in the *New York Times* in 2010: "Gay? Whatever, Dude." Blow interviewed Michael Kimmel, who explained how gender and sexuality interact in the cultural imagination of straight men in today's post-gay era: "Men have gotten increasingly comfortable with the presence of, and relative equality of, 'the other.'" This is why a gayborhood is no longer out of bounds. Furthermore, the ratio of single straight women to men in these spaces makes them especially attractive – minus all the personal discomfort that they would have to confront if they were overtly homophobic. Thus, cultural acceptance and assimilation have made gays and lesbians feel safer beyond the borders of the gayborhood while straights feel invited into it.[19]

By tracing the effects of the same triggers over time – history, community, sex and love, economics and politics – we have seen how urban sex cultures are transforming as the long arc of the moral universe bends toward justice. When we look at the city through the lens of sex cultures, we see that the demographic integration happening in gayborhoods is the spatial expression of acceptance. Culture is in the driver's seat here. The unprecedented visibility of gay people has made the idea of homosexuality fairly unremarkable – for both gays and straights – and a logic of cultural sameness is replacing the sense of sexual difference that prevailed in the cultural imagination of individuals who lived in the previous era. This mindset affects the choices that we all make about where to live and socialize. Just ask yourself if you think there's anything unusual about going to a gay bar with a bunch of your friends.

As more straights move into the gayborhood, gays and lesbians are moving out in droves. Some have even given up on pride parades, so radically reinvented is their cultural imagination. "We don't march in Pride, and we probably never will," a group of young gay men from Toronto told Aguirre-Livingston. "It's not that we hate gay culture; we just don't have that much in common with it anymore. To be a twentysomething gay man in Toronto in 2011 is to be free from persecution and social pressures to conform. It's also, in most ways, not about being gay at all." I doubt this means that the so-called new gays that Aguirre-Livingston is talking about (or the "post-gays," as we called them) are not proud

The City

of who they are – or that they are ashamed – but rather that they don't think very much about their sexuality. If some gay people say that they don't have a lot in common with gay culture anymore, then straights will no longer see the gayborhood as a restricted, minority-only space either. The gayborhood lives on, certainly, but, as homosexuality sheds the skin of its old cultural stigma, these urban districts are evolving into an elective, not exclusive, place for people to live, regardless of their sexual orientation.

Conclusions

All neighborhoods change, as do the cities that surround them, and the gayborhood is no exception. In this chapter, we've seen that culture shapes sex into sexuality in subtle and striking ways in the city, especially as time goes by (see table 1.3). The culture of the closet era was characterized by concealment (hiding who you were from family and friends), isolation (being disconnected from other gay people), feelings of shame, guilt, and fear (which stemmed from internalizing societal views about homosexuality), and duplicity (living a double life). Sexuality at this time found spatial expres-

Table 1.3 The queer metropolis in the closet, coming out, and post-gay eras

Sexual era	Historical time	Cultural imagination of sexuality	Expressions of urban sex cultures
Closet	1870 to World War II	Concealment; isolation; feelings of shame, guilt, and fear; living a double life	*Pre-formation*: "Scattered gay places"
Coming out	World War II to 1997	Being open and out about sexuality; having almost exclusively gay social networks; believing that "gay is good"	*Formation*: Gayborhoods form (post-WWII) and flourish (post-Stonewall)
Post-gay	1998 to the present	Acceptance of gays and lesbians by mainstream society; assimilation into mainstream society	*Transformation*: Gayborhoods de-gay and straighten

sion in "scattered gay places." The culture of the coming out era, in contrast, was typified by people being open and out about their sexuality; by constructing a world with almost exclusively gay social networks; and by believing that "gay is good" – to allude to a popular phrase coined by the activist Franklin Kameny in 1968, mirroring Stokely Carmichael's mantra "black is beautiful" (Valocchi 1999). As the nature of oppression changed in this next era, so too did the urban expressions of sexuality; we witnessed the birth of the gayborhood. Finally, the cultural ethos of the post-gay era represents a surprising reversal: being gay just isn't that big a deal anymore – nothing like what homosexuality meant in the closet era at least. What we see today is an acceptance of sexual minorities by mainstream American, British, and Canadian societies. Acceptance, in turn, prompts greater sexual integration, both within and beyond the gayborhood.

As we arrive at the final pages of this chapter, I would like to offer two words of caution. First, although there is a remarkable diversity of urban sex cultures, our public conversations about them often emphasize the cultural imagination of gay men. In doing so, we inadvertently erase the unique lives of lesbians. There is a long history of this erasure in scholarship, and awareness of it can help us to correct it. Castells (1983: 140) set the terms of debate when he wrote, "Lesbians, unlike gay men, tend not to concentrate in a given territory," and so they "do not acquire a geographical basis." The culprit was a key difference in how men and women relate to space. Castells explained: "Men have sought to dominate, and one expression of this domination has been spatial." Women, on the other hand, have "rarely had these territorial aspirations." When gay men struggle "to liberate themselves from cultural and sexual oppression, they need a physical space from which to strike out." This is because gay men are still men, and that is just what men do. "The same desire for spatial superiority has driven male-dominated cultures to send astronauts to the moon and to explore the galaxy." The situation is different for women. Lesbians "create their own rich, inner world," one that "attaches more importance to relationships." Drawing on an assumption of biological determinism, Castells concluded that lesbians are "placeless" and

The City

that "we can hardly speak of lesbian territory." Gender apparently accounts for patterns that sweep from gayborhoods to entire galaxies, but Castells painted a curiously barren landscape for lesbians.

A number of scholars have rejected the "simplistic assumptions" (Binnie and Valentine 1999: 176) that lesbians are placeless, that they lack a geographical basis, or that they are without territorial aspirations. Distinct lesbian geographies exist apart from the more visible, gay-male dominated districts. Consider first the Park Slope neighborhood of Brooklyn, where a local lesbian resident said, "Being a dyke and living in the Slope is like being a gay man and living in the Village" (Rothenberg 1995: 179). Consider next the tiny town of Northampton, Massachusetts. With its population of roughly 30,000, many consider it the most famous "lesbian mecca" and "haven" in the United States, to borrow descriptions from a 1993 *Newsweek* story: "Lesbians have a mecca, too. It's Northampton, Mass. a.k.a. Lesbianville, U.S.A. . . . Northampton has been a lesbian haven since the late 1970s. 'If you're looking for lesbians, they're everywhere,' said Diane Morgan," who coordinates an annual summer festival.[20]

Gender affects where we live – but why? Some scholars argue that men and women have different needs to control space, as we heard from Castells, while others stress women's lack of economic power (Adler and Brenner 1992). Although the gender wage gap (an indicator of economic inequality that is based on women's earnings as a percentage of men's) has narrowed, according to the US Labor Department's Bureau of Labor Statistics, women still earn on average less than men – 83 percent of what men earned in 2014.[21] Thus, persistent economic inequality explains why lesbian households cluster in lower-income areas. Cultural differences between gay men and lesbians also matter. Studies have shown that men are more influenced by sexual marketplaces and institution-building, whereas women are more motivated by feminism, countercultures, and informal businesses (Brown-Saracino 2011). Other researchers emphasize family formation. Female same-sex partner households are more likely to have children, and so they have different needs for housing (Bouthillette 1997). Lesbians are also more likely to live in rural areas (Kazyak 2012), while gay men select bigger

The City

cities. Finally, some lesbians reject gayborhoods due to a perception that they do "not particularly welcome women" (Pritchard et al. 2002:105). All these reasons constrain the connection between lesbians and particular neighborhoods, but they do not negate it. I encourage you to keep an open mind about how gender, sexuality, and the city interact together; don't assume that gayborhoods represent all facets of LGBT life.

Let's also turn a critical eye on the meaning of concepts like "acceptance" and "integration." These words sound as if they represent positive outcomes for gay and straight people alike, but we need to balance that view with an appreciation for the benefits that gayborhoods provide for sexual minorities. They incubate unique sex cultures, as we've seen, but also political perspectives, organizations and businesses, families, rituals, and styles of socialization in and around specific urban spaces. At the end of a long day, gayborhoods still promise an incomparable sense of safety – hate crimes against gay and transgender people continue unabated, sadly – and thus they symbolize a place where LGBT people can seek refuge from heterosexual hostilities and discrimination as these take insidious new forms. For instance, did you know that rental discrimination against gay people is more aggravated beyond the gayborhood than it is within it (Lauster and Easterbrook 2011)?

Gayborhoods offer more than just a protective shield. They also provide a platform from which gays and lesbians can organize themselves as a voting bloc, if they want to work within the system (recall the California Supreme Court case), or as a social movement if they wish instead to rally against it (we'll talk about this point in the next chapter). The personal is political, as we know, which is why gayborhoods represent a space of freedom for gays and lesbians to discover who they are without being censored by the closet or surveilled by straights. The more we look, the more we see that gayborhoods have a hand in nearly every aspect of modern life: from the municipal promotion of urban spaces to city planning and the shaping of real-estate values; from the institutional development of gay and lesbian communities to their civic engagement; and from pride parades to protests. Because the stakes are so high, it's important to ask whether the language of

The City

acceptance and integration applies equally to *all* non-heterosexual people. Who exactly are we talking about when we celebrate cultural sameness? And why do many straight people champion it? I wish we had time to dive deeper into these provocative questions, but alas there's only so much that we talk about in one chapter. I hope that you will not let this be the last sentence you read on the subject but, rather, let it be the spark of many new pursuits.

Case Study: Priced Out or Evolving Out?

Scholars and policy analysts who study urban sex cultures are uncertain about how to assess the relative effects of economic and political triggers of change. Consider three sets of numbers that clarify how economic forces shape sex cultures in the city. First, home prices increased on average by 23 percent in zip codes with high concentrations of gay male households and by 18 percent in those with high concentrations of lesbian households. This "'gayborhood effect' isn't just simply a product of the fact that same-sex households live in cities that have dynamic economies," wrote Chris Matthews in his review of a new study published by Ralph McLaughlin, a housing economist at Trulia who assessed the appreciation of home prices from 2012 to 2015. "When you compare the neighborhoods with high concentrations of same-sex couples to the broader metro areas where these neighborhoods exist, you still find higher prices in the so-called gayborhoods."[22]

Second, same-sex households in 2000 earned on average US$15,000 less per annum than their opposite-sex counterparts. The wealth gap persisted in 2010, when 20 percent of same-sex households were living in poverty compared to just 9 percent of heterosexual households. In addition, recent research from the Williams Institute at UCLA shows that gay and bisexual men earn 10 to 32 percent less than similarly qualified straight men – even after we control for education, race, occupation, and years of work experience.[23]

The City

Finally, straights will always outnumber gays. The most recent numbers from the Centers for Disease Control and Prevention (CDC) show that 1.6 percent of the population identifies as gay or lesbian and a further 0.7 percent identifies as bisexual.[24]

The trends above pose challenges for gay neighborhoods. These urban areas experience greater increases in housing costs, yet gays, lesbians, and bisexuals, who comprise a small proportion of the population, earn less than heterosexuals. From this perspective, gayborhoods are not sustainable – eventually, either there won't be enough people who can afford the housing or there won't be enough gay people to make it sufficiently "gay" – unless gay people never move or, for those who own their homes, they sell only to other gay people. Neither is plausible.

The statistics above are compelling, and many people cite them. But a common conclusion that the media make is that gayborhoods are "passé" for gays, as the *New York Times* declared in the opening case study, yet suddenly desirable for straights. This opens the door for a competing perspective that highlights the role of political and cultural factors.

❖ *How do you think that the lower wages of gay, lesbian, and bisexual individuals, along with escalating home prices in gayborhoods, will affect the future of urban sex cultures?*
❖ *Economic statistics are important for understanding urban sex cultures, but are they complete? Why at this particular moment do you think we are witnessing so much gay flight out of the gayborhood and straight immersion into it?*
❖ *The story in the* New York Times *implies that culture shapes sex differently based on a person's sexual orientation. What are your thoughts about how this works?*
❖ *A lot of people disagree about whether gay people are "priced out" of the gayborhood or if instead they are "evolving out," if you will, in a post-gay era. What do you think about this debate? Does it suggest to you that sexuality is similar to, or different from, the other social categories of race, class, and gender?*

The City

Questions to Consider

1. Why are gayborhoods an effective way to learn about sex cultures?
2. Why is history and chronology a useful tool? How does it reveal the cultural arguments that we care about in this book?
3. What does it mean to say that gay identity is "spatially constructed"?
4. How have urban sex cultures changed across the closet, coming out, and post-gay eras?
5. Debate the merits of the post-gay thesis. What reasons do we have to believe in it? Why might we remain skeptical?
6. Do sex cultures require oppression? Do they require geographic specificity?
7. Compare the changes that are happening in gayborhoods with those that are happening in ethnic enclaves such as Chinatown (do a quick search online). Does sexuality operate as a unique driver for an otherwise common process of urban change? Or are the changes in gayborhoods similar to those in ethnic enclaves?
8. Although sexual identity is multiracial, gayborhoods are often quite white. How do you think race informs the cultural imagination of sexuality?
9. In the opening case study, Amy Sueyoshi expressed discontent with straight people who kiss in gay bars. Why would she and other LGBT people feel uneasy about public affection between heterosexuals in queer spaces?
10. Find a newspaper article or blog post that focuses on a gay neighborhood near you. Apply any two concepts from this chapter to analyze the article.

2

Politics and Protest

Case Study: Straight Gays

From the Grammy-nominated song "Same Love" by the American hip-hop stars Macklemore and Ryan Lewis to the Austrian pop sensation Conchita Wurst, who won the Eurovision Song Contest; from shows like *Orange is the New Black* to *Transparent*; from RuPaul's drag race to Matt Bomer guest-starring on *American Horror Story* with Lady Gaga, and from Ellen to Neil Patrick Harris and Apple CEO Tim Cook – gay and lesbian (and even transgender) lives are becoming unstoppably visible in the mainstream.

But there's an urgent question we need to ask about the meaning of this cultural visibility: "When Did Gays Get So Straight?" The provocation leapt off the cover of *New York* magazine in the late 1990s. In the story, Daniel Mendelsohn argues that the way that gays define themselves – what we would call their cultural imagination – has moved from the "exoticized gay margin to the normalized straight center" (1996: 31). The community's substance and style are now "hard to differentiate from those of the straight mainstream" (ibid.: 26). Once upon a time, gay politics had a distinctive and defiant edge: activists enforced the right to have sex in public places and bath houses, debated the morality of forcibly outing others, and used dramatic, theater-as-politics tactics such as ACT UP's disruption of Easter service at St Patrick's Cathedral. At the dawn of the new millennium, however, gay politics focused conservatively on marriage and adoption rights, inclusion in the armed forces, and employment non-discrimination.

Mendelsohn describes these changes as the "heterosexualization of gay culture" or "the over-time acceptance of mainstream cultural norms by those who were once revolutionaries" (Mendelsohn 1996: 27). During the 1990s, gay culture suffered from "a classic assimilationist ailment (c.f., Jews): You can't take away what was most difficult about being gay without losing what made gay culture interesting in the first place . . . [Y]ou realize that, at least culturally speaking, oppression may have been the best thing that could have happened to gay culture. Without it, we're nothing" (ibid.: 31).

Oppression is like the blood that binds together a family of sexual minorities. "The outrageous, epithet-wielding sensibility that defined the gay cultural ethos made sense only when gays were 'chained to the gates,'" Mendelsohn observes. "The bitchiness, the irony, all of the brilliance came of repression . . . But as the difference between institutional 'inside' and the gay 'outside' began to erode, the offensiveness seemed less productive." Discrimination created distinct and vibrant sex cultures. As public acceptance of gay and lesbian lives increases, however, their sense of belonging to a common tribe, to a closely knit sex culture, is crumbling.

Writing for *The Guardian*, Peter Tatchell made similar observations and attempted to use them to untangle the relationship between equality and culture in the UK. "Accepting mere equality involves the abandonment of any critical perspective on straight culture," he argued. Nearly fifty years have passed since the Stonewall riots, and in both the US and the UK "there has been a massive retreat from [a] radical vision," Tatchell lamented.[1] Emine Saner, also writing for *The Guardian*, put the point in a global perspective. "[E]very advance [in LGBT rights] is accompanied by a backlash . . . [T]hat's happening on a global scale now – the advances that are being made in some parts of the world encourage a backlash in other parts of the world."[2]

Mendelsohn, Tatchell, and Saner's impressions echo accounts in the academy. Steve Seidman (2002) says that we're moving "beyond the closet." Urvashi Vaid (1995) queries the "mainstreaming of gay and lesbian liberation." Jane (Ward 2008b) develops the counterintuitive notion of "respectably queer" to analyze the domestication of radical politics. And, in my own writings, I talk about the advent of a new "post-gay" era (Ghaziani 2011).

❖ *Why do you think gay culture and politics have become less radical and more mainstream?*
❖ *Do you think that social change is possible when members of a minority group feel as if they are culturally similar to the majority? What role does feeling different play in politics and protest?*
❖ *What types of LGBT people are visible to you? What does their visibility tell you about the cultural imagination of sexuality?*

The rapid rate at which LGBT people have gained acceptance in Western countries such as the United States and the United Kingdom represents the most impressive civil rights triumph of a generation. Homophobia and horrific hate crimes still exist, of course, but they are no longer casually condoned; they're now criticized from across the political spectrum. How has the activism to accomplish these changes unfolded over the years? And how has the cultural imagination of LGBT people shaped the trajectories of their activism? There are many forms that politics and paths to liberation can take, each as multifaceted as the concepts of culture and sexuality. Thanks to a massive growth in recent scholarship, which Gamson and Moon (2004: 47) characterize as "at once queer and phenomenal," we can now grapple with the relationship between sex cultures, politics, and protest.

Since their earliest days, LGBT activists have gone back and forth on their strategies for how to change the world. Should we embrace what makes us unique and protest the heteronormative assumptions of existing institutions such as marriage? Or should we assert our common humanity with heterosexuals and integrate into societal structures, work with straight allies, and demand that the government stay out of our lives? This tension between "sameness and difference" occupied the attention of the writers in the opening case study. Asking it, as we will do in this chapter, gets to the heart of our cultural approach.

Earlier generations of scholars were blinded by their particular biases, and, for many of them, thinking about LGBT protest was "an afterthought," Warner (1993b: ix) remarked. They were limited by the assumptions they made about sexuality, the same ones that we discussed in the Introduction. If you believe that sex is biology, then you won't see the cultural expressions of LGBT sexuality. Moreover, if you think homosexuality is an aberration of that biology, then you most certainly will not ask questions about social justice and social change for sexual minorities (you wouldn't see them as "minorities" at all). If you endorse the view that sex is personal and private, then it won't occur to you to think about sexuality as the basis for marching in the streets. If you see sex as fixed, then you won't possibly imagine the interactions between sexuality and society. No surprise, then, that earlier scholarship didn't even try to tackle the topics that we'll cover in this chapter: the sex cultures of gay liberationists, lesbian feminists, queer activists, and marriage equality activists. Part of what makes it possible for us to do so today is our ability to conceive of the sexual self as created in the maelstrom that is culture. Our goal in these pages is to understand how activists think about the meaning of sameness and difference and how their cultural imagination about these ideas shapes the choices they make about how to change the world.

Sameness and Difference

That ongoing debate among LGBT activists is neither new nor unique to them. All activists must decide whether to magnify or mute the distinctions that rationalize their disadvantaged social position, but these "difference troubles" (Seidman 1997) have been especially pronounced among sexual minorities. Social scientists have characterized this tension in many ways: the "movement of gay politics between radical separatism and assimilation" (Seidman 1993: 131); "boundary defending" versus "boundary stripping" (Gamson 1995: 400); "identity for critique" (creates distance from straights by criticizing them and their institutions) or "identity for education" (a strategy that brings straights closer in by teaching them about a common humanity) (Bernstein 1997: 538); "debates of identity and difference" (Epstein 1999: 32); "a focus on similarities or absolute opposition" (Valocchi 2005: 1371); "assimilationist and liberationist approaches" (Rimmerman 2008: 5); a "community consciousness" that expresses "distinctions" or one that moves toward their "deemphasis" (Ghaziani 2008: 296); and "absolute opposition or a focus on similarities" (Moon 2012: 1371). Humanists have followed suit, writing about "sex radicals at one end and assimilationists at the other" (Warner 1999: 43–4), or about "repeated assimilationist tirades against more flamboyant in-your-face gay activists" (Duggan 2002: 177).

Scholars who study social movements use the concept of "cycles of contention" (Tarrow 1998) to describe the outbreak of protest across the political system by different constituents. The famed activism in the 1960s is an example of a cycle of contention. The decade included actions staged by anti-war and anti-nuclear, civil rights, free speech, feminist, student, environmental, and gay activists. Despite belonging to different movements, these groups shared an anti-establishment and countercultural ethos as they tried to redefine the meaning of the so-called American Dream. What is more helpful for our purposes is the concept of "political sex cultures." Political sex cultures represent bursts – we might even say waves – of activism which occur within the same movement. Plurality is an important part of this definition. The notion of *the* civil rights movement as a singular entity is a fiction, for example, because it conceals the diverse political sex cultures of African-Americans. In an essay for the *Boston Review*, Doug McAdam remarked that civil rights activism consisted of "a coalition of thousands of local efforts nationwide, spanning several

Politics and Protest

decades, hundreds of discrete groups, and all manner of strategies and tactics – legal, illegal, institutional, non-institutional, violent, non-violent."[3] Regardless of whether we are talking about civil rights or LGBT activism, political sex cultures are characterized by a rapid diffusion of activism, an increase in both its organized and spontaneous forms, organizational change and tactical innovation, the emergence of new collective identities, and intensified interactions among movement actors, countermovements, and state authorities. Thinking about political sex cultures will allow us to see social movements as perennial and diverse but still interconnected.

LGBT activism in the United States has persisted continuously in one form or another since its inception in the 1940s. Like all movements for social change, it has adjusted its targets and trajectories. Many scholars have mistaken these "turning points" (Blee 2012) as representing the death or birth of new forms of insurgency. To avoid making the same mistake, we will emphasize the effects of the changing cultural imagination of activists, especially their ability to draw on lessons learned in the past as they make decisions about the most effective goals and tactics to use in the present and what to anticipate in the future. We will review research on three political sex cultures, each of which has been critical to the movement's mass mobilization and its success over time: gay liberation and lesbian feminism, queer activism, and marriage equality. The first two are illustrations of mobilizing around a sense of difference. We will compare these earlier sex cultures with a third, the effort to legalize same-sex marriage, which represents a recent turn toward sameness. As LGBT activists deliberate whether to emphasize their similarities to heterosexuals or their differences from them, they redefine their cultural imagination, which includes the field of perceived threat, an understanding of how power works within it, and their appraisal of strategies, tactics, goals, and targets in response. Like it was in the city, culture again is in the driver's seat in this chapter. When we look at protest and politics in such a way, we witness the ever-changing ways that culture kindles sex into sexuality.

Politics and Protest

Gay Liberation and Lesbian Feminism

Most scholars date the origins of the modern gay rights movement to the Stonewall riots of 1969, when street queens, queers of color, butch lesbians, and others fought back against an increasingly common practice: the police would raid their spaces, sometimes to arrest gays and lesbians and other times to harass or embarrass them (Duberman 1993). Before the Stonewall riots, gay and lesbian groups adopted a cautious approach, seeking to normalize their sexuality by emphasizing what made them similar to heterosexuals (Adam 1995). World War II and the Cold War called attention to discrimination in the military, and the post-war crackdown on homosexuals in government employment – the "Lavender Scare," which lasted even longer and affected more people than the "Red Scare" (Johnson 2004) – cultivated a cultural imagination that affirmed same-sex desire. Gays and lesbians formed local networks and organizations, including both the Mattachine Society and ONE in Los Angeles and the Daughters of Bilitis in San Francisco (D'Emilio 1983). Although small in numbers, the "homophile movement," as it was called, sought to improve gay and lesbian lives by fighting discriminatory laws and practices through publications, conferences, research, and media appearances; by providing support for people with same-sex desires; and by resisting the longstanding cultural tropes used to explain homosexuality – as a sickness or a sin, invariably linked with criminality or deviance (Meeker 2006).

As social movements of all kinds gained traction in the 1960s cycle of contention, the efforts of the homophile movement to demonstrate that gays were respectable and just like heterosexuals seemed, well, polite. Gay liberation and lesbian feminism exploded onto the scene in the late 1960s and early 1970s as radical spin-offs of the era's increasing militancy, as more men and women embraced a cultural imagination that demanded their rights out loud (D'Emilio 1983). The Gay Liberation Front formed in New York shortly after Stonewall, and the spread of similar groups to different cities and college campuses across the country was the turning point that marked this transition – from respectability to liberation and from fitting in to standing out – as emblematic of bold new political sex cultures. Composed of loosely structured groups that were influenced by the New Left, anti-war, and Black Power movements, gay liberationists proclaimed themselves anti-capitalist, anti-imperialist, and revolutionary.

The flurry of activism was astonishingly radical yet, in hindsight, also surprisingly conservative. Gay liberation was dominated by white men; women and people of color struggled to play central roles in the movement. These white men asserted that being gay was something to be proud of, but the term "gay" itself created problems since, as Armstrong (2002: 144) found, "organizations composed of gay men could and did represent themselves as including both gay men and lesbians even when lesbian participation was minimal or nonexistent." Consciously or not, gay men took advantage of ambiguities in the word "gay" and rendered women invisible. In response, women demanded that all existing organizations change their name from "gay" to "gay *and* lesbian." This was a rhetorical strategy, but it had profound consequences for the cultural imagination of activists then and today. For example, the National Gay Task Force was founded in New York City in 1973, and it quickly became a leading voice in local politics. In later years, the leadership of the organization renamed the group to the National Gay and Lesbian Task Force, "a move that marked both the specificity of lesbian life and politics and the coalition between lesbians and gay men."[4] Including the word "lesbian" in organizational names like this signaled that women's experiences of being gay were not identical to those of men and, at the same time, that lesbian issues mattered just as much as the concerns of gay men (ibid.: 145). As gay liberation forced Americans to acknowledge the presence of an entire group of people who were too often ignored, so also did the challenge from lesbians force gay men to expand their cultural imagination.

Gay people of color had to confront biases within gay liberation and lesbian feminist projects. Unlike women, people of color did not have a space within which their racial and sexual identities were reciprocally and equally celebrated. They felt the sting of racism from within the mostly white gay community, and they confronted homophobia from communities of color. As a result, many gay men and lesbians of color struggled to manage the mutuality of their racial and sexual identities. Audre Lorde described her experience:

> I find I am constantly being encouraged to pluck out some one aspect of myself and present this as the meaningful whole, eclipsing or denying the other parts of self. But this is a destructive and fragmenting way to live. My fullest concentration of energy is available to me only when I integrate all the parts of who I am. (Quoted in Armstrong 2002: 150)

Gay liberation and lesbian feminism represent some of the earliest articulations of sexual difference by activists. Unlike the homophile movement's "strategies of respectability" (Stein 2000: 211) and its aversion to anything transgressive, these new activists were adamant that their sexual differences should be celebrated. Gay liberationists advocated coming out, authenticity, and pride (Stein 2012), while lesbian feminists promoted social and cultural separatism (Taylor and Whittier 1992). From the outset, activists did not define themselves as a minority group seeking civil rights. Rather, inspired by the radical ideas circulating in the 1960s cycle of contention, they viewed gay liberation as part of a network of groups working against interlocking oppressions. For example, the name "Gay Liberation Front" was inspired by and expressed solidarity with the "Vietnamese National Liberation Front" (Staggenborg 2011: 119). Gay liberationists insisted that society must free itself from the moral restraints of the church, the legislative restrictions that the state imposed, and the pathological classifications of medical professionals (Warner 2002). Activists also embraced the "prefigurative politics" that characterized radical movements of the 1960s more generally. This style of engagement inspired activists to create organizations and relationships that modeled (or "prefigured") the ideal, egalitarian, and democratic society that they wished to build (Breines 1989). This ethos quickly became part of the cultural imagination of gay liberationists and lesbian feminists, and it compelled them to reject the notion of "a uniform and monolithic movement." Jim Owles of the New York Gay Activists Alliance opposed organizing around such a principle of uniformity because it supported the myth that gay people are "all alike." He advocated for activists to unite around their diversity as a political resource and as a way to counter stereotypes (Armstrong 2002).

Urban sex cultures emerged in big cities during the "great gay migration" (Weston 1995) of the 1970s, as we saw in the last chapter. These spatially based sex cultures made it possible for activists to unify around a visible, militant, and diverse gay identity in major cities. In June 1970, activists organized the first "gay freedom day" parades in New York, Chicago, and Los Angeles to commemorate the Stonewall riots. These "pride parades," as we call them today, spread across the country as a form of collective action that gays and lesbians used to assert their identities and resist heteronormative cultural codes by public displays of their gender and sexuality (Bruce 2013). Over the next two decades, gay liberation groups would continue to spring up across the United States and challenge conventional ideas about sexuality and the nuclear family. These groups were typically short-lived on account of the endemic internal conflicts associated with mobilizing around a logic of difference (Adam 1995). Cross-dressers, drag queens, and transsexuals were more accepted by gay liberationists than they were by homophile activists, although not by much, and women and people of color continued to accuse the gay liberation movement of sexism and racism (Jay 1999). Women of color also challenged the assumption of a united collective identity among lesbian feminists (Stein 1997), as did bisexuals and transgender individuals who felt excluded from feminist efforts (Gamson 1997).

Despite mobilizing through separate networks and organizations – embodying their own political sex cultures, in other words – gay liberationists and lesbian feminists took a similar path. They each targeted the broader culture as the source of oppression, favored direct action, established free spaces to nurture a political consciousness (Evans and Boyte 1986), and championed coming out to promote the growth and political power of their communities. Visibility was a key tactic. Lesbian feminists created distinct

Politics and Protest

communities through music festivals, theaters, conferences, art, journals and small presses, record companies, and other businesses. The convergence of lesbian separatism and a growing women's counterculture spawned "cultural feminism," a strand of feminist thought that valorized women's difference from men, criticized heterosexuality as a form of internalized male domination, and promoted separation from men and relationships with women as a political strategy (Echols 1989). In a similar way, the chant "out of the closet, into the streets" shows how gay liberationists smashed open the doors of secrecy and silence to dispel stereotypes, assert a proud identity, and normalize homosexuality in everyday life (Humphreys 1972). Together, gay liberationists and lesbian feminists stimulated non-profit and commercial organizations, community newspapers and magazines, media visibility, and the development of gay neighborhoods, all of which nurtured the growth of future political sex cultures. The key to ensuring these generative outcomes was the expression of a public and celebratory gay and lesbian cultural imagination, even if it was mostly local and regional at the time.

Queer Activism

Gay and lesbian life during the 1960s and 1970s lacked a national fiber. Although there were different ways to imagine what it meant to be a sexual minority, many did so within the well-established though secluded gayborhoods that we saw in the last chapter. These urban districts provided freedom to "be gay," however one might choose (Escoffier 1998). As physically concentrated sites, gayborhoods allowed people to fuse sex with a shared culture – and eventually a political paradigm as well – as activists met and exchanged ideas about their collective experiences. It was in this cultural crucible that the popular slogan "We Are Everywhere" arose. Some attribute its origins to the 1960s radical hippie activist Jerry Rubin of the Youth International Party, or "yippies," who published a manifesto with this title in 1971. Gay liberationists traveled in similar circles with other New Left activists, and so

Politics and Protest

it didn't take long before gay and lesbian activists picked it up. They "printed up stickers so that a gay person who saw one, say in a conference room in the Pentagon, or a sorority house, would know that another proud gay person had been there" (Shenk and Silberman 1994: 308). Appropriating "We Are Everywhere" communicated something that many people knew instinctively but couldn't yet say with words: that the gay and lesbian cultural imagination was growing national.

Political organizing developed rapidly through the 1970s as gays and lesbians became collectively visible through their annual freedom day parades and through individual acts of coming out. Their physical presence, along with an effervescing feeling of being everywhere, created a demand for a symbol that could embody their cultural imagination. In 1978, a San Francisco native, Gilbert Baker, embraced the challenge. Responding to the request of the San Francisco Gay and Lesbian Freedom Day Committee, Baker and thirty volunteers hand-dyed and hand-stitched two flags for the June 25, 1978, San Francisco Freedom Day Parade. The flag contained eight horizontal stripes, each a different color, producing an effect that resembled a rainbow. Baker's design earned him the affectionate nickname "the gay Betsy Ross" (Ghaziani 2008).

The concept for the new flag was aesthetic but also deliberate; each color was a symbol of its own. Hot pink represented sex, red stood for life, orange for healing, yellow for the sun, green for serenity with nature; turquoise symbolized art, indigo harmony, and violet spirit. The colors combined to affirm community diversity, united under a single symbol. Practical factors such as costs and production constraints (hot pink wasn't commercially available then) resulted in the dropping of hot pink and turquoise, and royal blue replaced indigo. Thus, 1979 witnessed the birth of what we recognize today as the primary symbol of gay pride: a six-striped (red, orange, yellow, green, blue, and violet) rainbow flag, sometimes referred to as "the freedom flag." The flag diffused rapidly across the country – indeed, across the globe – and became the most prominent cultural symbol for gay pride.

During the next decade, activists confronted a number of menacing threats, including those posed by the religious right,

Politics and Protest

the Supreme Court's criminalization of sodomy in the *Bowers v. Hardwick* (1986) case, and life-threatening challenges posed by the spread of HIV, especially the Reagan administration's slow response to the crisis (Gould 2009). The president avoided using the word "AIDS" in a public address for the first six years of the epidemic, and, even then, he refused to acknowledge that gay men were dying in disproportionate numbers.

As government officials denied the growing public health crisis, and as stigma and discrimination against people with HIV/AIDS worsened, gay and lesbian activists took matters into their own hands with direct actions. Although the disease disproportionately infected men, lesbians were vital in the movement, and decades of feminist advocacy for women's health was an important inspiration for AIDS activism (Schneider and Stoller 1995). Feminist beliefs about control over your body, resistance to medical authority, patient inclusion in medical decision-making, and discriminatory practices in health care fueled the formation in 1987 of the AIDS Coalition to Unleash Power (ACT UP) in New York City. The potent combination of community development, diverse voices, and exogenous threats provided a turning point in the cultural imagination, one that renewed gay rage and motivated activists to assert their differences aggressively from straight people.

Queer activism emerged in this explosive context. It took shape in organizations such as Queer Nation, ACT UP, the Lesbian Avengers, Transgender Nation, and the North American Bisexual Network, all of which were based on the notion of social movements as utopian "nations" and of activists as embodying "peoplehood" (Walker 1997: 505). Characterized by an in-your-face style of confrontational protest, queer activists blended material targets such as pharmaceutical companies with cultural targets such as silence and stigma (Gamson 1989). They pursued a program that we might call "cultural provocation" and a "theatrical politics of parody," using everything from street parades to graffiti art (Warner 1993a), while also relying on legal suits and op-ed pieces to confront doctors, biomedical researchers, and scientists about their treatment of AIDS (Epstein 1996). Signature actions of queer activists included kiss-ins, mall takeovers, infiltrating straight bars, dressing in drag and camping it up, distributing flyers and countercultural zines in urban neighborhoods, medical outreach and education about HIV/AIDS, and spray painting sex-positive graffiti in public spaces (Berlant and Freeman 1993). Participating in queer protest events affirmed the value of a militant cultural imagination.

Queer activism was in close conversation with academic "queer theory," a framework which emerged in the 1980s in conferences at elite American universities (Seidman 1996). Queer theorists oppose invariant sexual categories, arguing that binary labels such as gay or straight, male or female, masculine or feminine are ways that society regulates sex and gender. This is why queer theorists rally around Foucault's insight about the transition from sex to sexuality that we considered earlier: the modern homosexual was born as a culturally specific "species" in 1870 when sodomy was redefined from an act to a disposition. Queer theorists hold that the process of lumping and splitting the social world into dichotomous expressions is inconsistent with the fluid and continuous nature of sexuality, including our attractions, behaviors, and identities. Research by Peter Hennen (2008) shows that effeminacy and homosexuality were wed in opposition to masculinity and heterosexuality in the eighteenth century, despite the fact that masculinity, even today, doesn't require a male body (Halberstam 1998). Because our existing categories of sex, gender, and sexuality imperfectly map onto people's lived experiences, some queer theorists push to expand our cultural imagination by identifying multiple categories (such as asexual, bisexual, or polyamorous) and arguing that sexuality is a continuum (think about Kinsey's research, for example). Others call for reconceptualizing the logic that we use to create the categories themselves. This deconstructionist impulse has a long history in the social sciences (Green 2007), and it motivated queer theorists to focus on discursive struggles, rather than electoral politics, as their favored form of protest.

Queer protest embodies contradictory logics. Activists work to bring together people who feel perverse, odd, deviant, and different while affirming their common identity as being on the fringe or periphery of the mainstream. This contradiction is codified in the name of the activist group Queer Nation. Whereas the word "queer" denotes difference, "nation" emphasizes sameness. Queer activists who feel like they belong to the group Queer Nation are "torn between affirming a new identity – 'I am queer' – and rejecting restrictive identities – 'I reject your categories' – between rejecting assimilation – 'I don't need your approval, just get out of my face' – and wanting to be recognized by mainstream society – 'We queers are gonna get in your face'" (Bérubé and Escoffier 1991: 14). Thus, Queer Nation exemplifies the promises and pitfalls that activists confront if they attempt to balance sameness (we are queers, and we comprise a nation united) and difference (we reject your categories and cultural forms) in just one group.

Queer activism embodied a set of collective norms about sex and sexuality – or political sex cultures, as we are calling them. Activists shared a radical ethos with gay liberationists and lesbian feminists, but they differed in their approach by destabilizing and blurring the boundaries of sexual identities. Josh Gamson (1995: 390) calls this the "queer dilemma," an idea which highlights the difficulties in advocating simultaneously for sameness and difference. In examining the San Francisco Gay Freedom Day Parade which had as its theme "The Year of the Queer," Gamson found that participants tried to recognize a wide variety of sexualities, called attention to intersecting forms of oppression, and endeavored to break apart the binaries. His analysis shows that it can be "as liberating and sensible to demolish a collective identity as it is to establish one" (ibid.: 402). Queer activists have had to delicately balance these opposing logics that at times were only thinly shared; some struggled for acceptance by the mainstream while others pushed for a radical rejection of heteronormativity.

As individuals, queer activists perceived the world in multifaceted ways. Their cultural imagination embraced anger and parody, most importantly, but they also celebrated a militant definition of difference and promoted the effervescent qualities of radical activism. Through their signature actions, queer activists demonstrated that bodies are not just biological masses, they are not privately managed entities, and they are not fixed for all time. Queer bodies became the frontlines of their public protests. Queer activism also revealed that cultural sources of oppression, such as stigma and stereotypes, media representations, and public opinion, are effectively addressed by exposing the falsehood of sexual binaries. The most visible group, Queer Nation, emerged in the late 1980s but faltered by the mid-1990s because it was unable to present a viable organizational infrastructure around which other movements could rally (Ward 2008b). Thus, there are some words of caution which we should consider. Changing laws and public policies requires activists to create legible identities with solid boundaries, regardless of whether those signal sameness or difference. Like queer theory, the political sex cultures of queer activists needed to address the "very concrete and violent institutional forms" that made their sexuality "a basis for discipline, regulation, pleasure, and political empowerment" (Gamson 1995: 400). This required them to couple sex with cultural critique and then locate their emergent cultural imagination in specific laws, policies, and institutions.

Marriage Equality

Nothing better illustrates the tension between sameness and difference than the battle for marriage equality. The campaign for it did not begin with mainstream organizations but from couples who simply wanted to wed. Some of them brought lawsuits as early as the 1970s, while others expressed their mutual commitment through public rituals (even if the government didn't recognize their gestures as legal). Many activists believed that LGBT people contended with such an oppressive climate, even into the early 1990s, that the pursuit of same-sex marriage was unthinkable (Chauncey 2004). Since 1974, for example, the religious right has sponsored over 200 anti-gay ballot measures challenging gay rights at the state and municipal levels. Almost 70 percent were successful, making LGBT people the target of the largest amount of discriminatory legislation directed at a single group in recent US history (Stone 2012). Though these defeats made mainstream

Politics and Protest

acceptance seem illusory, they also created a moral shock, one that molded a new cultural imagination that motivated activists to mobilize around the legal goals of relationship recognition through such national organizations as the Human Rights Campaign, the National Lesbian and Gay Task Force, the Lambda Legal Defense and Education Fund, and the National Center for Lesbian Rights, as well as local and state groups formed to fight these incessant ballot initiatives (Boutcher 2010).

The LGBT movement put marriage on its national agenda for the first time in 1987 at the third March on Washington for Lesbian and Gay Rights (Ghaziani 2008). Couples, Inc., a Los Angeles-based organization fighting for legal recognition for same-sex partners, organized The Wedding, a ceremony that celebrated gay and lesbian relationships and demanded that such partnerships receive the same rights as married heterosexual couples. Although several thousand couples participated, it was the most controversial event of the march. Echoing feminist critiques, and foreshadowing the queer position on marriage that would emerge after the march, critics argued that The Wedding promoted traditional monogamous relationships and patriarchal family forms that were inconsistent with the sexual freedom espoused by gay liberationists, and that it would redirect the movement toward a mainstream, "homonormative" agenda (Duggan 2003). Despite the ambivalence toward marriage that activists expressed, however, the HIV/AIDS crisis and the lesbian baby boom of the 1980s led increasing numbers of lesbians and gay men to a growing awareness of their need for legal rights and relationship protections.

The marriage campaign gained momentum six years after the march on Washington, when activists jumped into the fray surrounding a legal case filed in 1993 by same-sex couples seeking marriage licenses in Hawaii. In *Baher v. Lewin*, the Hawaii Supreme Court ruled initially that banning gays and lesbians from marriage violated the equal protection clause of the Constitution. The possibility that lesbians and gays might obtain the legal right to marry catapulted same-sex marriage to the top of the right's political agenda, resulting in the 1996 federal Defense of Marriage Act (DOMA), which restricted marriage to "one man and one

Politics and Protest

woman" and allowed states and the federal government to refuse to recognize same-sex marriages performed in other states. Appeals mounted by the right eventually led the Hawaii Supreme Court to rule that same-sex couples didn't have the legal grounds to marry, and the legislature passed its own state-level DOMA in the form of a constitutional amendment.

In the meantime, same-sex couples filed copycat suits in other states. Activists in Vermont scored a victory in 1999 when the state Supreme Court ruled, in *Baker v. State of Vermont*, that same-sex partners must be granted the same benefits as married heterosexual couples. The Court ordered the legislature to remedy the situation, and the result was a compromise that granted all the benefits of marriage but denied symbolic equality by creating the separate term "civil unions" exclusively for same-sex relationships (Bernstein and Burke 2013). The passage of anti-gay initiatives increased after the Hawaii and Vermont cases, and over the next decade the right placed DOMA initiatives on the ballot in thirty-five states. The feverish jousting between the LGBT movement and the religious right countermovement had the unintended consequence of extracting gay and lesbian issues from the cultural margins, where queer activists operated, and placing them at the center of politics and public discourse (Fetner 2008).

On the defensive against a seemingly all-powerful foe, and betrayed by the federal government with DOMA, in 2004 LGBT activists increased the pace of collective action to promote marriage equality. That year, Massachusetts became the first state to legalize same-sex marriage, creating additional opportunities for mobilization by the LGBT movement and their opponents. Activists also invented an innovative new direct action tactic intended to capture more public attention. Same-sex couples began showing up at licensing counters across the United States, demanding marriage licenses, and holding weddings in city halls and other public places. The largest protest took place in San Francisco in February 2004, when Mayor Gavin Newsom directed the city to issue marriage licenses to same-sex couples (Taylor et al. 2009). During the month-long "winter of love," more than 4,000 same-sex couples married at City Hall, creating a public spectacle that gripped media attention. The San Francisco protest led to a series of lawsuits opposing the weddings, and the California Supreme Court voided them all in August – but a groundswell of support for marriage equality quickly resurfaced. Four years later, the California Supreme Court reversed its earlier decision and ruled it unconstitutional to exclude same-sex couples from marriage, making it possible for 18,000 same-sex couples to wed during what activists called the "summer of love." In the same year, however, opponents introduced Proposition 8 (Prop 8 for short) to ban those marriages in the state. Prop 8 was the most heavily funded anti-gay ballot initiative ever mounted by the right. Their vitriolic media campaign, which attempted to influence the cultural imagination of Americans more broadly, portrayed same-sex parents as a danger to children and their marriage as a threat to tradition (Oliviero 2013). Prop 8 passed in November 2008 with 52 percent of the vote, ending same-sex marriage in California.

The passage of Prop 8 was a game changer for LGBT activists. By fighting it and other ballot initiatives in southern and heartland states, movement organizations that had debated but deliberately avoided visibility strategies now focused on publicly claiming a gay or lesbian identity (Stone 2012), signaling a major shift in their political sex cultures. After the Prop 8 defeat, LGBT groups mobilized through emotion-laden direct action tactics, suggesting a powerful continuity with queer activist sensibilities. These tactics included wedding protests organized in shopping malls and parking lots; "courageous conversations" that involved coming out to friends, neighbors, and co-workers; and storytelling by gay and lesbian couples who tried to educate the public about the discrimination their families faced (Taylor et al. 2009). In these public education campaigns, the national organization Freedom to Marry and other groups abandoned their strategy of framing marriage as a civil right (Hull 2001), which had failed to win public support in the campaign to defeat Prop 8, and switched to a less oppositional frame: marriage as an equal right to love and commitment (Moscowitz 2013). This is a good example of how sameness ascended in the place of difference in the political sex cultures that formed around the fight for marriage equality.

Politics and Protest

Changes in the broader political context at this time gave LGBT activists and movement organizations greater access to the courts and the support of elite allies, including Barack Obama, who in 2012 became the first sitting president to support same-sex marriage. The accumulation of support provided an opening for activists to mobilize the law and public opinion in support of marriage equality, and, as the name they gave to their effort implies, marriage equality relied on a strategic articulation of sameness. Public opinion followed suit and began to shift in favor of marriage equality; by the late 2000s, more than half of the US population was in support of it (Powell et al. 2010). The right swayed the cultural imagination of the American public in the short term, but their hostile worldview proved unsustainable.

In 2013, the US Supreme Court invalidated Prop 8, and same-sex marriages resumed in California. At the same time, in *United States v. Windsor*, the Court struck down Section 3 of DOMA, which defined marriage under federal law as the union of one man and one woman, as unconstitutional. The case was brought by an elderly lesbian who, after her partner died, would have been left homeless since, unprotected by federal policy, she could not afford the taxes on their house. During the months leading up to the trial, national organizations promoted a "post-gay" collective identity (Ghaziani 2011) that deepened their feelings of sameness with straights, thereby creating a reciprocal bridge with the cultural imagination of the larger American population. A frequent tactic that activists used in court cases like this was to seek support from allies, including women's and civil rights activists, academics, medical and professional associations, and businesses, all of whom filed amicus briefs, or legal petitions to influence judicial decisions.

United States v. Windsor set the stage for numerous state lawsuits sponsored by LGBT organizations that resulted in legalized same-sex marriage in thirty-seven states. Several other states, mainly in the South but also the Midwest, refused to lift their bans, and the US Supreme Court agreed to hear four cases challenging them, in Kentucky, Michigan, Ohio, and Tennessee. In a historic ruling on June 26, 2015, the Court found that bans on marriage equality were unconstitutional and ruled that gay and

Politics and Protest

lesbian couples have the same right to marry as other US citizens. This prompted President Obama to tweet #LoveWins, echoing the movement's own language of cultural sameness. The case in question, *Obergefell v. Hodges* (2015), was brought by an Ohio man who rushed to marry his dying partner inside a medical transport plane on the tarmac of Baltimore airport, where same sex-marriage was legal. Because of its ban, the state of Ohio refused his request to be listed on his husband's death certificate.

The fight for marriage created a rift among activists who espoused different political perspectives. For gay liberationists, lesbian feminists, and queer activists, marriage was an oppressive institution that undermined sexual freedom and an unabashedly queer cultural imagination, and it symbolized the mainstream movement's desire to normalize gay and lesbian identities in order to fit into US society, rather than fundamentally restructure it (Bernstein and Taylor 2013). The groups who celebrated queerness and thus difference all felt silenced by national and state organizations' use of tactics such as shoring up collective identities with hard boundaries, fund-raising around it, political messaging and lobbying to normalize it, and litigating as the primary tactic for social change (Warner 1999).

Bernstein and Taylor (2013) suggest that the debate over marriage boiled down to three major concerns: marriage would assimilate gays into the heterosexual mainstream and dilute their cultural distinctions; emphasizing similarities between gays and the straight majority would depoliticize their sex cultures; and the movement's emphasis on marriage would benefit the sex cultures of white, middle-class, cisgender gay couples, thereby further marginalizing poor queers, queers of color, bisexuals, and transgender people. One of the most vocal opponents, Lisa Duggan (2003: 188), condemned the campaign for marriage as "a strategy for privatizing gay politics and culture for the new neoliberal world order," putting LGBT people behind a white picket fence where they would no longer challenge heteronormativity. Although queer opponents have been outspoken in their objections to marriage, research suggests that the majority of the LGBT community is less ambivalent (Hull and Ortyl 2013).

Politics and Protest

As with earlier waves of protest, relatively little research has focused on the participation of women in marriage equality, despite the fact that lesbian individuals and organizations played central roles in both advocating and opposing same-sex marriage. Some scholars suggest that the traditional association of women with marriage, weddings, and parenting gave lesbians a heightened symbolic role in marriage equality activism. In her study of couples who married in the 2004 San Francisco wedding protest, Katrina Kimport (2014) found that the meaning of marriage varied significantly based on gender and parenthood. Lesbians made up 57 percent of the couples who wed, and they outnumbered gay male couples by nearly two to one in states where marriage became legal. Lesbians were also more likely than gay men to be parents, and couples with children offered social recognition of their families as a reason to marry, although this was somewhat less true for people of color for whom marriage was not as essential in defining a family. At the same time, lesbians were also more likely to use feminist critiques to express ambivalence about marriage.

Marriage was the central and most controversial issue of the LGBT movement in the first decade of the twenty-first century. The growing organizational leverage of activists, their use of the courts, and their framing of marriage as an equal right to love and commitment shifted the cultural imagination of activists away from a lens of difference, a desire for societal transformation, and sexual liberation; instead, national organizations and activists emphasized the similarities between themselves and the heterosexual mainstream. The resulting controversies among activists that we've seen around this most recent wave of protest illustrates a point worth repeating: sex cultures, like the cultural imagination of the individuals who participate in them, are never singular or static.

Conclusions

We used debates about sameness and difference to examine the political sex cultures of gay liberationists, lesbian feminists,

Politics and Protest

queer activists, and activists who fought for marriage equality. Conversations about whether LGBT people are similar to or different from heterosexuals shaped the cultural imagination of activists who participated in these groups, which in turn directed their choice of strategies, tactics, and identities. Gay liberation and lesbian feminism successfully created a collective and celebratory public identity that they saw as comparable to racial and ethnic ones. After these movements declined, the cultural imagination of a new group of queer activists expanded to reflect the interests of bisexuals, transgender individuals, and others who resisted normative societal prescriptions about gender and sexuality. Finally, the recent wave of marriage activism highlighted the staying power of sameness among a current generation of activists. In each of these political sex cultures, we see the cardinal point of this book: culture shapes sex into sexuality in ways that have synchronic and diachronic effects.

The discussion above, and throughout the chapter, suggests that we need to distinguish the idea of "sex cultures" from the "cultural imagination." Sex cultures are collective, the product of a group. We each belong to sex cultures – at least one but likely more. In the process of mobilizing for change, LGBT people experience the effervescent qualities of activism as they interact with other activists, straight people, the government, and countermovements. All of this shapes their understanding of what it means to be a sexual minority, as does the surrounding context of mobilization, which includes a set of norms about social justice and inequality that defines the place and promise of sexuality. Consider the contrast between the Lavender Scare and Obama tweeting #LoveWins as one example. Now that we have repeatedly attached the word "cultures" to the word "sex," we begin to see an emerging pattern. Sex is not just something we do with our bodies. It is not always a personal and private matter. It is not universal and fixed for all time. Sex cultures are powerfully social, and they are wrapped in a dense web of meanings. They are also political – hence our use of the phrase "political sex cultures" in this chapter. By contrast, a cultural imagination is something that we harbor individually and that we bring to the table in our conversations with others. It is shaped by more than one person, much like the sociological imagination, but it is a way of seeing the world (and politics in this case) that each of us has within ourselves. It is a filter, if you will, that brings into focus the many meanings we perceive as we navigate and negotiate our place in the world.

Despite recent attention to LGBT activism by social scientists and humanities scholars, there is still so much more for us to learn. First, we know more about queer politics and lesbian feminism than we do gay liberation and contemporary movements. As a result, we have scant knowledge of LGBT mobilization using conventional indicators such as protest events (how often is there a march or rally?), media coverage (how much attention does the group receive, by which paper, and where in it is the story published?), individual recruitment (how do we get people involved in the movement?), and the birth of new organizations (how can we explain the emergence of new groups?). In addition, we need to recognize that the sameness/difference tension is not unique to LGBT activism but applies to other movements as well. Compare the language of Martin Luther King's "I Have a Dream" speech with what we've heard from the Black Lives Matter movement. Dominant paradigms in social movement theory have failed to acknowledge that shifts in the cultural imagination are a key element of protest waves. As we continue thinking about political sex cultures, we must keep in mind that sameness and difference are not oppositional outcomes; they lie on a continuum from one to the other. Once we acknowledge this insight, we can ask how, unlike in the case of Queer Nation, a logic of difference can be viable in an era of marriage equality. Finally, published research that pays attention to turning points and multiple protest waves stresses the centrality of human agency in activism. We need more dialogue to assess what incites the turning points themselves, to determine whether certain sex cultures have more formative consequences, to analyze the relationship between turning points and the cultural imagination of activists, and to trace the impact of all of this on laws, policies, and public opinion.

Case Study: What Does Victory Mean?

On June 26, 2015, the United States become the twenty-first country in the world to legalize same-sex marriage. *Obergefell v. Hodges* ended a battle that had been brewing in the states for forty-five years. Justice Anthony Kennedy wrote the 5–4 majority opinion:

> No union is more profound than marriage, for it embodies the highest ideals of love, fidelity, devotion, sacrifice, and family. In forming a marital union, two people become something greater than once they were. As some of the petitioners in these cases demonstrate, marriage embodies a love that may endure even past death. It would misunderstand these men and women to say they disrespect the idea of marriage. Their plea is that they do respect it, respect it so deeply that they seek to find its fulfillment for themselves. Their hope is not to be condemned to live in loneliness, excluded from one of civilization's oldest institutions. They ask for equal dignity in the eyes of the law. The Constitution grants them that right.

The decision was "a crowning achievement but also a confounding challenge to a group that has often prided itself on being different," noted Jodi Kantor, writing for the *New York Times*, in her aptly titled essay "Gay Culture's Outsider Element Fades as Marriage Rights Arrive." Kantor explained the conundrum: "The more victories that accumulate for gay rights, the faster some gay institutions, rituals, and markers are fading out. And so, just as the gay marriage movement peaks, so does a debate about whether gay identity is dimming, overtaken by its own success." The film critic John Waters conceded the same in his 2015 commencement speech at the Rhode Island School of Design: "Refuse to isolate yourself. Separatism is for losers. Gay is not enough anymore."[5]

Kantor spoke with celebrated gay and lesbian public intellectuals who offered similar observations about the paradoxical contributions of oppression. Andrew Sullivan wondered, "What do gay men have in common when they don't have oppression?" The historian Eric Marcus similarly mused, "There is something wonderful about being part of an oppressed community." Finally, Lisa Kron, who wrote the book and lyrics for the Broadway musical *Fun Home*, reflected, "The thing I miss is the specialness of being gay. Because the traditional paths were closed, there was a consciousness to our lives, a necessary invention to the way we were going to celebrate and mark family and mark connection. That felt magical and beautiful." All these sentiments have an uncanny resemblance to the questions that Mendelsohn asked nearly twenty years earlier in his essay "When Did Gays Get So Straight?" (see the opening case study).

Although the marriage decision was a huge win for gay and lesbian rights, it does not mean that the struggle is over, any more than it signals the erasure of a cultural imagination based on difference. "We can pass all of the laws we want and talk about public policy until we run out of air, but until our society stops thinking of queer people as deviant or corrupt or sinful or in any way less than non-queer people, nothing is going to change," said Noah Michelson, founding editor of *HuffPost Queer Voices*.

More than a year after the Supreme Court decision, many battles remain unfinished, including adoption rights, which equal marriage does not resolve, workplace discrimination, conversion therapy, housing discrimination, acceptance in sports and politics, health risks, restrictions on gay men that prevent them from giving blood, anti-gay harassment and violence, hate crimes, suicide, homelessness, and transgender rights. The view of gay people as culturally and sexually different from straights persists. "It's probably the most difficult thing we face," Michelson continued. He explains how to overcome it:

> The only way to do it [challenge it] is to come out as queer whenever we can. And once we're out, we need to talk openly and honestly about our lives and who we love and how we have sex. It's only after we've challenged and changed the most basic and fundamental viewpoints about who we are that we can really begin to think about true liberation and true equality.[6]

Politics and Protest

After the *Obergefell* decision, LGBT Americans were left wondering about the meaning of their so-called victory. The historian Timothy Stewart-Winter wrote in the *New York Times*,

> The graver danger comes not from the religious right, but from the risk that our newfound clout will blind some of us to the struggles of others. More gays are insiders than ever before; a gay man leads Apple, one of America's most valuable corporations. A lesbian, Tammy Baldwin, Democrat of Wisconsin, was elected to the Senate in 2012. Prominent Republicans, libertarians, financiers and chief executives have given their names, time and money to the cause of same-sex marriage.[7]

Stewart-Winter cautioned not to overstate an argument of cultural sameness, since "many more gay and transgender Americans are permanent outsiders. Some churches are doubling down on anti-gay rhetoric, which fuels family rejection and contributes to youth homelessness. Violence against transgender Americans is on the rise. Gay people in prison remain subject to rape and abuse. Rates of new H.I.V. infections are rising among young black men." LGBT movements can learn from other groups here. "Just as feminists learned after the 19th Amendment was ratified in 1920, a social movement that throws most of its weight in pursuit of a single policy may falter and stagnate when it achieves a resounding victory."

What does Stewart-Winter think we should do? He offers a history lesson:

> The gay movement has stood for valuing all families – including those led by single parents, those with adopted children, and other configurations. It has stood for other ideas, too, that risk being lost in this moment's pro-family turn: that intimacy, domesticity and caretaking do not always come packaged together; that marriage should not be the only way to protect one's children, property and health; that having a family shouldn't be a requirement for full citizenship; and that conventional respectability shouldn't be the only route to social acceptance.

Politics and Protest

In other words, there should be room for difference at the table.

❖ *What are the advantages and disadvantages of an approach that emphasizes the similarities between a minority group and the majority? Consider next the advantages and disadvantages of an approach that emphasizes difference. What can these strategies accomplish?*
❖ *Does acceptance from the mainstream of society cause minority sex cultures to wither? What are your thoughts about the relationship between oppression and culture more generally?*
❖ *From a global perspective, the repression of gays is far from over. In Russia, President Putin has passed numerous anti-gay laws, including legislation that punishes people who distribute information considered "propaganda of non-traditional sexual relations." The country can also arrest and detain foreign citizens believed to be gay – or even "pro-gay."[8] In February 2014, the president of Uganda signed an anti-gay bill into law that punishes gay sex with life imprisonment. Consider as well that homosexuality is punishable by death in five countries: Iran, Saudi Arabia, Yemen, the Islamic Republic of Mauritania, and Sudan. What can activism that is based on a logic of sameness accomplish in such hostile contexts? What can activism that is based on a logic of difference accomplish in hostile contexts?*

Questions to Consider

1 What do scholars mean when they talk about a tension between "sameness and difference" in LGBT activism?
2 What are "political sex cultures"? Why is this manifestation of the more general sex cultures concept useful for us?
3 What is the difference between the cultural imagination and sex cultures?
4 Compare gay liberation and lesbian feminism, queer activism, and marriage equality. What do these political sex cultures

teach us about how the cultural imagination affects politics and protest?
5 Why is it important for organizations to include the word "lesbian" in their name? Why is it not enough to just say "gay"?
6 What types of actions did queer activists pursue? What was their goal?
7 What did the fight for marriage equality symbolize to queer activists?
8 What new direct action tactic did same-sex couples create to capture public attention about marriage equality?
9 Changing the cultural frame of marriage equality helped activists to win public support. Describe the shift that they made.
10 Find a newspaper article or blog post that focuses on a social movement other than the ones we considered in this chapter. What evidence can you find of the sameness/difference tension?

3

Heterosexualities

Case Study: Straight Men Kissing

During a 2012 soccer playoff game against Germany, Oliver Giroud from France scored the first of two goals that would declare the French team the victors. A teammate of Giroud's, midfielder Mathieu Debuchy, "grabbed his head with both hands and kissed his teammate," reports *The Local*, France's English newspaper, in an article with a double-entendre headline, "French Kiss Celebrates Victory Over Germany." A photograph of this straight man-on-man action accompanied the article.[1]

The sociologist Eric Anderson and his colleagues find that young straight men in England are redefining the meaning of a kiss: it is no longer an expression of erotic behavior, which would mark them as gay, but rather a means of homosocial bonding. "Kissing happens all the time in football," one of his interviewees told him. "Loads of guys kiss on the lips after scoring a goal" (Anderson et al. 2012: 424).

A 2015 poll of 1,632 young British men and women aged eighteen to twenty-four similarly found that the cultural imagination of heterosexuality is diversifying for this generation. Only 46 percent self-identified as "completely heterosexual" and 6 percent as "completely homosexual." Everyone else

Heterosexualities

Table 3.1 Percentage of adults identifying as heterosexual/homosexual or bisexual by age group (measured by self-placement on the Kinsey scale)

Age	Heterosexual or homosexual	Degrees of bisexuality
18–24	52	43
25–39	67	29
40–59	81	16
60+	89	7

Source: created with data from YouGov, 2015.

adopted some shade of bisexuality. In contrast, 67 percent of those aged twenty-five to thirty-nine, 81 percent of those aged forty to fifty-nine, and 89 percent of those aged sixty and above identified as completely heterosexual.[2]

Writing for *The Guardian*, Rebecca Nicholson says that the hard binary between gay or straight is crumbling. "Sexuality now falls between the lines. Identity is more pliable, and fluidity more acceptable, than ever before." To make this vivid, Nicholson interviewed a 23-year-old woman from Sussex who described herself as "bisexual homoromantic," by which she meant, "It means I like sex with men and women, but I only fall in love with women." She noted that many of her friends "talk about their sexuality in terms of behaviour these days, rather than in terms of labels. So they'll say, 'I like boys,' . . . rather than saying, 'I'm gay.'"[3]

In the United States, *The Voice* judge and American country superstar Blake Sheldon publicly admitted to having a "man crush" on his co-judge and Maroon 5 frontman Adam Levine. "I want to kiss him. I want to kiss him so bad," said Sheldon, who cannot imagine why anyone – male or female – would feel differently. "Can you honestly tell me that you don't have a little bit of a crush on Adam? He's sexy," added Sheldon, who is happily married to a woman.[4]

❖ *How would you explain the phenomenon of straight men kissing each other, and straight women who do the same,*

> *using our three assumptions? What would an argument about bodies, biology, and nature sound like? How about one that emphasized privacy and individualism? And fixity and universality?*
>
> ❖ *What do you think the phenomenon of straights kissing each other signifies about the cultural imagination of heterosexuality?*
> ❖ *The number of people who describe themselves as "exclusively heterosexual" has been decreasing with each generation. Have you discovered the same thing among your friends? How would you explain this using a cultural framework?*
> ❖ *What does it mean for a man to say that he "likes boys" instead of "I'm gay"? Why do you think that he is talking about his sexuality in terms of behavior rather than identity and culture? Does his assertion reinscribe the assumptions that we've worked so hard to challenge?*

So far, we've talked about two facets of queer worlds – the gayborhood and activism – in order to understand sex cultures and how they operate. These discussions, I hope, have introduced you to a set of new ideas and have given you the tools that you need to analyze them as cultural phenomena. Now we are ready to widen our lens to something that I'm guessing you rarely stop to think that much about: heterosexuality. We will articulate the assumed (try asking a friend: "When did you choose to be straight?"), mark the invisible (we speak freely of gay and lesbian cultures; do straights have cultures too?), and flip our perspective from the sex cultures of minority groups to the majority.

In 1990, the historian Jonathan Ned Katz published his boldly titled essay "The Invention of Heterosexuality." Five years later, he expanded it into a groundbreaking book with the same name (Katz 1995). Nothing like it had existed before. The beauty of Katz's approach was his inversion, if you will, of popular arguments about the social construction of *homo*sexuality. That notion of homosexuality as created by culture has been one of the bedrocks of this book, and it is one of the most indispensable insights that emerge from our

Heterosexualities

cultural approach to the study of sexuality. A famous example of a social constructionist is Michel Foucault, who, as we have seen, declared that "the homosexual as a species" was born around 1870 (Foucault 1978: 43). Another example is provided by Adrienne Rich, who asserted that all women exist on a "lesbian continuum" (Rich 1980). Similarly, David Halperin's historical research revealed an antiquity populated by "molles" (soft or unmasculine men who depart from cultural norms of manliness by embracing femininity) and "tribades" (masculine women who are eager to have sex with other women) (Halperin 1993), while George Chauncey time traveled to early twentieth-century New York City, where he uncovered a world filled with "trade," "husbands," "wolves," "fairies," "third-sexers," and "punks" (Chauncey 1994). All these pieces have shown us how homosexuality is historically fabricated.

But Katz dove into the sex cultures of *hetero*sexuality and challenged an idea that many people accept, even now, without a second thought: heterosexuality – that attraction, behavior, and identity which exists between a man and a woman – is as "old as procreation, ancient as the lust of Eve and Adam." It is, we mistakenly believe, "unchanging, universal, essential: ahistorical" (Katz 1990: 7). His provocation should by now sound familiar, as it underlies the assumptions that we discussed in the Introduction. To borrow from Katz himself: "Biology does not settle our erotic fates . . . Just as the biology of our hearing organs will never tell us why we take pleasure in Bach or delight in Dixieland, our female or male anatomies, hormones, and genes will never tell us why we yearn for women, men, both, other, or none" (ibid.: 29). Katz proposed an alternative thesis that is compatible with our pursuits in this book. Heterosexuality is a fairly recent invention, located in specific moments in time, and it has organized arrangements between men and women in ways that we would say are best understood as cultural. It is "a word and concept, a norm and role, an individual and group identity, a behavior and feeling, and a peculiar sexual-political institution" (ibid.: 28) – all of which are densely packed with meanings.

More than twenty years have passed since Katz published his essay and book, but his ideas about heterosexuality remain

Heterosexualities

richly resonant and intellectually unmatched. Add to his clout a sensitivity to constructionist viewpoints, and we can recognize his work as synergistic with our interest in sex cultures. Thus, we will use his arguments to anchor the present chapter. We will begin with a brief review of his points to make sure we've calibrated our thinking. Katz offers a periodization that ends in 1982. This creates a propitious opportunity for us to use our cultural approach and analyze how the sex cultures of heterosexuality have evolved over the last thirty-five years in ways that neither Katz nor anyone else could have anticipated.

The Invention of Heterosexuality

Katz divided the history of heterosexuality into seven periods, starting in 1820 and ending in 1982 (figure 3.1). In his work, Katz excavated published references to the word "heterosexual" as a rhetorical device to determine how its meanings were invented and adjusted over time. Our review of his ideas will also emphasize the role of language and speech in the construction of heterosexual sex cultures. Once we turn our attention to filling in the blanks

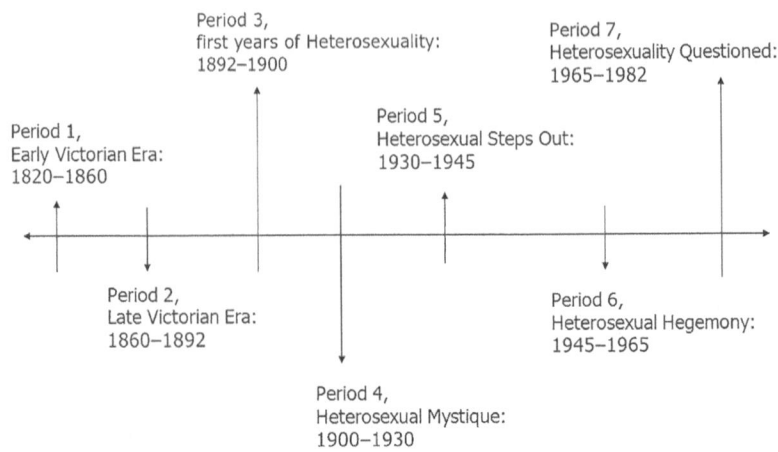

Figure 3.1 Heterosexual history

Heterosexualities

between 1982 and the present, however, we will broaden the methodology and also investigate the cultural pivots (or "turning points," as we called them in the previous chapter) that have infused sex with a set of meanings that have produced many different forms of heterosexuality.

Period 1: Before Heterosexuality
Early Victorian True Love (1820–1860)

As an erotic being, "the heterosexual did not exist" (Katz 1990: 11) in the English language before 1820. At this time, middle-class white Americans characterized their cultural imagination by gender-based standards of "true womanhood" and "true manhood." The defining features of this period were purity, propriety, and a lust-free "true love" that manifested in marriage and its sacred obligation to procreate. "Proper" men (also called "manly men") and proper women (who were "womanly women") were defined not by Eros but by their distance from it. Desire was legitimate, but only if it furthered the goals of procreation (this standard applied more strictly to women than men, who were allowed to live "closer to carnality"). Thus, men and women were "procreators," not "erotic beings or heterosexuals," Katz said. The Victorian concept of "truth" linked "'sex-biology' with 'sex-psychology,' so that feelings were thought of as female or male in the same sense as a penis or clitoris: anatomy equaled psychology" (ibid.: 12). The primacy of gender gave rise to the "invert," a medical classification that applied to all cases of gender deviance. While there were some state sodomy laws on the books, they proscribed sex acts in which anyone could conceivably engage.

Period 2: Late Victorian Sex-Love (1860–1892)

Like magic, heterosexuality didn't just "appear out of the blue" (Katz 1990: 11). The cultural imagination of sexuality changed in the 1860s as poets, academics, and activists began using the term "sex-love" to replace "true love." The shift allowed them to per-

Heterosexualities

ceive a new "eroticized universe," and it redefined the relationship between men and women as lustful. For example, when Walt Whitman published the third edition of *Leaves of Grass* in 1860, his new version contained a section called "Calamus," where he offered a detailed description of acts that Katz called "erotic communion." Whitman named "amative relationships" between men and women (what we today call heterosexuality), but he also talked about "adhesive intimacies" between men or between women (homosexuality, as we label it). He thus became the first American to name distinctly these sex cultures. In a utopian stroke of the pen, Whitman also positioned same-sex eroticism alongside heterosexual desire; for him, both were healthy expressions of sexuality.

A few years later, in Germany, the sodomy-law reformer Karl Kertbeny also tried to classify different sex cultures. In a private letter he wrote in 1868, Kertbeny first coined the words "heterosexuality" and "homosexuality." Katz described this moment as "the debut of the modern lingo." The discovery of this archival evidence was decisive because it refuted the assumption that heterosexuality is universal and timeless. Kertbeny used the word "homosexual" in public for the first time in 1869 in an effort to reform sodomy laws, and he first used "heterosexual" in public in 1880 in a defense of homosexuality. Katz regarded this as "one of sex history's grand ironies": Kertbeny designed his neologisms to advance the cause of homosexual emancipation.

In the United States, as we saw in our discussion of the city, economic changes meant that most family households transformed from being producers to consumers. As people became accustomed to buying things, the body became a part of the economy, one that was oriented toward not only consumption but also pleasure. During this time, the medical profession ascended in power and authority. Katz explained the effects: "Medical men, in the name of science, defined a new ideal of male–female relationships that included, in women as well as men, an essential, necessary, normal eroticism" (1990: 13). As this perspective gained traction, it ushered an era of "Normal Love." The Normal Woman and the Normal Man were finally allowed to feel some pleasure.

Heterosexualities

Period 3: The First Years of Heterosexuality (1892–1900)

The words "heterosexual" and "homosexual" traveled from Germany to the United States in 1892, when they first were used in a pioneering journal article by the Chicago doctor James Kiernan. He used the term "heterosexual" differently than we do today, however: these were people with "psychical hermaphroditism," "inclinations to both sexes," and those who resorted to "abnormal methods of gratification." Kiernan's heterosexuals were effectively bisexuals who masturbated! They were "definitely not exemplars of normality," Katz pointed out, given their "double deviance from both gender and procreative norms" (1990: 14).

Kiernan published his article in May 1892, and it contained one of the earliest uses of the word "homosexual" in American English (Kertbeny's use was the first ever, but it was in German). "Pure homosexuals," Kiernan argued, were people whose "general mental state is that of the opposite sex." He defined them by a gender-inverted state of mind. Also in 1892, Richard Krafft-Ebing's influential tome *Psychopathia Sexualis* was translated into English in the US. Unlike Kiernan, Krafft-Ebing focused on Eros and defined "hetero-sexual" as an "erotic feeling for a different sex" and "homo-sexual" as an "erotic feeling for a same sex." Krafft-Ebing also included a third category of "psycho-sexual hermaphroditism" to characterize "impulses toward both sexes." His view of sexuality departed from the prevailing and overriding goal of procreation, and it shifted the cultural imagination of sexuality by integrating biological sex, gender, and procreation alongside pleasure and the pursuit of happiness.

Period 4: The Heterosexual Mystique (1900–1930)

Falling birth rates, rising numbers of divorces, and other social anxieties, such as the flappers of the 1920s and women entering the workplace, prompted nervous doctors to redefine heterosexuality as "a procreant urge linked inexorably with carnal lust." These medical professionals created what Katz called "the mystique of

Heterosexualities

heterosexuality" – a new aspect of the cultural imagination that included an urgent emphasis on hedonism which was designed to affix pleasure onto our "baby-making capacity." The sexes were reified as opposite in nature, and their attraction to each other was presumed universal, natural, and inevitable (even though it was clearly manufactured). Dr Sigmund Freud was the most influential "hetero-mystique maker." In his book *Three Contributions to the Theory of Sex*, Freud regarded heterosexuality as a state of sexual "maturity," while the homosexual was "fixated" and "immature" (Freud 1910). Katz concluded: "In the name of Freud and popular psychology, heterosexuality would be proclaimed throughout the land as, simply, perfection" (1990: 18). Here, we see some of the earliest articulations of the assumptions about sex which we know have lingered ever since.

At the same time, early feminist declarations of "women's moral superiority cast suspicions of lust on women's passionate romantic friendships with women," Katz noted, and the possibility of sensual desire between women birthed "a menacing female monster, 'the lesbian.'" The attention to gender differences – what Katz called "physiological and gender dimorphism" – was a functional, if conservative, response to the many societal disruptions that characterized these years. This was especially true for men, who felt like they were losing control over their work, social roles, and power to control that fairer sex, who were supposed to have eyes only for them.

Period 5: The Heterosexual Steps Out (1930–1945)

In the years before World War II, the concept of heterosexuality emerged from the "rarified realm of a few doctors" and spread into the mainstream. On April 30, 1930, the *New York Times* printed the word "heterosexual" for the first time, in a review of Andre Gide's *The Immoralist*, and thus made it "a love that dared to speak its name." The review described the character in the book as shifting "from a heterosexual liaison to a homosexual one." This one-liner is the earliest known print reference to what was becoming a widely acknowledged, if still confusing, hetero-

Heterosexualities

sexual/homosexual binary. The slang abbreviation "hetero" also appeared for the first time in this period – in Eileen A. Robertson's 1933 novel *Ordinary Families* – while the racy 1940 Broadway musical *Pal Joey* included a song titled "Zip" with the following lyrics: "I don't like a deep contralto / Or a man whose voice is alto / Zip! I'm a heterosexual." Katz registered these trends as a "historically new, self-conscious, public proclamation of a heterosexual identity" (1990: 20). As it was reformulating, the cultural imagination of heterosexuality was growing deeply skeptical of "purity" because it bred distrust in the opposite sex.

Period 6: Heterosexual Hegemony (1945–1965)

The upheavals and tumult of World War II triggered a regression to Victorian-era norms. An emerging "cult of domesticity" forced women inside the home while valorizing their expected roles as mothers and caregivers. The cultural imagination in this moment of uncertainty insisted that men be masculine, breadwinning fathers who worked outside the home. The feminine female and masculine male were celebrated as "prolific breeders," and the homosexual was chastised as a "sad symbol of 'sterility.'" These new social norms allowed heterosexuality to soar to a powerful hegemonic status. It was talked about more than ever, and, perhaps more than ever before, it was also considered the "normal" and "natural" way to be (hearing this, we might wonder whether the assumptions of sex are harder to shake during unsettled times). Ironically, the dominance of heterosexuality diversified its expressions: liberals expanded the boundaries of permissible sex to include non-procreative, premarital, and extra-marital acts.

With the publication in 1948 of *Sexual Behavior in the Human Male*, Alfred Kinsey permanently complicated the hetero or homo binary by introducing the idea that sexuality lay on a scale from 0 ("exclusively heterosexual") to 6 ("exclusively homosexual"), with varying degrees of bisexuality in between – where most people fall. "The world is not to be divided into sheep and goats," he famously asserted. "It is a fundamental taxonomy that nature rarely deals with discrete categories." The hetero/homo binary is

Heterosexualities

not natural, in other words. We created it because the binary helps us to classify and simplify an exceedingly complex world. "Only the human mind invents categories and tries to force facts into separated pigeon-holes. The living world is a continuum" (Kinsey et al. 1948: 639, 656). Although Kinsey questioned the validity of terms such as "normal" and "abnormal," Katz argued that his continuum "reaffirmed the idea of a sexuality divided between the hetero and the homo" (1990: 22). Kinsey expanded the era's cultural imagination of sexuality by introducing the notion of a continuum, but he didn't fundamentally alter it because of the end points.

Period 7: Heterosexuality Questioned (1965–1982)

In Katz's final interval, growing voices of the counterculture, especially feminists and gay rights activists, launched an antiestablishment attack and an "unprecedented critique of sexual repression in general" – and heterosexuality in particular. The cultural imagination buzzed with the rhetoric of resistance, including Christopher Isherwood's "heterosexual dictatorship" that demanded a singular sexual standard (Isherwood 1997), Adrienne Rich's "compulsory heterosexuality," which the Brussels Tribunal on Crimes Against Women officially recognized as a means of oppression (Rich 1980), and Lillian Faderman's notion of "heterocentric," an adjective she used to condemn the erasure of homosexuality and of lesbians in particular (Faderman 1999a). The chorus of criticism put heterosexuality in distress and on the defensive.

The Ongoing Invention of Heterosexuality

By 1982 – ninety years after heterosexuality was invented in the US – the *New York Times* was regularly publishing stories about "a heterosexuality in crisis," one that was losing "its old certainty, its unquestioned status." Sexuality had gone from an aspect of human life that was rarely discussed to one that was rarely left alone. For us, the implication from Katz's history is clear: people

Heterosexualities

have always made assumptions about sex and sexuality. A closer look at history belies those assumptions, and Katz's book was a shock precisely because he lifted the veil behind which so many of us had gotten comfortable.

Katz's ideas were pervasive in the previous pages. They had to be, of course, since we anchored our discussion in his highly influential work. Now that we've reviewed it, we can take his insights and creatively extend them to the present. We have no reason to believe that heterosexual sex cultures have ceased to evolve. So, let's pick up where he left off and examine the ongoing invention of heterosexuality. What has happened in the past thirty-five years? I will propose three additional periods. To carve them out, I have broadened Katz's methodology and moved away from an exclusive examination of published references to the word "heterosexual." In what follows, we will also consider the social forces that provided pivot points in the way culture shapes sex into heterosexuality.

Period 8: Heterosexuality Revitalized (1982–1990)

On July 3, 1981, the *New York Times* ran a story about a medical oddity – "Rare Cancer Seen in 41 Homosexuals" – that would change the course of history. This was the first public mention of what would later become known as AIDS. The paper noted that "the cause of the outbreak is unknown" and that "no cases have been reported to date outside the homosexual community."[5] The limited observations and widespread uncertainties compelled the CDC to provide the first name for the disease: Gay Related Immune Deficiency, or GRID. The name mistakenly connected the syndrome with homosexuality, and its early circulation stigmatized gay people in ways that would linger for years, if not decades (Shilts 1987). The lack of information about the disease catalyzed other pernicious names. Some in the medical community called it ACIDS, for Acquired Community Immune Deficiency Syndrome, a term that conjured horrific images of the disease's impact. Others preferred CAIDS, for Community Acquired Immune Deficiency Syndrome. According to Randy Shilts, "The 'community . . .' was

Heterosexualities

a polite way of saying gay; the doctors couldn't let go of the notion that one identified this disease by whom it hit rather than what it did . . . By now, somebody was dying almost every day in America from an epidemic that still did not have a name" (Shilts 1987: 138).

On July 27, 1982, the CDC linked the disease to blood as new cases were reported outside gay and bisexual men, and it was renamed to what we call it today: Acquired Immune Deficiency Syndrome, or AIDS. Three months later, at a White House briefing, a reporter asked Press Secretary Larry Speakes about the new disease. "What's AIDS?" Speakes asked. Larry Kinsolving, the reporter, replied, "It's known as the gay plague." The room erupted in laughter. "I don't have it," Speakes retorted. "Do you?" Again, everyone present in the room laughed out loud. Speakes continued his mockery and implied that Kinsolving must be gay simply because he had knowledge of AIDS. The press secretary finally admitted that nobody in the White House, including President Reagan, knew anything about the epidemic.[6]

We must view the response to AIDS against a backdrop of a homophobia that was designed to revitalize the cultural dominance of heterosexuality, a way to reverse its retrenchment in the prior period. Moralists railed that AIDS was "God's punishment" for homosexual sodomy, a virulently religious expression of the fixity and universality assumption. Pat Buchanan harnessed the assumption of biological determinism to slander the community in the *Washington Times*: "The poor homosexuals; they have declared war upon nature, and now nature is exacting an awful retribution."[7] The conservative William Buckley, in a 1986 *New York Times* article, endorsed mandatory HIV testing and the forcible tattooing of HIV-positive gay men "on the buttocks, to prevent the victimization of other homosexuals."[8] The measures that many public officials recommended throughout the 1980s embodied an understanding of gays as outsiders, a group of people with an unnatural and unhealthy sexuality. Shilts (1987: 228) says that it was "virtually an article of faith among homosexuals that they would somehow end up in concentration camps." Polls from 1985 show that 72 percent of Americans favored mandatory HIV testing and that 51 percent supported quarantining people with AIDS. This association of AIDS with gay men allowed the federal government both to ignore the disease and to stoke public hysteria about it. Congressional staffers joked that NIH really stood for "Not Interested in Homosexuals," and it wasn't until June 1987 – an alarming six years into the epidemic – that President Ronald Reagan finally used the word "AIDS" for the first time in a public address. His homophobia blinded him to the reality that AIDS was not a gay disease – and it never could be. "Viruses do not respect social identity boundaries," Armstrong (2002: 173) cleverly notes. The only way conservatives could condemn the gay community so vehemently is by having a clear sense of their own moral superiority, a collective self to contrast with the stigmatized "other." Homophobia, therefore, can fuel its own brand of sex cultures.

Conservatism, religiosity, and anti-gay attitudes saturated American society at this time. A striking example is a policy from the *New York Times* which prohibited printing the word "gay" unless it was in the official name of an organization or part of a direct quote. It wasn't until June 15, 1987, that the paper declared that the words "gay" and "lesbian" were "fit to print." The Reagan administration's conspiracy of silence was encouraged by the religious right, a hateful group which viewed gays as a blemish upon American "family values" and a threat to the social order. Robert J. Billings and Jerry Falwell's Moral Majority (founded in 1979), along with fundamental Christians more generally, were given credit for Reagan's landslide victory in 1980. "Moral Majority" became a household name in no time as analysts heralded Falwell and his fundamentalist followers as "the most important new political force to emerge in America in decades." The Moral Majority exerted influence on matters of politics and policy through 1989, when the organization disbanded, only to be replaced in the same year by Pat Robertson's "Christian Coalition," a more venomous countermovement that has jousted with gays and lesbians ever since (Kaiser 1997: 273).

Consider also the Supreme Court's decision in *Bowers v. Hardwick*. After having spent all night at work, Michael Hardwick, a gay bartender in Atlanta, grabbed a beer as he left

Heterosexualities

the bar in the early morning hours of July 5. Patrolman Keith Torrick spotted him throwing his bottle in the trash and gave him a ticket for public drinking. The officer warned Hardwick that he would be arrested if he missed his court date. Hardwick showed up on time, paid a fine, and assumed he had put the matter to rest. A month later, on August 3, 1982, with the unintended assistance of a friend who was sleeping off a hangover on the couch, Torrick entered Hardwick's home with an arrest warrant for a ticket that Hardwick had paid.

The patrolman searched for Hardwick once he was inside his apartment. Torrick eventually walked into a candle-lit bedroom and reported being "shocked" and "grossed out" to find Hardwick and a male guest engaging in mutual fellatio. The officer announced that Hardwick was under arrest, to which he rightfully retorted, "What are you doing in my bedroom?" Torrick handcuffed Hardwick and his guest and took them both to the station, where the officer, Hardwick recalled, "made sure everyone ... knew I was there for cocksucking." He was charged with violating Georgia's state sodomy law: "(a) A person commits the offense of sodomy when he performs or submits to any sexual act involving the sex organs of one person and the mouth or anus of another ... [and] (b) A person convicted of the offense of sodomy shall be punished by imprisonment for not less than one nor more than 20 years" (Engel 2001: 117).

Anticipating the complexities of the case, the district attorney dropped all the charges. Hardwick still fought back and filed a suit in a federal district court where he argued that the state of Georgia had violated the due process guarantees of the Fourteenth Amendment of the US Constitution. He hoped that a higher court would rule sodomy laws unconstitutional, since he had a right to engage in consensual sexual activity in the privacy of his own home (think about how he is using the assumption of privacy). "I realized that if there was anything I could do, even if it was just laying the foundation to change this horrendous law, that I would feel pretty bad about myself if I just walked away from it."

The case moved to the Supreme Court, which decided it on March 31, 1986. The bitterly divided justices upheld the state

Heterosexualities

statute in a 5–4 vote and ruled that sodomy laws did not violate any fundamental rights under the Constitution. The majority opinion and dissent showcase a battle about the cultural imagination of sexuality in the 1980s. Was this case about the right to privacy? Or a right to engage in sodomy? In delivering the opinion of the Court, Justice White affirmed the latter: "[R]espondent would have us announce . . . a fundamental right to engage in homosexual sodomy. This we are quite unwilling to do . . . [I]n Constitutional terms there is no such thing as a fundamental right to commit homosexual sodomy." Drawing on assumptions of biology and universality, Chief Justice Burger concurred: "'The infamous crime against nature' [is] an offense of 'deeper malignity' than rape, a heinous act 'the very mention of which is a disgrace to human nature.'" From his perspective, "to hold that the act of homosexual sodomy is somehow protected as a fundamental right would be to cast aside millennia of moral teaching." *Bowers* thus deepened the scarlet letter of homosexuality and bolstered the normative status of heterosexuality; in so doing, it implied that sex and sexuality were neither shaped by context nor subject to change.

Justice Blackmun, who wrote the majority decision in *Roe v. Wade*, along with Brennan, Marshall, and Steven, filed a dissenting opinion that championed privacy. "This case is . . . [not] about 'a fundamental right to engage in homosexual sodomy,'" Blackmun began. "The statute at issue . . . denies individuals the right to decide for themselves whether to engage in particular forms of private, consensual sexual activity." Privacy, for Blackmun, "embodies the 'moral fact that a person belongs to himself and not others nor to society as a whole.'" This case was about "the right to be let alone" (Kaiser 1997: 319–20). This is an intriguing example about how the assumptions we make about sex are not always or even inherently problematic. In this case, a Supreme Court justice used privacy to promote equality for gays and lesbians.

The majority and concurring opinions in *Bowers* did not use the word "heterosexual" at all. In their dissent, however, Justices Blackmun, Brennan, Marshall, and Stevens argued that Georgia displays an "apparent willingness to enforce against homosexuals

Heterosexualities

a law it seems to not have any desire to enforce against heterosexuals." The curious absence of the word "heterosexual" by the Supreme Court justices exemplifies what Janet Halley (1993: 90) describes as "*the* salient characteristic of the class." In defining the contours of homosexuality (does the Constitution guarantee a fundamental right to engage in homosexual sodomy, Justice White asked?), the majority opinion of the Court allowed heterosexuals to remain unacknowledged (not once did White use the word "heterosexual"). In theoretical terms, this suggests that heterosexuality remains the default characteristic "for people who have not marked themselves or been marked by others as homosexual" (ibid.). Yet it is a "compulsory" (Rich 1980) "political regime" that regulates homosexuality as the "other" by defining itself as natural, taken for granted, and universal (Ingraham 2006: 238). To restate the important point: legally defining a class of homosexuals in *Bowers* also involved "the far less visible" practice of defining a class of heterosexuals. The two are "coextensive" or "diacritical," according to Halley (1993: 83); they acquire definition in relation to each other. Based on Halley's argument and the *Bowers* decision, we learn that straights renewed their confidence and cultural dominance during these years by "dropping silently out of the picture." Therefore, silence is a form of speech (Sedgwick 1990), and we must remain vigilant to ways of *not saying* something. Sex cultures are made by inaction and assumption as well as by action and protest.

To make this concrete, imagine that you are a gay teenager living in the 1980s. You hear about AIDS on the nightly television news, and you see the media vilifying gay people day after day. Next you read about the *Bowers* decision. How likely are you to come out of the closet? How would you feel about sex – and gay sex? The threat of being expelled from the norm – from the class of heterosexuals and all the privileges that its members reap – will bribe you to comply with a self-righteous morality and cultural imagination that stipulates heterosexuality as "coherent, stable, exclusively loyal to heterosexual eroticism, and pure of any sodomitical desires or conduct" (Halley 1993: 90). That notion of coherence and purity, as we'll soon see, is a fiction.

Heterosexualities

Period 9: Heterosexual Anxieties (1990–1996)

"Something happened in the 1990s, something dramatic and irreversible," John D'Emilio (2002: ix) reflected. "The world finally did turn and notice the gay folks in its midst." This decade witnessed a significant increase in front-page coverage of gay issues. Headlines captured debates about whether homosexuality was born or bred (*Time*, September 9, 1991, and *Newsweek*, February 24, 1992); about gays in the military (*Newsweek*, February 1, 1993); and general interest covers such as "The Future of Gay America" (*Newsweek*, March 12, 1990) that endeavored to get to the bottom of "what America thinks." Meanwhile, the *New York Times* acknowledged that gays could be just "The People Next Door."

The surge in visibility of gays in the media induced anxieties for many straight people – and with that anxiety came both subtle and strong forms of backlash. Clinton's negotiations on whether gays should serve in the military, the compromise that produced "Don't Ask, Don't Tell," provides one example. According to the policy, the Pentagon would not ask soldiers and recruits if they were gay, and those who self-identified would have to remain closeted both on and off base. If they dared to disclose their non-heterosexual orientation, they risked a dishonorable discharge. The policy passed despite numerous reports published between 1957 and 1994 that found little to no evidence for claims of security risks and diminished military performance, readiness, and morale. Bruce Bawer lambasted the policy, saying that it would "write into law the institutions of the closet." He explained, "While heterosexuals would continue to enjoy their right to lead private lives and to discuss those lives freely, gays would be allowed to remain in the armed forces only so long as they didn't mention their homosexuality to anyone or have relationships on or off base" (Bawer 1993: 117). Don't Ask, Don't Tell manipulated our assumptions about privacy; it leveraged the belief that what we do in our own bedroom is no one else's business as a cloak for homophobia. An editorial published in the *New Republic* elaborates: "The most demeaning assumption about the new provisions is that they single out the deepest moment of emotional intimacy – the private sexual act – as that which is most repugnant. Its assumption about the dignity and humanity of gay people, in and out of the military, in public and in private, is sickening" (Rimmerman 1996: 120). Although the compromise intended to serve gays better, in the years following codification, discharge rates spiked. Even President Clinton declared the policy a failure.

Another manifestation of straight anxieties in this period was the "Special Rights" campaign initiated by the religious right. Conservatives had condemned gay people for a long time, but in this campaign they tested a new approach that warned against providing "preferential treatment." Discrimination against gays wasn't the same as that against other minorities, the right argued, since gays choose to live a sinful life. Just as the Supreme Court did not confer a "fundamental right to sodomy" in its 1986 *Bowers v. Hardwick* decision, so too should the government not confer "special rights" to a group of people who have elected a certain lifestyle. Thus, homosexuality became a pathology and foil against the gold standard of heterosexuality. What is interesting about this campaign for us is that the idea of gays choosing their sexuality hints that it is infused by culture rather than being biologically ordained.

Colorado's Amendment 2, a constitutional provision that nullified all existing protections for gay people and banned future anti-discrimination measures for them, became the stage on which the special rights debate was fought. Amendment proponents encouraged the government to "permanently exclude sexual orientation protections" (Fetner 2008: 98). During nine days of testimony, they presented evidence that tried to assess "all that was known about gay people – from ancient history through the latest scientific research – to determine where and how gay people fit into the body politic." The strategy unleashed a raging debate on the origins of homosexuality and the nature of civil rights claims. Do gay people deserve them? Or are they asking for special rights? How do we distinguish the two? Claiming to represent the majority of Americans, the right argued that homosexuality was morally wrong and unnatural. Gay activists responded by saying that they constituted a minority. Being gay was orthogonal to morality, they rebutted, and those in the straight majority could not dictate private matters such as the right to love, nor could they deprive any minority group, including gays, of their civil rights. In a 53 to 47 vote using a ballot initiative, Coloradans approved Amendment 2 in 1992.

By debating the merits of the special rights frame, Americans were doing nothing less than considering the cultural contours of homosexuality. In the year leading up to the passage of Amendment 2, *Newsweek* ran a cover story that showed the face of an infant, with the headline "Is This Child Gay? Born or Bred: The Origins of Homosexuality." The article cited the research of a neuroscientist, Simon LeVay, who found that the hypothalamus, a tiny area in the brain, controlled sexuality. If gays were born that way, then they were entitled to legal protections based on an indisputable minority group status and claims to equal (not special) rights. According to LeVay, "A genetic component in sexual orientation says, 'This is not a fault, and it's not your fault.'" Some scientists took issue with his interpretations. "Of course it [sexual orientation] is in the brain," retorted John Money in response to LeVay's finding that gay men's hypothalamus were similar in size to that of straight females. "The real question is, when did it get there? Was it prenatal, neonatal, during childhood, puberty? That we do not know."[9]

The born versus bred debate, alongside the special rights debacle, created divisions among gay activists. Some felt the search for a cause implied that homosexuality was defective and thus something that could be cured or fixed. Keen and Goldberg (2000: 44) noted,

> In our rush to embrace biological explanations because of their political utility, let's not forget that an earlier generation of gay rights advocates, in Germany in the first part of the twentieth century, argued tirelessly for a congenital explanation of homosexuality. They believed it would promote tolerance. Their efforts came to naught after Hitler's rise to power when the Nazis decided that these congenital "defectives" ought to be eliminated for the sake of the master race.

Heterosexualities

The *Newsweek* story cited a comparative study of four countries in which researchers found that those people who believed that homosexuality was biological in nature were the least homophobic. Therefore, being born gay would make it unfair to discriminate "for being true to nature's ways" (D'Emilio 2002: 159). These debates were never resolved – indeed, they persist to this day. Their tenacity teaches us the vastness of the cultural imagination and the complex ways in which assumptions about sex mingle with culture to produce sexuality.

Heterosexual angst climaxed on September 21, 1996, with the passage of the Defense of Marriage Act (DOMA). As we saw in the last chapter, DOMA sought to "protect" the heterosexual institution of marriage from a very specific homosexual threat. It defined marriage as "a legal union of one man and one woman as husband and wife" and specified that the word "spouse" "refers only to a person of the opposite sex who is a husband or wife." The legislation also allowed states to refuse to recognize a same-sex marriage that was legally performed in another state. DOMA was designed to quarantine same-sex marriage. I call this moment the apex of angst because it screamed so loudly about "protecting" heterosexual values that it ultimately revealed the uncertainty of those who were championing them. The bill was devastating to gays and lesbians and forced a number of ugly legal fights. But it also hinted at a fascinating vulnerability, the cracks in the veneer of cultural dominance. No longer were the sex cultures of heterosexuality and normative masculinity the standard, so deeply taken for granted that they could wield power by silently dropping out of the picture. Now, those sex cultures had to be vigorously articulated and defended.

Many scholars locate the onset of the legal battles over marriage to a case in Hawaii, as we saw in the last chapter, which was brought by two lesbian couples and one gay male couple. Each of the couples applied for a marriage license. After being denied, they filed a lawsuit against the state. Three years later, in May 1993, the Supreme Court of Hawaii decided *Baehr v. Lewin* and declared that denying marriage licenses on the grounds of same-sex application violated the equal protection clause of the state's constitution

Heterosexualities

that outlawed sex-based discrimination. In "the ruling that roiled America" (Sullivan 1997: 104), Hawaii's Supreme Court established a legal precedent for marriage equality. The Court decreed, "We hold that sex is a 'suspect category' for purposes of equal protection." If the plaintiffs were heterosexual couples, they would be allowed to marry. Sex, therefore, was a suspect category. *Baehr* dictated that the state must show a compelling interest in prohibiting same-sex marriage. The Hawaii Supreme Court remanded the case back to the trial court. Although the decision was not final, it was the first time in US history that a court placed same- and opposite-sex couples on an even field. Gays celebrated; straights panicked.

In a commentary entitled "The Marriage Fight Is Setting Us Back," D'Emilio (2006) made a pointed observation about how the fight for marriage flared heterosexual anxieties. "The battle to win marriage equality through the courts has done something that no other campaign or issue in our movement has done: it has created a vast body of new anti-gay law." By the time DOMA was signed, same-sex marriage cases "overshadowed all other gay-related legislative issues." A total of twenty-five anti-gay measures were signed into law, of which only seven did not relate to the issue of same-sex marriage. One prominent gay rights organization concluded, "Without question, same gender marriage occupied the center stage in the 1996 state legislative sessions. Last year, anti-gay forces chose one central issue to rally their troops around the country. That issue was marriage" – which became a contested symbol for the imperiled sanctity of heterosexuality.[10]

Period 10: A Renaissance of Heterosexualities (1996–2016)

By the late 1990s, a story in the *New York Times* asked, "Gay or Straight? Hard to Tell." David Colman, the reporter, explained in the paper's Sunday style section how hard it had become to differentiate straight men from gay men:

> As gay men grow more comfortable shrugging off gay-identified clothing and Schwarzeneggerian fitness standards, straight men are more at

Heterosexualities

ease flaunting a degree of muscle tone seldom seen outside of a Men's Health cover shoot. And they are adopting looks – muscle shirts, fitted jeans, sandals and shoulder bags – that as recently as a year or two ago might have read as, well, gay.

Straight men appear gayer, and gays are routinely mistaken as straight. "The result is a new grey area that is rendering gaydar – that totally unscientific sixth sense that many people rely on to tell if a man is gay or straight – as outmoded as Windows 2000." Colman intuited that the meanings of sexuality were becoming so complex that the existing binaries of gay or straight would no longer suffice. "What's happening is that many men have migrated to a middle ground where the cues traditionally used to pigeonhole sexual orientation – hair, clothing, voice, body language – are more and more ambiguous." How do we make sense of these blurred lines? What neologisms can help us to keep up with these cultural trends? "Call it what you will: 'gay vague' will do. But the poles are melting fast." Nearly a decade later, the *Globe and Mail* in Canada remarked on the same development in the title of its story "Who's Gay? And Who's Just Gay-Vague?" Micah Toub interviewed Eric Anderson, whom we met in the opening case study. Anderson explained that the gay vague trend has given straight men "much more freedom to choose activities – sports, music, entertainment – that we desire without being marginalized, without being called a fag and beaten up because you'd prefer to watch *Glee* than football." "Gay vague" is a surprisingly resonant symbol of our current day, and it shows how the cultural imagination of heterosexuality is broadening in breathtaking ways.[11]

The current period is characterized by a renaissance of heterosexualities – in the plural to be sure. New terms abound, including "gay vague," that signify new sex cultures. This international "menaissance," as both the *Boston Globe* in the US and *The Observer* in the UK called it in 2006,[12] is a cultural phenomenon that has rehabilitated ways of being straight. So "homoflexible" is today's heteroworld that a straight man can be in a relationship with another man without being gay. In a 2002 story entitled

Heterosexualities

"Standing Straight," Samuel Reiss teases, "Two guys in a relationship. Gay, right? Wrong! These three male couples explain what it's like to be together when one is a homo and the other insists that, under any other circumstances, he is a bonafide breeder boy." Reiss recounts the cool and comfortable heterosexual men who shrug, "I'm just a heterosexual in a male relationship" (Reiss 2002). Four years later, *The Advocate* magazine ran a story titled "Seeking Straight" with a lascivious byline: "As many gay men know, 'straight' men can be had." The journalist observed, "There is greater acceptance of pansexual behavior among straight men ... Men who are self-identified as straight are more willing to explore their homosexual side. It's less of a taboo" (Edozien 2006).

And who can forget the "metrosexual"? Mark Simpson coined the word on November 15, 1994, in *The Independent*, a national newspaper in the UK. The "metrosexual man," said Simpson, is "the single young man with a high disposable income, living or working in the city (because that's where all the best shops are), [and] is perhaps the most promising consumer market of the decade." The word gained traction after Simpson reused it in a 2002 *Salon* article, where he elaborated, "He might be officially gay, straight or bisexual, but this is utterly immaterial because he has clearly taken himself as his own love object and pleasure as his sexual preference."[13] The 2003 reality television series *Queer Eye for the Straight Guy* wed the idea to American popular culture. That same year, the *New York Times* became the first American newspaper to print the word, in a story titled "Metrosexuals Come Out." The article defined metrosexuals as "straight urban men willing, even eager, to embrace their feminine side ... Having others question their sexuality is all part of the game."[14] The conceits of metrosexuality are clear enough: pleasure tops sexual object choice, and gender inversion is unrelated to sexual orientation. Metrosexuality is a performance that gives straight men permission to experiment with gender expression, like using skin care products or dressing impeccably, that have traditionally been associated with gay men. Think David Beckham, who has become a global icon for metrosexuality. Ultimately, the metrosexual revels in a cultural panache, even if he doesn't articulate his thinking as sociological. He, more

Heterosexualities

than any other manifestations of the expanded heterosexual canon, sees culture as a thing to play with and identity as consisting of hats he can try on and take off as he pleases.

After metrosexuality came "bromance" – a word that combines "brother" and "romance" to designate a close but not sexual relationship between two straight men. Dave Carnie is credited with coining the term in his skateboard magazine *Big Brother*,[15] even though mainstream American journalists had been wrestling with similar questions of homosocial intimacy for a while. On April 10, 2005, the *New York Times* ran a story inquisitively titled "What do you call two straight men having dinner?" The answer: a "man-date," defined as "two heterosexual men socializing without the crutch of business or sports. It is two guys meeting for the kind of outing a straight man might reasonably arrange with a woman."[16] On October 26, 2006, *USA Today* characterized the same phenomenon as a "male-ationship" or a "bromance," a pop cultural obsession that came of age by innovations in "the whole culture of masculinity."[17] Just as *Queer Eye* popularized "metrosexual," Hollywood films such as *I Love You, Man* and *The Hangover* spread the appeal of this sex culture into living rooms across the world.

While metrosexuality expanded opportunities for straights to leave behind the shackles of masculinity in their dress and affectations, bromances have expanded the possibilities for how they interact. Bromantic relationships permit intimate friendships between straight men in a way that "simulates ancient notions of Greek and Roman brotherhood; a time in which men's homosocial bonds were culturally prized" (Anderson 2011: 81). As we saw in the opening case study, the country superstar Blake Shelton told MTV News that he had a "man crush" on the Maroon 5 frontman Adam Levine, yet no one accused him of being a closeted gay or bisexual man.

Scholarship on heterosexuality has flourished alongside these commentaries. The "declining significance of homophobia" (McCormack 2012) has caused the poles between gay and straight to melt, and heterosexuals have become more self-conscious about their sexual identities as a result. This might be a third expression, beyond the cycling between taken for granted and anxiety, which occurred in earlier periods. I use the word "self-conscious" to emphasize a set of cultural norms that permit straight men to curate their identities in new ways. In our "post-closeted cultural context," as James Joseph Dean calls it, "straights can neither assume the invisibility of gays and lesbians, nor count on others to always assume their heterosexuality." They also cannot assume that "other straights are homophobic or intolerant of gays and lesbians" (Dean 2014: 3). Living in such a moment motivates straights to define explicitly the meaning of their sexuality in ways they have not felt forced to do in the past. The result is a pluralizing of the heterosexual cultural imagination.

As straightness declines in its assumed status, more heterosexuals are adopting a "politically gay" identity. Meyers (2008: 169) describes this group as "commitment-based" straight activists, unlike the "experience-based" gay activists. He shares an interview that another scholar conducted with a woman who was asked "if she's ever done it with a woman." Grinning, she replied, "No, and I get teased because I haven't." Would she ever, the interviewer probed? "Well, I've fantasized about it. Hey! It's never too late." Meyers suspects that heterosexuals who share social networks with the LGBT community use language such as this to demonstrate their cultural sensitivity and "avoid flaunting their heterosexuality" (ibid.: 171). Popular examples of straight allies include Brad Pitt, Kathy Griffin, and Beyoncé.

In a different study, Grzanka, Adler, and Blazer (2015) show how greater societal acceptance of sexual minorities has compelled straight allies to think closely about the meaning of sexual attraction, behavior, and identity. The participants in their study reflected on a range of issues, including the origins of an ally identity, the emotional experiences of being an ally, and the efficacy of straight ally activism. A pattern emerged across topics of conversation: "being an ally is less a pre-scripted role to be taken on and more of a nascent identity" (ibid.: 176), one that is informed by other aspects of our identity, such as our age, generational cohort, religion, social class, and upbringing. This is why there is "no singular definition of [a] straight ally" (ibid.), much like heterosexuality itself. The nascent concept provides evidence of our cultural approach at work. In contrast to the silent, unspoken dominance of heterosexuality for so long, the notion of straight allies is about *not* taking that identity for granted – being more aware and articulate about the assumptions that heterosexuals make.

Straight allies affect social change in "passive" and "active" ways. Passive activism entails promoting "moral standards of respect and empathy toward LGBT individuals," whereas active engagement is characterized by "purposeful and organized efforts to bring about social transformation" (Grzanka et al. 2015: 177). One of the most visible institutional arenas for active engagement among straight allies is the Gay–Straight Alliance (GSA), or similarly named organizations increasingly common in high schools and universities across the United States and Canada. One study compared the experiences of students who attended high schools that offered such groups with those students who studied at schools without them (Fetner and Elafros 2015). The researchers found that sexual minorities at both schools reported experiences of harassment and hearing anti-gay comments. This tells us that homophobia still exists, even in a post-closeted world. However, students at GSA schools say they receive more support from their teachers and administrators than students who attend high schools that do not have them. Students in the latter group indicate that their teachers and administrators actively oppose LGBT equality. GSA students also report more friendships that cross lines of sexual orientation, as compared to non-GSA students, who report feeling more isolated and withdrawn.

These friendships are sometimes quite beautiful. At one high school in Nevada in 2015, a straight senior student, Jacob Lescenski, asked his gay best friend, Anthony Martinez, to prom. With the help of his friends, Lescenski created a banner to propose to his friend: "You're hella gay, I'm hella str8, but you're like my brother, so be my d8?" CNN interviewed Martinez, who said that it was the "sweetest, coolest thing that has ever happened." Although Lescenski was a bit nervous at first, he let go of his anxieties: "If it made Anthony happy, and fulfilled his dream of going to prom with a guy, and I had a date to prom myself, nothing else mattered."[18] For these guys, friendship came first – and without all the baggage of being anti-gay or homophobic.

Straight women allies sometimes adopt separate terms. Those who are attracted to other women emotionally and politically but not sexually call themselves "political dykes" (Taylor and Whittier 1992: 115) or "heterodykes" (Clausen 1990: 445). This modern identity is consistent with an observation that Adrienne Rich made decades earlier in her famous essay "Compulsory Heterosexuality and Lesbian Existence." According to Rich (1980), all women exist on a "lesbian continuum," regardless of whether they identify as a lesbian. The continuum specifies diverse ways in which women can identify and relate with other women, not all of which require attraction and sex. Like other social constructionists, Rich suggests that sexuality is a matter of choice and affiliation rather than bodies and biology. In doing so, she raises the provocative possibility that *all* women are lesbians, even those who are in heterosexual relationships.

In addition to forming alliances with gays and lesbians, straights, especially women, are practicing their sexuality in fluid ways. In her influential work, the psychologist Lisa Diamond (2003) asks if women who identify as gay, lesbian, or bisexual later relinquish that identity. To find out, she interviewed eighty women, aged eighteen to twenty-five, three times over a five-year period. Over one-fourth of her sample changed the label they used to define their sexual identity. Half these women returned to heterosexual identity, while the other half stopped using any labels at all. For Diamond, these results confirm that "sexual fluidity" is real. "One of the fundamental, defining features of female sexual orientation is its fluidity," she asserts, by which she means that women's sexual responsiveness depends on the situation in which an individual finds herself (Diamond 2008: 3). Many women acknowledge their "capacity for diverse, fluctuating desires and experiences." One woman said, "I think I've become more comfortable in looking at [sexuality] as a continuum" (Diamond 2003: 358). This is why Anne Heche can fall in love with Ellen DeGeneres despite having been exclusively heterosexual in her past.

Heterosexualities

In her research, Diamond takes great care to dispel three misunderstandings. First, sexual fluidity does not mean that all women are inherently bisexual (or lesbian, as Rich asserts). Women have different degrees of sexual fluidity; some experience stable patterns of desire while others do not. Second, sexual fluidity does not mean that there is endless variation in women's erotic desires but, rather, that some of them can experience a wider variety of sexual feelings and experiences. Finally, sexual fluidity does not mean that people can change their sexual orientation on a whim or that it's entirely a choice. It means that sexual orientation is not the only factor that determines the object of attraction for women. Even when women report a change in their erotic attractions and behaviors, "they typically report that such changes are unexpected and beyond their control. In some cases they actively resist these changes, to no avail" (Diamond 2008: 11). In offering these arguments, Diamond refutes the assumption of fixity while acknowledging the experiential difficulties in doing so.

In recent years, we have begun to see similar evidence in men – who now cuddle, kiss, and even have sex with each other without anyone challenging their heterosexuality. In their study of male student athletes at a British university, Anderson and McCormack (2015) found that 93 percent loved to cuddle and spoon with other men, and a whopping 98 percent of respondents said that they had slept in the same bed with another man at least once. Some did this for practical reasons – lack of bed space in a cramped dorm room – while others did it to "feel close" to their friends. This new form of "homosocial intimacy" (emotional and physical but non-erotic affections between straight men) is redefining "heteromasculinity" among straight men [the cultural conflation of heterosexuality with masculinity and homosexuality with femininity; the latter is also known as the "effeminacy effect" (Hennen 2008: 9)]. Now, they can "share beds with other men without risking their socially perceived heterosexual identity" (ibid.: 215). In earlier decades, cuddling and spooning were considered homoerotic behaviors, and they were "excised from same-sex interactions through homophobic stigma" (ibid.: 216). The social reconstruction of heteromasculine sex cultures in modern times allows these

Heterosexualities

previously forbidden expressions. "It's just not a big deal," one of Anderson and McCormack's respondents said (2015: 221). Another described his "cuddling arrangement" with his best friend: "I feel comfortable with Connor and we spend a lot of time together. I happily rest my head on Connor's shoulder when lying on the couch or holding him in bed . . . We have a bromance where we are very comfortable around each other" (ibid.). A third just shrugged his shoulders and said, "I love a quick cuddle." His friend agreed: "We very often have hangover cuddles and naps together . . . I really enjoy it! Seriously, I do it all the time."

None of this is to say that "homohysteria" is dead. This aspect of the cultural imagination of heterosexuality describes a "fear of being homosexualized" (Anderson 2011: 87) or a compulsion among straight men to avoid homosexual suspicion. Homohysterical straight men distance themselves from culturally stigmatized gay identities. Times of high homohysteria entail mass cultural suspicion, and they promote singularity; straight men align their sexual identity as heterosexual, their gender identity as heteromasculine, and their behavior as exclusively heterosexual. The phrase "no homo" is an example. The rapper Cam'ron coined the phrase in East Harlem in the late 1990s, and it merged into mainstream hip-hop culture by way of a song by Lil Wayne in 2008. A writer in *The Guardian* notes that "straight men now feel the need to say 'no homo' when discussing emotions." Saying "Dude, you're so awesome. No homo. Lol"[19] is an example. In moments of lower homohysteria, heterosexuality becomes plural as straight men experience more freedom of gender and sexual expression (Anderson 2011: 80). Gay vague is an apt example.

Not only do they cuddle and spoon, some straights also kiss each other. The phenomenon of women doing this at parties and bars is by now ubiquitous, "from Katy Perry's hit song, 'I Kissed a Girl,' to Tyra Banks online poll on attitudes toward girls who kiss girls in bars, to AskMen.com's 'Top 10: Chick Kissing Scenes" (Rupp and Taylor 2010: 28). Madonna's lip-locking moment with Britney Spears and Christina Aguilera during the 2003 VMA music awards is another instance. Women do this for many reasons, including seeking attention from men; experimentation,

Heterosexualities

sexual fluidity, and bi-curiosity; and as a means to explore their authentic same-sex desires (Rupp and Taylor 2010).

Men do it too. In a study of 145 straight male high-school and university students in Britain, Anderson, Adams, and Rivers (2012) found that 89 percent of the men in their sample had kissed another male friend on the lips. This finding of "simple kissing" (ibid.: 424) excludes kissing one's father, kissing a man on the cheeks, or kissing someone because of an athletic team initiation of fraternity hazing. All the men indicated that "this behavior was a regular occurrence among undergraduate populations" (ibid.). One respondent said, "I kiss guys on the pitch. Guys I don't even know. And I'm not the only one" (ibid.: 425). The practice extends off the athletic field as well. "Kissing happens on nights out, yeah. It happens all the time," one man confessed (ibid.). These young men have reinvented their cultural imagination by stripping same-sex kissing of its homosexual significance. "It's like shaking hands," one man explained – but then quickly added, "Well, it's more than that, but it's the same attitude." Another man mused, "It's a feeling, an expression of endearment, an act that happens to show they are important to you." Yet another said affectionately, "It's an 'I love you mate' type of kiss" (ibid.).

In addition to brief kisses that happen in the moment, 37 percent of the sample reported sustained same-sex kissing – or making out. "I kissed a guy with tongues for about 3 or 4 seconds, so that some girls would do the same. You know like in the movie American Pie 2, you go, we go, you go, we go!" The young men in the study were aware that this type of kissing was culturally taboo. To get around the stigma, they again redefined kissing between straight men as "homosocial bonding" (Anderson et al. 2012: 424), "platonic heteromasculine affection" (ibid.: 426), and a form of intimacy. One man explained, "It's not sexual. You just do it for fun." Another clarified, "I mean, it's sexual, but it's not sexy [read: erotic]." However, these men were aware that others may not perceive their kissing as non-sexual. "Of course," one man nodded. "Yeah, two guys with their tongues in each other's mouths. But I guess it just doesn't matter" (ibid.: 427). The statements provide strong evidence for radical changes in the cultural imagination of heterosexuality. "Today's young men are freer to express love, fear and weakness to each other," Anderson said in an interview to the media about his work.[20] Historically, the sex cultures of heterosexuality have been based on a particular understanding of power: the man will be the head of the household, masculine, and in charge of his wife. The ability to be vulnerable, as these young men express, is a huge leap.

I suspect that guy-on-guy action is less visible in the United States than it is in Britain for two reasons. First, the sight of affection between men provokes a visceral disgust among straight Americans (both men and women). This reaction is called "the ick factor," or a "primary disgust" that some straight people feel with gay male sex, especially anal sex. To this day, the ick factor is used as a legal defense to support discrimination.[21] The philosopher Martha Nussbaum offers "projective disgust" as a second reason why men kissing is a practice that is less culturally supported in the US. Affection between men prompts an irrational fear of contamination: viewing two guys kissing will soil the moral and sexual purity of the straight man, who is now forced to imagine participating in gay sex acts. Nussbaum explains:

> Projective disgust has its origin in a discomfort with one's own body and its messier animal aspects, including sexuality, and that, in a defense mechanism, disgust is then projected outward onto vulnerable groups [such as gay men] who are characterized as hyperphysical and hypersexual. In this way, the uncomfortable people displace their discomfort onto others, who are then targeted for various forms of social discrimination.

She cites integrated drinking fountains, lunch counters, and swimming pools as an example from the civil rights movement. Lesbian relationships were never the object of disgust in the same way. Quite the opposite: "girls kissing other girls can be a turn-on for men in our culture, as the girls who engage in it well know" (Rupp and Taylor 2010: 30).[22]

The most stunning research findings in recent years show straight men going all the way – while maintaining a legible heterosexual identity. A recent study conducted by the CDC in

Heterosexualities

the United States found that more than 3 million men who self-identify as straight have sex with other men. A survey from New York City found that one out of every ten men who say they are straight occasionally have sex with other men. Of these, 70 percent are married to women. These studies highlight the complexities of sexual orientation – and straight sex cultures, specifically. The deeper we look, the more we see crisscrossing combinations of sexual identity, attraction, and behavior. "Same-sex encounters aren't about romance or sexual attraction and desire" for these straight-identifying men who have sex with other men, notes Joe Kort (2008). The motivation is "sexual and physiological arousal – 'getting off' with another who's male and accessible."

In the past, a single same-sex act would define a person wholly as gay. This is called the "logic of the closet": same-sex sex among heterosexuals is evidence of their repressed homosexuality and their failure to be honest about their true non-heterosexual identity. According to this view, men who have sex with other men are really just closeted gay men who are constrained by a culture of homophobia. Inspired by similar arguments about racial identity, Anderson (2008: 105) calls this the "one-time rule of homosexuality":

> Borrowing from the one-drop theory of race ... in which a dominant White culture once viewed anyone with even a portion of Black genetic ancestry as Black, I call the behavioral component of this model [one in which "the only way to be considered heterosexual is to avoid *any* same-sex sexual act *and* to avoid admitting same-sex sexual desire"] the one-time rule of homosexuality. I do so because one same-sex sexual experience is equated with a homosexual orientation in masculine peer culture, ruling out the possibility of men engaging in recreational same-sex sex without being homosexualized by their behavior.

Anderson interviewed sixty-eight self-identified heterosexual men aged eighteen to twenty-three who once played high-school football and then later become cheerleaders in American universities. Forty percent of his sample had sex with another man, yet this did not challenge their heterosexuality. "One time, me and

Heterosexualities

[my teammate] Trevor had a threesome with a girl. Yeah, well, I actually had a threesome with [my teammate] Drew, too." Jeff, the respondent, said that he also "made out" with another teammate, Ian, and once "jacked him off a bit too." Jeff still considers himself straight. "I'm not attracted to them," he explained. "It's just that there has to be something worth it. Like, this one girl said she'd fuck us if we both made out. So the ends justified the means. We call it a good cause." Patrick, one of Jeff's teammates, agreed: "There has got to be a reward. If I have to kiss another guy in order to fuck a chick, then yeah it's worth it. It's a good cause" (ibid.: 109). The "good cause argument" separates having sex with another man (or sexual behavior) from erotically desiring him (or sexual attraction). As young straight men do this, they "reproduce heterosexual privilege," Anderson argues, since "the good cause scenario retains the subjectivity of heterosexual desire and the need for a woman's sexual presence (and her request for their same-sex sexual behaviors)" (ibid.). His respondents, like many Americans today, separate their sexual identity from the labels we have long used. "I'm not into labels, and I don't think anybody is 100% anything, but I consider myself straight," one man explained. "I'm just not a homophobe."

Jane Ward (2008a) calls the phenomenon "dude sex," which she defines as "getting the kind of sex that all straight men want from women, but can only get from other men: uncomplicated, emotionless, guaranteed. "Str8 [a shorthand for straight] dudes get drunk, watch heterosexual porn, talk about 'pussy', and maintain a clear emotional boundary between each other that draws upon the model of adolescent friendship, or the presumably 'harmless,' 'proto-typical' circle jerk" (ibid.: 421). The conventional view of straight guy-on-guy action is that it occurs in moments of desperation and deprivation – think prisons, the military, and fraternity hazing rituals. Homosexual acts in such instances are isolated and situational, an erratic blip on an otherwise reliable heterosexual radar. There is nothing meaningful about it. According to Ward (2015: 7), "When heterosexual men *do* engage in homosexual sex, and if they are not immediately presumed to be in the closet, these practices are treated as momentary aberrations."

Heterosexualities

Ward finds that straight men draw on whiteness to establish heterosexual authenticity in a context of seducing other men. Her data consists of 125 ads from the "Casual Encounters" section of Craigslist in Los Angeles. Seventy-one percent of these ads made references to race. Of these, 86 percent were placed by white men. Ward argues that sexual contact between white men does not undermine their claims to heterosexuality provided that it exploits some racial strategies. For example, "white bros and thugs" (Ward 2008a: 422) appropriate terms of hip-hop masculinity, such as "sup" and "hit me up," to communicate that their sex will be "casual, meaningless, and embedded in heterosexual male culture" (ibid.: 423). Many men present themselves in their ads as surfers, jocks, and skaters; they wear flip-flops, tank tops, and shorts, all of which are "archetypes of white heterosexual masculinity" (ibid.: 424). One ad read as follows:

> Seeking a MASCULINE JACK OFF BUD to STR8 PORN – 29. Hot masculine white dude here . . . looking for another hot white dude to come by my place, and work out a hot load side by side. Straight porn only. Prefer str8, surfer, etc. Not usually into gay dudes. (Ibid.: 425)

Here's another ad:

> *Straight Dude Drunk and Horny* . . . *Any str8 bud wanna jack? – 27.* Here's the deal. Went out drinking and clubbing, thought I'd hook up with a chick, but didn't pan out. I'm buzzed, horny, checking out porn. Is there any other straight dude out there who would be into jacking while watching porn? . . . I'd rather hook up with a chick, but none of the CL [Craigslist] chicks ever work out. (Ibid.: 420)

Ward dives into this "heteroflexible" (aka, "I'm straight but shit happens") world of whiteness and male sexual fluidity in her book, where she examines "elephant walks" in fraternities and "crossing the line" rituals in the military. She introduces us to pledges who get naked and grab one another's penises and young men who stick their fingers up each other's anuses. In Ward's view, homosexual contact is a "ubiquitous feature of the culture of straight white men" (Ward 2015: 7), but these acts don't signal a

Heterosexualities

gay identity for them. Consider what a fraternity brother yells as he drags pledges out of bed early in the morning:

> Get up! Let's go! You aint seen shit! It's called the initiation. It's an important tradition. We're gonna teach you honor, community, and brotherhood! You want be part of this fuckin' fraternity, you're gonna fuckin' touch each other's dicks! . . . You wanna be a man, be a brother, keep going, suck that dick! (Ibid.: 177)

Media reports call this a "bro-job," or "when a straight guy gives another straight guy a blowie not in a meaningful sexual way but in a friendly, NSA [no strings attached], I'm-just-doing-you-a-little-favor, totally *not* gay sort of way."[23] Ward quotes an interviewee from another study, a navy lieutenant, who clarified the difference between gay sex and straight identity: "On submarines they have a joke that 'it's only queer if you're tied to the pier.' In other words, out at sea sex is okay, but once you're in port, you can't talk about that or they'll throw you out for it" (ibid.: 163).

From Craigslist to frats and the military, what matters is whether a man imagines himself culturally as a gay person or a straight person. This will affect how he will have sex with another man: "how he will set the scene, the narratives he will use to describe what is happening and why, the time and place the sex occurs, and whether it will be possible to imagine that the sex was never actually 'sexual' at all" (Ward 2015: 35). Such performances allow white men to "normalize and exceptionalize" their sexual behavior and "smooth over" inconsistencies (ibid.: 21). After having sex, a man will defend his heterosexuality by saying he was repulsed, the incident was experimental, or he was operating under conditions of extreme stress and duress. But homosexual acts still end up being a common feature of heterosexuality – so common, in fact, that Ward argues heterosexuality actually *requires* homosexual contact.

Ward's study has bold implications for the one-time rule of homosexuality – it is losing its stiff grip. Men can have sex with other with men while ensuring mutually legible heterosexual identities. There are caveats, however. Race is the first. We excuse the same-sex behavior of white men more readily than men of color, especially black and to a lesser extent Latino men, whom we assume are on the "down low" (Phillips 2005) – or in the closet on account of greater levels of homophobia and homohysteria in their respective communities. Whiteness and racial double standards are at play in these bro-jobs. Second, Ward's men do not conceptualize their behavior as erotic or even sexual. They call it "fucking around," she explains in an interview with *Next* magazine. "We're joking. We're drunk. This is hazing. It's not sexual." Put differently, "If you're a straight man, and you're so balls-out and you're so brave, this is something you might do just to show that you can," she adds. "You stand up unbroken, still heterosexual, even after letting another dude suck your dick."[24] The actor Tom Hardy is an example. When asked if he had ever had sex with men, Hardy replied,

> Of course I have. I'm an actor for fuck's sake. I'm an artist. I've played with everything and everyone. But I'm not into men sexually. I love the form and the physicality but the gay sex bit does nothing for me. In the same way as a wet vagina would turn someone else into a lemon-sucking freak. To me, it just doesn't compute.[25]

Finally, what makes a man straight is not the *absence* of sexual contact with other men but an *investment* in a culture of heteronormativity. Their cultural imagination defines heterosexuality as "natural, normal, and right ... It is the desire to be sexually unmarked and normatively gendered. It is a desire not simply for heterosexual sex and partnership, but for all of its concomitant cultural rewards" (Ward 2015: 35). Heterosexuality is part of a worldview and way of life, not just what you do with your body.

The contemporary landscape of heterosexuality is populated with provocative new terms: bromances, bro-jobs, cuddling arrangements, dude sex, the down-low, gay vague, heterodykes, heteroflexible, homosocial intimacy, lesbian continuum, menaissance, man-date, male-ationship, metrosexuals, platonic heteromasculine affection, political dykes, and sexual fluidity. These and others explode the assumed singularity of heterosexuality. They also show that race and gender interact to inflect heterosexualities with different meanings. What it means to be straight, just like

Heterosexualities

its coextensive companion what it means to be gay, is much too culturally complex to fit into a small number of neatly compartmentalized categories.

Conclusions

Men and women have been having sex since the beginning of time. So then how do we understand the assertion that heterosexuality has a history? Hanne Blank (2012), author of *Straight: The Surprisingly Short History of Heterosexuality*, offers an answer:

> We can talk about there being a history of heterosexuality in the same way that we can talk about there being a history of religions. People have been praying to God for a really long time too, and yet the ways people relate to the divine have specific histories. They come from particular places, they take particular trajectories, there are particular texts, and individuals that are important in them. There are events, names, places, dates. It's really very similar.[26]

Scholars such as Blank – and Katz, who has inspired us so much in this chapter – offer important take-away lessons: there is nothing natural, private, or fixed about heterosexuality. A more apt perspective directs us to think about the sex cultures (the collective norms about sex and sexuality) of heterosexuality and the cultural imagination (the meanings individuals use to make sense of the world in certain ways) of those who participate in them.

Sociologists have "not always been able to see straight" (Fischer 2013: 501); heterosexuality has been invisible to them for a long time as topic of study. Many scholars have just assumed its existence, probably because heterosexuality provided the baseline of a "normal, natural, healthy" sexuality. In this chapter, we have turned a critical eye on it, insisting that heterosexuality is a construct whose many meanings have been culturally invented over and over again. Our perspective is evocative of an area of scholarship called "critical heterosexuality studies." As I have done in this book, scholars who work in this area challenge our accumulated assumptions: that heterosexuality is natural and inevitable and

Heterosexualities

normative, that it is ahistorical and fixed and universal. We've brought a unique approach to the table by examining the sex cultures of heterosexuality as they are expressed in institutions (recall early medical classifications or more recent efforts in the military and the courts), meanings (think about terms such as "gay vague" and "bromance"), practices (the lesbian continuum and dude sex), and identities (consider the politically gay identity and straight allies).

Our awareness of sexuality has slowly, and often only grudgingly, expanded over the last 150 years. Today, especially in the academy, much of our efforts are geared toward studying those groups who have been ignored or oppressed. Thus, research on sexuality has focused disproportionately on gender and sexual minorities. Just as important, as I hope this chapter has shown you, is studying that which is common and modal – heterosexuality. I prefer words such as "common" and "modal" to "normal," which is how many people talk about heterosexuality. The very notion of a norm is a historical fabrication, but the only way to recognize that is to explore those ideas, like heterosexuality, that are so obvious, so entrenched, that we don't even see them. You might say that the greatest benefit of a cultural approach is to make us aware of those things that we didn't realize we already know.

Case Study: How Do We Define "Straight"?

"With a more normalized homosexuality, heterosexuals may have less to define themselves *against*," the sociologist Dawne Moon (2008: 192) argues. A quick peek at a couple of current events shows us how hard it has become to figure out what exactly it means to be "straight."

Current Event 1, Naked Rowers

In 2014, the University of Warwick men's rowing team decided to fight anti-gay bullying by getting naked. They produced a calendar of their squad posing in nude and often homoerotic scenes. They agreed to donate 10 percent of all profits from every product they sell (which includes films) to a charity called Sport Allies devoted to fighting homophobia and bullying. The rowing crew and their calendars received international attention. One journalist wrote, "Straight men take notice, if you are comfortable in your own skin, there should be no issue sharing moments with other men without having to be labeled gay, queer, homo or any other derogatory name commonly used in today's macho world."[27] As time passed, the rowers heard from a lot of gay men who adored their calendars. One of the guys on the team explained how they reacted to the attention: "Did we mind having gay fans, some of them asked? We didn't even understand the question. Why would we mind?" His teammate agreed, "Nobody should be afraid of anyone else's sexuality." A third added that they aspired to be "men who are not afraid to be themselves, to embrace people of every gender and sexuality, and to show our affection for each other."[28]

❖ *What are your thoughts about the Warwick Rowers? Can straight guys really pose nude in homoerotic scenes? Are these guys really just closeted gay men?*
❖ *Do you think American or Canadian university students could produce a calendar like this?*

Current Event 2, Straight Pride

In 2012, an anonymous user formed a public group on Facebook whose purpose was to designate July as "Heterosexual Awareness Month." The mission of the group was "to promote, celebrate, and protect heterosexuality." Participants hoped to organize a "straight pride day" to show their support and solidarity for heterosexuality.[29] Three years later, on July 25, a Seattle-based activist, Anthony Rebellow, staged a "heterosexual pride parade" in the city's Capitol Hill gayborhood (of all

Heterosexualities

places!). He invited more than 2,000 people on Facebook to join him "in the name of equality [and] equal rights ... to celebrate our right to be heterosexual, and to encourage younger heterosexuals that they should be proud of their heterosexuality." A meager 169 people responded "yes" to the event – but only one person showed up to the first-ever Seattle Heterosexual Pride Parade: Rebello himself. As he walked heterosexually through the gayborhood, passing rainbow flags and gay-owned businesses and many curious residents, Rebello held a cardboard sign that read "Straight Pride" while clutching a handful of balloons.[30]

- ❖ *What are your thoughts about heterosexual pride? Did it form for the same reasons as gay pride? Why do you think no one attended?*
- ❖ *Why would Rebello take his straight pride parade through the streets of a gayborhood?*
- ❖ *What do the Warwick Rowers and Straight Pride suggest about the sex cultures of heterosexuality today?*

Questions to Consider

1 How did people talk about heterosexuality before the word was invented?
2 Why does Katz say that early heterosexuals were "definitely not exemplars of normality?"
3 What does it mean to say that heterosexuality is "coextensive" or "diacritical" with homosexuality?
4 Katz turns to texts to trace the history of heterosexuality. What are the strengths and limitations of this methodology? How would arguments about the invention of heterosexuality be different if we adjusted our focus?
5 Starting with "true love" in the first period of heterosexuality, create a list of all the variants of heterosexuality. Define each. How are they similar? How are they different?
6 What other examples of heterosexualities can you come up with?

Heterosexualities

7 What is the relationship between homohysteria and the cultural imagination of heterosexuality?
8 Compare male and female heterosexualities. Are they both equally fluid?
9 Consider a question that Katz himself asks: Would human freedom be enhanced if we paid no attention to the biological sex of the people we were attracted to, and if we had no names to differentiate between same-sex attraction and opposite-sex attraction?
10 Find an article online that addresses a term about heterosexuality that we did not cover in this chapter. Which one did you select? What does it does it teach us about the cultural imagination of heterosexuality?

4
Studying Sexuality

Case Study: Gaydar

Jerry Seinfeld, the wisecracking comedian of the quotidian, once quipped, "I am not gay. I am, however, thin, single, and neat. Sometimes when someone is thin, single, and neat, people assume they are gay because that is a stereotype. They normally don't think of gay people as fat, sloppy, and married" (quoted in Cox et al. 2016).

Sexuality, unlike race or gender, is not visible on the body; we rely on clues to infer it. Enter gaydar. This neologism combines "gay" with "radar" to mean an intuition that people use to speculate about a person's sexual orientation. Today, gaydar is a staple of pop culture. But for decades, perhaps even centuries, before we started talking so openly about whether another person was gay or straight (and certainly before the words "homosexual" and "heterosexual" entered our lexicon), people hinted at their sexuality in cryptic ways. Historians have unearthed numerous instances of how people used cultural codes surreptitiously to communicate their sexuality.

American men in New York in the early 1900s wore a red necktie as a "subtle signal" to disclose their homosexuality to "those in the know" (Chauncey 1994: 52). Between the 1930s

Studying Sexuality

and 1960s, British gay men developed a secret language called "Polari" that they used to out themselves and find similar others. One man might say, "Vada the eek dear. Don't tell me you haven't seen her. She's been trolling round here for years." This would be inscrutable to an outsider, but the insider will hear, "Look at that face. Don't tell me you haven't seen him. He's been walking around here for years."[1]

Screenwriters used coded words to describe homosexual characters. A real boarding-school afternooner, someone who eats his dinner in a restaurant, a fellow who walks down the shady side of a street, a gentleman of the piers, an individual who is a sunset lover or the son of a moon, someone who salutes another flag, rides the carousel, gives a careful handshake, is fond of his mother, or an avowed bachelor – if you heard any of these phrases to portray a character in a movie that was made before 1970, there's a good chance that they described a gay man.[2] A real shadows girl or an evening girl, someone who prefers the hour just after dusk, a gal with her own library card, who pays her own way, is well read, scholarly, and independent-minded, a woman who is standoffish, incurable, keeps her hands in her pockets, and stands up on a night train, a shirts-and-trousers female, or a real pal who carries her own purse – in classic films, all of these phrases characterized lesbians.[3]

Cultural codes communicate sexuality without requiring us to say it out loud. People adopt them so that they can be *read by others* as gay. Gaydar is culture's companion, an alleged ability to detect and decipher those codes so that we can *read others* as gay. Gaydar makes cultural codes legible and intelligible to us. But is it real or just a myth? Cox et al. (2016: 168) put the question about the validity of gaydar into perspective: "The very notion of gaydar would require that gay men and lesbians each possess some common essence that differentiates them from their straight counterparts and makes their orientation perceptible." Whether this essentialist position about gaydar is compatible with a cultural approach is up for debate.

Studying Sexuality

Some studies find that people can assess the sexual orientation of a stranger with above chance accuracy just by looking at photographs of their faces. One team of researchers created an experiment that involved more than one hundred undergraduate students. Those who were in the experimental group saw ninety-six randomly ordered faces of gay men, straight men, gay women, and straight women, and they were asked to judge their sexual orientation. The researchers found that participants were better than chance alone at reading men's sexual orientation (57 percent accuracy) and even better at reading women's sexual orientation (65 percent accuracy). They concluded, "Naïve perceivers can, in fact, read sexual orientation from unknown others' faces" (Tabak and Zayas 2012: 3). This happens astonishingly fast – within 50 milliseconds, in some cases (Rule and Ambady 2008).

Other researchers added descriptive statements alongside the facial photographs. Among examples of these "gay-stereotypic," "straight-stereotypic," and "stereotype-neutral" statements were the following: he is a hairdresser, he is fashionable, he likes musical theatre, he plays football, he drives a pickup truck, he likes cars, he likes to travel, he is outgoing, and he likes listening to music. Adding stereotypes about sexuality next to a person's face affects our gaydar – or at least what we think is our gaydar. "Orientation is not visible from the face," they rebut. Their findings suggest a counterargument: people rely on stereotypes to infer the sexual orientation of others. The researchers also found that participants stereotyped more frequently if they believed that gaydar was real but less when they were told that "gaydar is an alternate label for stereotyping" (Cox et al. 2016).

❖ *What do you think is the relationship between gaydar and the cultural imagination?*
❖ *Now that you have received some training in a cultural approach to the study of sexuality, how would you respond to Cox et al.'s assertion about a "common essence"? What is gaydar if not an expression of essential differences between gays and straights?*

Studying Sexuality

❖ *A commentary on Polari suggests that the language is "no longer necessary. British laws and society have changed dramatically since the middle of the twentieth century. Now, as one aficionado said, it's purely a celebration of a lost culture."[4] Having read this statement, recall our discussions about the city and protest, especially when we talked about a "post-gay" era. Do we need cultural codes – and gaydar to read them – in countries that have high levels of acceptance for sexual diversity?*
❖ *Now recall our discussion of heterosexualities, especially the ascendance of gay vague, metrosexuality, bromances, and sexual fluidity in men and women. What do you think it means if a straight man or a straight woman sets off your gaydar?*

Studying sexuality and culture is not easy. Both concepts are "chameleon-like" and can take "many shapes and forms" (Binder et al. 2008: 8). According to the American Psychological Association, sexual orientation includes sexual attraction (about whom do you fantasize physically, emotionally, and romantically?), behaviors (with whom do you experience arousal, genital contact, and orgasm?), and identities (how do you self-identify, and what labels do you use to describe yourself?).[5] That these three aspects of sexual orientation do not always line up, as we have already seen, muddies the matter.

Think about who you've had sex with. Laumann, Gagnon, Michael, and Michaels (1994) found that, among women who had had at least one female sex partner since they were eighteen years old, only 28 percent had been involved over the past year in exclusively same-sex partnerships. For men, 42 percent who had had a male same-sex partner since age eighteen had exclusively same-sex sex over the year before they conducted their survey. The study also found that about half of American men who reported same-sex sexual contact had had both male and female partners in the past year of the study. The same was true for almost two-thirds of the women the authors surveyed. Another way to think about these findings is to compare the lifetime figures for *any* homosexual contact with the lifetime figure for *exclusive* homosexual contact. Only one in every fifteen men with homosexual experience has had an exclusive portfolio of such behavior, while the same is true for only one in every twenty-one women. What do these small numbers of people who are "exclusively" gay or lesbian mean? How can we incorporate the numbers into our cultural imagination?

As with so many aspects of life, the answers you find are shaped by the questions you ask. In general, measuring sexual attraction will provide the greatest prevalence of homosexuality in a population, whereas measuring gay, lesbian, or bisexual self-identification will produce the lowest. People who indicate that they are attracted to someone of the same sex are two to three times greater in number than those who claim a non-heterosexual identity (Laumann et al. 1994: 301). Based on these and other similar findings, Michael (1994: 182) concludes, "Far more women and men experimented with homosexuality than currently identify themselves as lesbians or gays. It seems likely that many try it and then go back to being heterosexuals, neither desiring others of their own gender nor finding the idea of homosexual sex very appealing."

Sexuality is fluid. It is not always stable or consistent over the course of our lives (Diamond 2008). The implications of this plasticity for studying sexuality – or, I should say, for attempting to study it – are staggering. A person who is classified as gay or lesbian in one study may not be construed that way in another. If we define homosexuality by same-sex behavior, then we will omit gay virgins while including self-identified straight men who trade "bro-jobs" with other men (Ward 2015). If homosexuality is defined by a person who proclaims an identity label such as "gay" or "lesbian," then we will exclude those people who experience same-sex arousal or behavior but do not identify as gay, lesbian, or even bisexual. In the biological and health sciences, a single instance of same-sex behavior automatically places an individual in the "homosexual" category, "with little regard for the sexual context, what constitutes sex, the desirability of enjoyment of sex, or the frequency of sex" (Savin-Williams 2006), not to mention that person's label of choice at any given time.

Studying Sexuality

Culture as a concept presents similar challenges when we try to study it. It is "one of the two or three most complicated words in the English language" (Geertz 1973: 87). Debates rage over what the term means, and these trickle down to confusion over how to study it. A classic definition for culture in the humanities references "the best that has been thought and known" (Arnold [1869] 1949), while social scientists use the same word to mean "that complex whole which includes knowledge, belief, art, morals, law, custom, and any other capabilities and habits acquired by man as a member of society" (Tylor [1871] 1958). Seeking parsimony, some sociologists say that the word "culture" specifies one or more of four ideas: beliefs, expressive symbols, norms, and values (Peterson 1979). This dizzying array of definitions across disciplines prompted Gary Alan Fine (1979: 733) to describe culture as "an amorphous, indescribable mist which swirls around society members." But this raises a conundrum: If culture, like sexuality, is a chameleon that can blend into its surroundings and shift its appearance, then how do we observe it? Or, as I have asked elsewhere (Ghaziani 2009): how do you measure mist?

In this final chapter, we will tackle the challenges associated with studying sexuality. We will organize our inquiry around one of the most frequently asked questions in the field, wondered about by experts and everyone else: How many people are gay? The point of these pages, I hasten to add, is not to answer once and for all this vexing question. If sexuality is fluid, as research shows, then the search for an answer, one that is fixed and final, puts us in danger of subscribing to the same assumptions that we've worked so hard to debunk. Besides, we care about culture, not demography. Throughout this book, we have seen how culture binds with sex to produce sexuality in the city, in politics and protest, and how culture cultivates plural expressions of heterosexuality. Rather than discuss yet another facet of sexuality (the possibilities are endless!), we will tilt the frame to its scientific study, that process which has produced the knowledge that we've been absorbing all along. We will study the study of sexuality.

It is time to see how researchers (especially those who use surveys) collect data about sexuality – and how we need a cultural imagination to make sense of that data. My choice to focus on certain methodological strategies is deliberate. Surveys, experiments, and other quantitative techniques are explicitly concerned with how to represent the social world and provide observational grounding to it (and let's not forget that the question of estimating the size of the gay and lesbian population is a numerical inquiry). Things like the experiments in the opening case study or surveys like Gallup and the census are the outcome of meticulous efforts to coordinate theoretical concepts with representational procedures. To ensure that the ideas in this chapter are relevant to as many people as possible, I will focus on measurement (perhaps unexpectedly, you might think). The topic captures curiosities that are shared by scientific and humanistic "styles of knowing," since measurement expresses the "continuum of quality and quantity" (Mohr and Ghaziani 2014: 229, 234). Exactly how to convert something as complex as "sexuality" – and especially its meanings – into "observable analytic units" (Ghaziani 2014a: 375) is undeniably a cultural enterprise. Our approach will reveal that science, like sexuality, is constantly shifting and evolving; it, too, is far from fixed or monolithic. Thus, "How many gay people are there?" is a really just a question that I am using, along with several related puzzles about overestimation, composite concepts, writing survey questions and response categories, measuring the closet, and measuring the transgender population, to pull back the curtain and expose some of the "tricks of the trade" (Becker 1998).

How Many People are Gay or Lesbian?

If you had to guess, what percentage of people would you say are gay or lesbian? Stop reading and think about it for a minute. Chances are that you're wrong (sorry). Recent research shows that we routinely *overestimate* the size of the non-heterosexual population. "The American public estimates on average that 23% of Americans are gay or lesbian," notes the Gallup organization in its 2015 report on the measurement of social issues.

Studying Sexuality

Table 4.1 Guestimates of the gay and lesbian population (percentages)

	Mean	Less than 5%	5% to <10%	10% to <15%	15% to <20%	20% to <25%	More than 25%	No opin.
2015	23	9	11	14	7	20	33	6
2011	25	4	9	17	9	17	35	8
2002*								
Men	21	8	11	16	9	15	25	16
Women	22	7	14	12	7	17	24	19

*Asked of a half sample with wording, with separate questions:
Just your best guess, what percent of men in the United States today would you say are homosexual or gay?
Just your best guess, what percent of women in the United States today would you say are homosexual or lesbian?
Source: Copyright © 2015 Gallup, Inc.[6] All rights reserved. The content is used with permission; however, Gallop retains all rights of republication.

Thirty-three percent of the public estimates the size of the population at more than 25 percent. Younger people guess higher than those who are older. Men and women make similar guesses, and the numbers have remained stable since Gallup first asked the question in 2002. Table 4.1 reports the results that the Gallup organization received in response to the following question: "Just your best guess, what percent of Americans today would you say are gay or lesbian?"

Nearly everyone is wrong! Only 9 percent of Americans correctly estimate the size of the gay and lesbian population at somewhere under 5 percent. Why do people overestimate, despite the availability of actual data that shows far fewer numbers? Part of the explanation comes from Americans' general misunderstanding of social statistics. Similar errors arise in their estimation of racial and ethnic populations. Gallup remarks, "Americans estimate that a third of the U.S. population is black, and believe almost three in 10 are Hispanic, more than twice what the actual percentages were as measured by the census." The better educated you are, the lower your estimates. Therefore, lack of experience with seeing demographic data and interpreting those numbers accounts for some of the reason why people provide overestimates.

Studying Sexuality

Table 4.2 Estimates of the US gay and lesbian population by age, gender, and education

	Mean estimate %
18 to 29	28
30 to 49	24
50 to 64	21
65+	20
Men	19
Women	27
Postgraduates	15
College graduates	17
Some college	25
High school or less	28

May 6–10, 2015
Source: Copyright © 2015 Gallup, Inc. All rights reserved. The content is used with permission; however, Gallop retains all rights of republication.

Table 4.3 Estimates of the US gay and lesbian population by political party and ideology

	Mean estimate %
Democrats	25
Independents	24
Republicans	19
Social liberals	24
Social moderates	24
Social conservatives	21
Same-sex marriage should be valid	25
Same-sex marriage should not be valid	21

May 6–10, 2015
Source: Copyright © 2015 Gallup, Inc. All rights reserved. The content is used with permission; however, Gallop retains all rights of republication.

Younger people, women, and Democrats make higher guesses than those who are older, men, and Republicans (tables 4.2 and 4.3). This distribution of responses suggests that another factor is at play besides education and familiarity with statistics. What do younger people, women, and Democrats have in common? What distinguishes them from older folks, men, and

Studying Sexuality

Republicans when it comes to how they estimate the size of the gay and lesbian population? The Gallup organization didn't ask these questions. Instead, it explored the effects of education levels, as we heard, and the media as well. The pollsters conclude: "The overestimation may also reflect prominent media portrayals of gay characters on television and in the movies . . . and perhaps the high visibility of activists who have pushed gay causes."[7] The problem is that this should apply equally to younger *and* older people, women *and* men, Democrats *and* Republicans. One hypothesis for the demographic difference is that those who are more liberal in their attitudes toward homosexuality will offer greater estimates about the size of the gay and lesbian population.

Figure 4.1 lets us test this proposition. It shows responses to Gallup surveys which asked about support for same-sex marriage at two points in time: 1996 and 2015 (the question was still hypothetical, since the survey was administered in May 2015, more than a year before the US Supreme Court legalized same-sex marriage in *Obergefell v. Hodges*). Although support had risen across the board, there are notable differences within groups. Women reported greater rates of support than men, younger people more than older cohorts; university graduates were more supportive than those who did not graduate, and Democrats were significantly more supportive than Republicans. These are also the groups that estimated greater prevalence rates for homosexuality (Gallup did not ask how different racial/ethnic groups estimate prevalence or how it varies across regions). Thus, we might hypothesize that, if you support a minority group, you will have an inflated perception about its size. A social justice-oriented cultural imagination may be the mechanism that explains this relationship.

Another hypothesis is that our estimates about the prevalence of homosexuality will vary depending on whether we ask about sexual/romantic attraction or arousal; sexual behavior, acts, and contact; or sexual identity. Researchers call variables such as sexuality "composite measures" (Babbie 2012) because they consist of multiple components. To study them, we need to ask questions that capture each slice of the larger concept. Imagine what would happen to our understanding of sexuality if we asked

Studying Sexuality

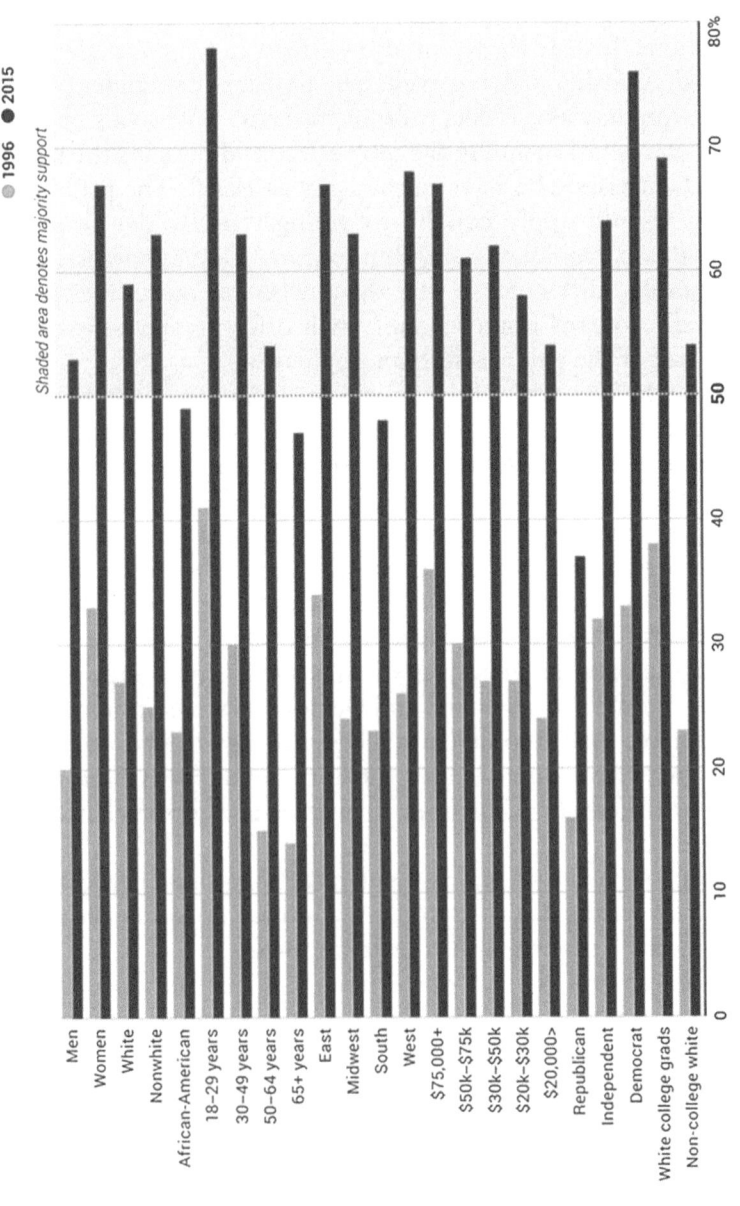

Figure 4.1 Support for same-sex marriage, 1996 and 2015

Source: Brownstein (2015); © 2015 The Atlantic Media Co., as first published in *The Atlantic Magazine*. All rights reserved. Distributed by Tribune Content Agency.

Studying Sexuality

questions *only* about a person's attractions and fantasies, or if we inquired *only* into sex acts, or if we relied *only* on self-reports of identity. Our knowledge about the "new gay" twentysomethings who frown upon gayborhoods, queer critics of marriage equality, bromances, straight girls kissing, and other sex cultures would be partial and limited. We need to make multiple observations because sex cultures, the ways of life that we create based on expressions of our sexuality, are themselves many-sided.

Table 4.4 identifies the three major components of sexual orientation and shows sample questions that we can ask to learn about them. Based on this information, Savin-Williams (2006: 40) advises us to be precise when we study sexuality: "The three components are imperfectly correlated and inconsistently predictive of each other, resulting in dissimilar conclusions regarding the number and nature of homosexual populations. Depending on which component is assessed, the prevalence rate of homosexuality in the general population ranges from 1 to 21%." As we can see in figure 4.2, the responses also vary by cohort (youth, young adult, and adult) and country (we'll revisit cross-national trends later).

The different measures for sexual orientation are not interchangeable. They do not measure the same thing nor do they produce the same results. Asking about attraction returns the highest prevalence rates of homosexuality, as I mentioned earlier. The numbers are two or three times as high as those we find by asking about same-sex behavior or self-identification as gay, lesbian, or bisexual. Savin-Williams (2006: 41) remarks, "The majority of individuals attracted to their own sex or engaging in same-sex sexual behavior do not identify as homosexual." This finding was so powerful that journalists circulated it beyond the academy. "Survey language affects how people answer polls about sexuality," notes Arit John, writing in 2014 for *The Atlantic*. For his story, John inquired into the obstacles that Gallup faces. "Measuring sexual orientation and gender identity can be challenging since these concepts involve complex social and cultural patterns."[8] This is why composite measures are valuable: they provide holistic insights about sex cultures.

Studying Sexuality

Table 4.4 Definitions of sexual orientation and sample questions

Component	Definition	Questions
Sexual/romantic attraction	Attraction toward one sex or the desire to have sexual relations or to be in a primary loving, sexual relationship with one or both sexes	"On a scale of 1 to 4, where 1 is very appealing and 4 is not at all appealing, how would you rate each of these activities: . . . having sex with someone of the same sex?" (Laumann et al. 1994: 293) "Have you ever had a romantic attraction to a male? Have you ever had a romantic attraction to a female?" (Udry and Chantala 2005: 484)
Sexual behavior	"Any mutual voluntary activity with another person that involves genital contact and sexual excitement or arousal, that is, feeling really turned on, even if intercourse or orgasm did not occur." (Laumann et al. 1994: 67)	"Have you ever had a relationship with someone of your own sex which resulted in sexual orgasm?" (Eskin et al. 2005: 188)
Sexual identity	Personally selected, socially and historically bound labels attached to the perceptions and meanings individuals have about their sexuality	"Pick from these six options: gay or lesbian; bisexual, but mostly gay or lesbian; bisexual; equally gay/lesbian and heterosexual; bisexual, but mostly heterosexual; heterosexual; and uncertain, don't know for sure." (D'Augelli et al. 2001: 252) "Do you think of yourself as heterosexual, homosexual, bisexual, or something else?" (Laumann et al. 1994: 293)

Source: Copyright © 2006 by Savin-Williams. Reprinted by permission of Sage Publications, Inc.

Studying Sexuality

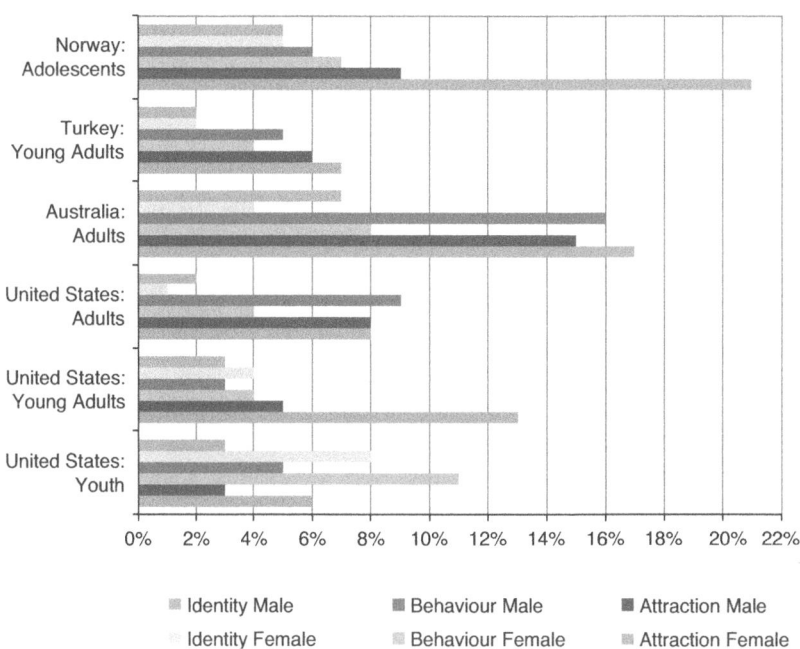

Figure 4.2 How many people are gay?
Source: based on data from Savin-Williams (2006).

Sexuality and Surveys

What, then, is the actual size of the gay and lesbian population, and how do we best determine it? As the story in *The Atlantic* implied, surveys are the go-to instrument to find answers. They are an efficient way to collect a sample that can represent the entire population (now might be a good time to freshen up on probability theory). Imagine for a moment that you wanted to create a survey and distribute it at your university or your workplace. Based on what you have learned so far, what questions would you ask? Would you ask about self-identity? If so, how many categories would you include? Or would you ask about the frequency of same-sex behavior? Or sexual attraction? If you incorporated all

141

these measures, how would you manage the inconsistencies that Savin-Williams (2006) warned you about – people who experience same-sex attraction and have experienced same-sex contact, for example, but who self-identify as heterosexual?

Several population-based surveys across the world include questions that researchers use to estimate the number of gays, lesbians, and bisexuals (GLBs), and they allow us to explore more deeply the cross-national variation that we encountered earlier. Given the complexities of measuring sexual orientation, it's no surprise that our estimates for the percentage of adults who identify as GLB vary considerably (figures 4.3 to 4.7).

Figure 4.3 reports the results of nine international surveys that describe the prevalence of GLB-identified adults. Five surveys were based in the United States, and the others were in Canada, the United Kingdom, Australia, and Norway. The lowest numbers come from Norway, while the highest numbers come from the United States. In general, non-US surveys estimate lower percentages of non-heterosexual self-identification (ranging from 1.2 to 2.1 percent). Estimates from the US range from 1.7 to 5.6 percent. If we averaged these surveys, we would conclude that 1.7 percent of adults in the United States self-identify as gay or lesbian, 1.8 percent as bisexual and 0.3 percent as transgender. This means that there are about 9 million GLBT Americans. Estimates of the prevalence of same-sex behavior produce different counts. About 8.2 percent of survey respondents (19 million Americans) report that they have engaged in same-sex contact at some point in their lifetime, and 11 percent (25.6 million Americans) acknowledge feeling some same-sex sexual attraction (Gates 2011).

Another way to think about estimating GLB-identified adults is to poll members of just this group, rather than all adults in a population, and ask about their specific identities (figure 4.4). In most surveys, the number of adults who say they are gay or lesbian outnumbers those who call themselves bisexuals (60 versus 40 percent, respectively). The National Survey of Family Growth found the opposite: only 38 percent identified as gay or lesbian compared to 62 percent as bisexual. The National Survey of Sexual Health and Behavior and the Australian Longitudinal

Studying Sexuality

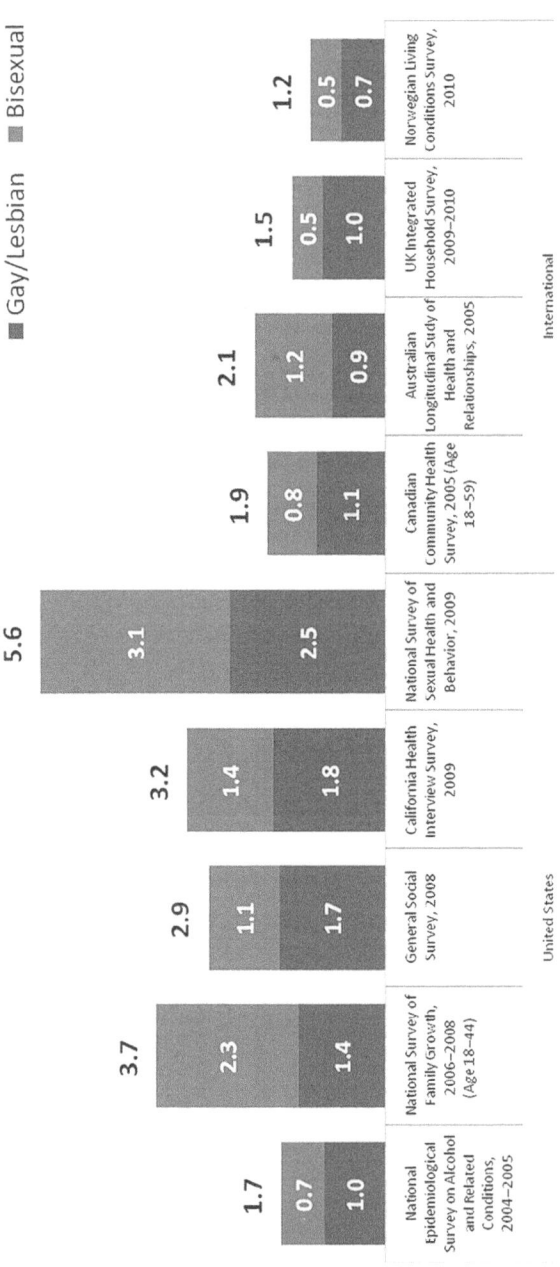

Figure 4.3 Percentage of adults who identify as lesbian, gay, or bisexual, 2005–2010

Source: Gates (2011) with permission from The Williams Institute.

Studying Sexuality

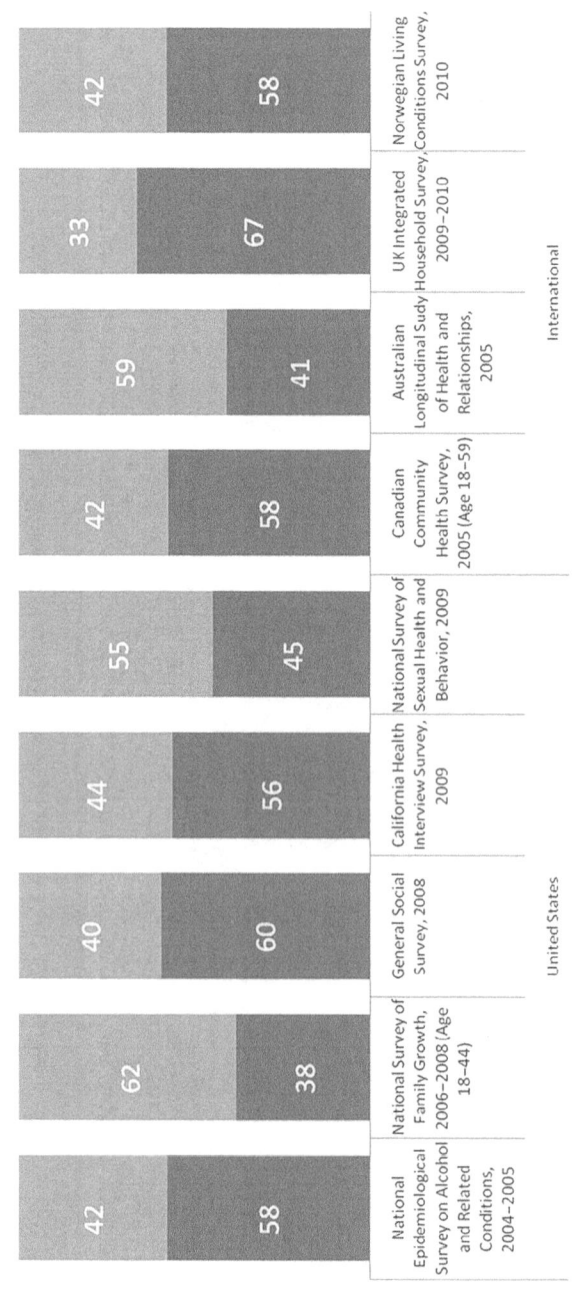

Figure 4.4 Percentage of adults who identify as gay or lesbian versus bisexual

Source: Gates (2011) with permission from The Williams Institute.

144

Studying Sexuality

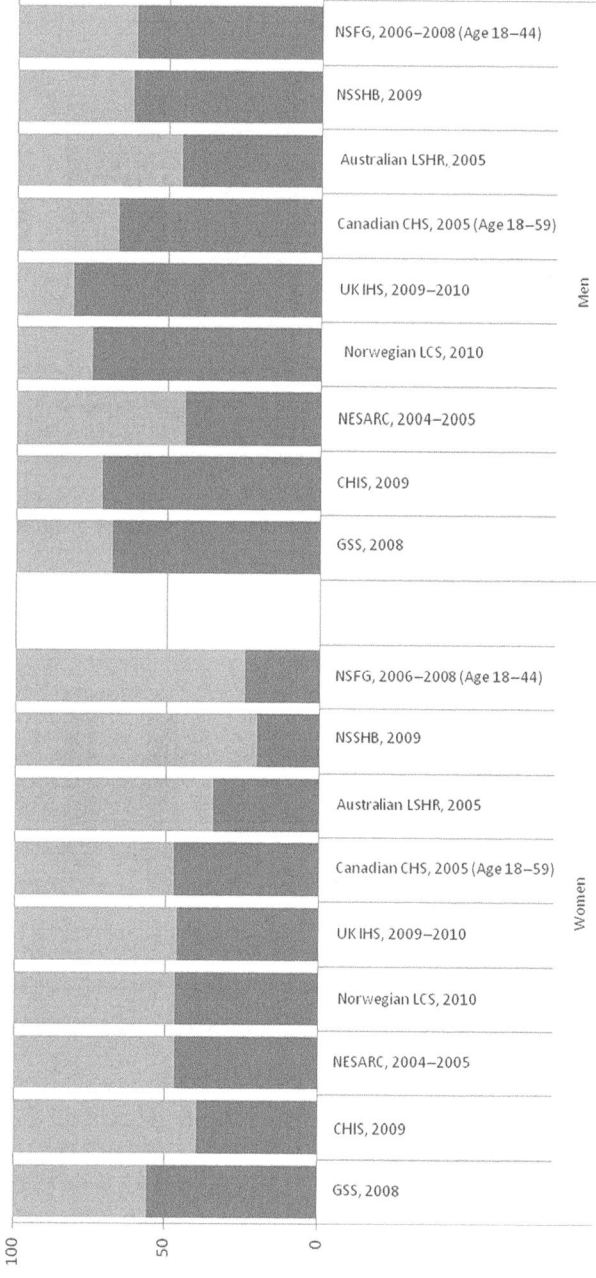

Figure 4.5 Self-identification by sex (percentages)

Source: Gates (2011) with permission from The Williams Institute.

145

Studying Sexuality

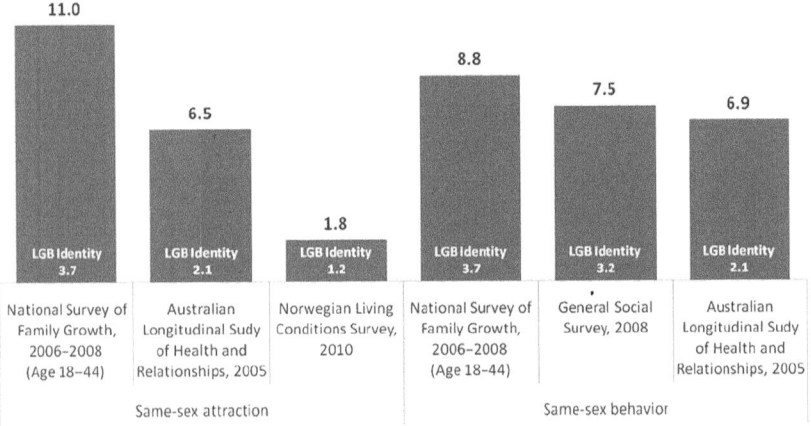

Figure 4.6 Percentage of adults who report any same-sex attraction and behavior

Source: Gates (2011) with permission from The Williams Institute.

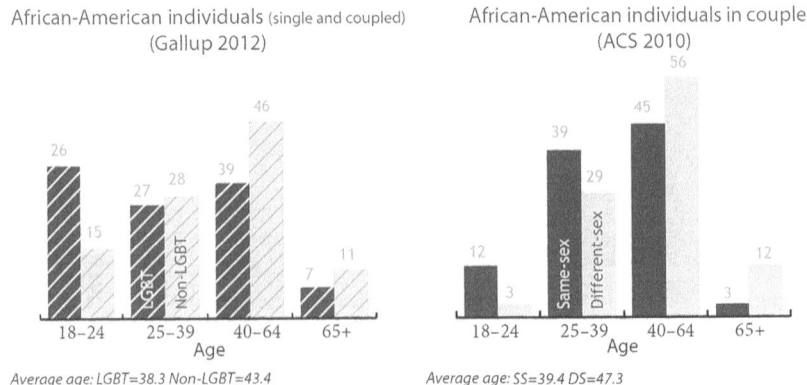

Figure 4.7 African-American individuals (single and coupled) (percentages)

Source: Kastanis and Gates (2013a) with permission from The Williams Institute.

Study of Health and Relationships found a similar pattern of greater bisexual identification.

What about gender differences? Figure 4.5 shows that women are more likely than men to identify as bisexual. This implies that the relationship between attraction, behavior, and identity varies

Studying Sexuality

by gender. That women identify as bisexual more often than men might inspire us to compare the sex cultures of female fluidity (recall the work by Lisa Diamond from the last chapter) with those of dude-sexing men (recall Jane Ward's scholarship). We might hypothesize that same-sex behavior is more likely to affect the adoption of a non-binary identity for women than it is for men because men are able to engage in sexual acts without triggering a change in their cultural imagination.

Figure 4.6 explores the intuition of our hypothesis and shows what happens when we ask separately about sexual behavior and attraction. Adults are two to three times more likely to say that they are attracted to a person of the same sex or that they have had same-sex sexual *contact* than they are to identify as gay, lesbian, or bisexual. Gates (2011: 7), who complied these studies into a concise report, offers a useful mental exercise to put the numbers into perspective: "These analyses suggest that the size of the LGBT community is roughly equivalent to the population of New Jersey. The number of adults who have had same-sex sexual experiences is approximately equal to the population of Florida while those who have some same-sex attraction comprise more individuals than the population of Texas."

An "intersectional approach" (Crenshaw 1991), one that stresses the connections between different facets of our identities (such as race and sexuality), provides more texture to our knowledge about sex cultures by showing that the meanings of sex and sexuality are a product of "intersecting patterns" (ibid.: 1243). A mistake that some researchers make is to overlook the sex cultures of people who are black *and* gay or Latino *and* lesbian. Thus, we need to account for "multiple grounds of identity" (ibid.: 1245) when we think about sex cultures. The 2012 Gallup Daily tracking survey shows that approximately 3.7 percent of African-American adults (or 1,018,700 individuals) self-identify as GLBT. On average, GLBT African-American individuals are younger than the non-GLBT African-American population and African-Americans in same-sex couples (figure 4.7).

The same survey also shows that about 4.3 percent of Latino/a adults (or 1.4 million individuals) self-identify as GLBT. Similar

Studying Sexuality

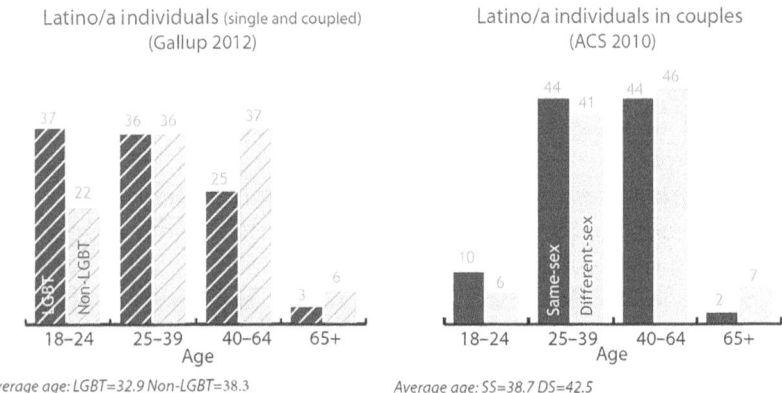

Figure 4.8 Latino/a individuals (percentages)

Source: Kastanis and Gates (2013b) with permission from The Williams Institute.

to the findings for African-Americans, GLBT Latino/a individuals are younger than both the non-GLBT Latino/a population and Latinos/as in same-sex couples (figure 4.8).

That there is a significant difference between rates of same-sex attraction and behavior, and that there are additional differences based on race and gender, should be where we begin, not end, our conversation. What do these differences tell us about the pathways that produce sex cultures? Having sex with someone of the same sex "means" something different – it has more cultural gravitas – than being attracted to someone of the same sex. We know this to be true because others believe it as well; it is part of our sociological imagination (recall this idea from C. Wright Mills). Think for a moment about how many more things you desire in your life (your attractions) than those on which you act (your behaviors). You probably wanted to be twenty different things when you grew up; chances are, you picked one or two. When we apply this logic to sex cultures, we can appreciate that they sometimes form around perspectives that are widely shared. Remind yourself about the lesbian feminists who were committed to separatist politics or those Victorians who subscribed to a model of true love. Sex cultures also arise to accommodate those people who go against the grain of the public – hence the straight men who freely trade bro-jobs, even if the dominant or "hegemonic" (Gramsci 1971) cultural imagination of heterosexuality enforces the "one-time rule of homosexuality" (Anderson 2008). Finally, sex cultures form in response to intersectional expressions, the ways in which sexuality is inflected by our race or gender. This explains why the culture of dude sex is a white male phenomenon, whereas black men who do the same thing are dismissed as being "really gay" and just on the "down low" (see Ward 2008a for more on this point). Thus, there are many paths through which the meanings we associate with sexual attraction, behavior, and identity coalesce into sex cultures.

What is the closet? Who's in it? How do we measure it?

The problems of studying sexuality are aggravated by the enduring stigma of homosexuality – regardless of how "post-gay" we think we are. In any and every survey, we have to account for the fact that fear or shame might prevent some people who self-identify as GLB from being honest in their responses; we would then underestimate the size of the population. Thus, our task is twofold. Not only do we need to figure out how to engineer our surveys so that the answers we receive give us the most honest data, but we also need to figure out who is not being honest with us. How do we measure people who don't want to be measured?

To increase the validity of our estimates of the GLB population, we need to find ways of measuring the size of the closet. Gates (2012: 702) explains, "[H]ow might we measure the closet? In essence, we are attempting to measure a population that, by definition, does not want to be measured." First, we need to define the closet. Gates summarizes an approach that many people take: the closet consists of people "who are discordant with regard to recent behavior and identity, along with those who intentionally hide their LGB identity" (ibid.: 704). Earlier, Savin-Williams (2006) provided clues for how to capture the first part – the inconsistencies between behavior and identity (see table 4.4). But what

Studying Sexuality

about the second part – those people who hide? The 2008 General Social Survey included several questions that the Williams Institute commissioned about the decision of respondents to disclose their sexual identity. Analyses of those responses reveal that "0.3 percent of adults self-identify as LGB but indicate that they have never told anyone about their sexual orientation – even though they identified as LGB on the survey." For Gates, this group "represents a direct measurement of the closet" (2012: 703).

What happens when we measure the closet *indirectly* by comparing responses that people offer about their sexual behavior from those they report about their sexual identity? Untangling the components of sexual orientation may help us open the closet. Gates discovered the following: "If we consider those who have had any same-sex behavior since age eighteen and then add those who self-identify as gay, lesbian, and bisexual, we find that about 7.7 percent of adults either self-identify as gay, lesbian, or bisexual or report that they have had a same-sex sexual encounter." Two-thirds (5.2 percent) of this group consists of people who report having had same-sex sexual contact yet still self-identify as heterosexual. "This could represent one estimate of the closet," according to Gates (2012: 703). When we narrow our definition of the GLB population to those who self-identify or have had a *recent* same-sex encounter, then the gap between behavior and identity shrinks. Only 1 percent of adults have had same-sex contact in the last five years but do not self-identify as GLB. Combined with the 0.3 percent of adults who intentionally hide their sexual orientation, this suggests that 1.3 percent of adults are in the closet (representing 37 percent of the GLB population). If we include only sexual behavior in the past year and add those people who are consciously concealing who they are from others, then only 1 percent of adults are in the closet (or 30 percent of the GLB population). Here, as before, the implications for how we define our concepts (and which components we measure) are alarming. "As a proportion of the LGB community, the closet under the latter two definitions is half of what it would be when compared to an LGB definition that includes lifetime same-sex sexual behaviors" (ibid.: 704).

Studying Sexuality

This strategy for how to measure the closet is clever but inconsistent with some of the newest research on heterosexuality. Remember the following argument from Ward (2015: 7) that we heard in the previous chapter: "When heterosexual men *do* engage in homosexual sex, and if they are not immediately presumed to be in the closet, these practices are treated as momentary aberrations." For Ward, men who identify as heterosexual but have sex with other men are neither latently homosexual nor in the closet. She argues that homosexual contact is a "ubiquitous feature of the culture of straight white men" (ibid.) – and it has nothing to do with gay or even bisexual identity.

To remedy persistent misconceptions that men who have sex with other men are "actually gay or bisexual but refuse to accept those identities," epidemiologists more than two decades ago created the behavior-based category of MSM, which stands for "men who have sex with men" (Carrillo and Hoffman 2016: 1). In avoiding a conventional identity-based category, the goal of epidemiologists was to find better ways of counting "non-gay-identified MSM" without automatically assuming that they are closeted gay men. The category conjures sex cultures from a group of people whom we might not have otherwise identified as distinct. It also unscrambles sexual behavior from sexual identity and makes it easier for us not to conflate these two aspects of sexuality.

The language of MSM never caught on beyond academic and medical circles. Terms such as "heteroflexible," "mostly straight," and "bicurious" have become more popular within and beyond the academy. These neologisms expand the definition of heterosexuality (and reduce the size of the closet) by incorporating same-sex desires and practices into the sex cultures of straights. In their study of 100 straight-identified men who use the "Men4Men" section of Craigslist, Carrillo and Hoffman (2016: 5) found that half confirmed during an interview that "the labels 'straight' and 'heterosexual' fully describe them." Twenty-three adopted words that evoked heteroflexibility, and twenty-six revealed that in private they might call themselves bisexual – but they quickly added that they would never openly adopt such an identity because they preferred to maintain "a public identity as straight" (ibid.).

Many of these men were "convinced that they are significantly different from strictly bisexual or gay men" (ibid.: 6).

The men in Carrillo and Hoffman's study defended their cultural imagination as heterosexual, despite their sexual interest in men, in one of four ways. First, they emphasized that they are "primarily attracted to women, which is a cornerstone of their ability to identity as straight" (2016: 6). In effect, they downplayed their attractions to men. Second, some of the participants said that sex with other men "is not comparable in any way to having sex with women in terms of pleasure, meaning, or significance." These men reported feeling "odd" after they orgasm, and they do not experience "the same afterglow that I would have with a woman . . . the feel good feeling after sex" (ibid.: 8). The third strategy that men use to justify their pursuit of sex with other men without compromising their heterosexuality has to do with relieving the pressures of masculinity. One man said, "I'm a good father. I'm a good husband in providing material things for my wife . . . I'm in charge in a lot of places . . . There's times when I don't want to be in charge, and I want someone to be in charge of me . . . it's kind of submitting to another guy or being used by another guy" (ibid.: 9). Finally, some men said they have sex with men as a way to "spice up" their sex lives with women. For instance, one man said that his girlfriend told him "it would be hot to see me with a guy" (ibid.: 10). These arguments show us that we can increase the elasticity of heterosexuality as a category (and thus reduce estimates of the size of the closet) when we allow for the possibility of same-sex contact within it. Demanding consistency across sexual attraction, behavior, and identity constrains our understanding of the composition of sex cultures.

What You Learn Depends on What You Ask

So far, we have used the puzzle of "how many people are gay" as a guide to think about measuring sexuality in surveys, the inconsistencies among the components of sexual orientation, how our other identities shape our experiences of sexuality (what we

Studying Sexuality

called "intersectionality"), variation across countries, and how to estimate the size of the closet. Our conversation has implied a concern about the power of words. Thus, in this short section, we'll shift our inquiry away from estimating the size of the GLB population and ask a question that's been rumbling beneath the surface this entire time: Why does it matter which words we use when we write a survey? Specifically, does it make a difference if we ask about "homosexual relations" or "gay and lesbian relations" when we write our questions? The answer is yes. A 2010 CBS/*New York Times* poll first asked 500 respondents how they felt about allowing "homosexuals" to serve in the US military. Next, they asked a different set of 500 respondents how they felt about "gays and lesbians" serving in the US military. Figure 4.9 shows the results.[9]

How do Americans feel about gays in the military? The answer: it depends. When we ask about "homosexuals," 51 percent of Americans support allowing them to serve in the military, including 34 percent who say they strongly favor that position. Ten percent say that they somewhat oppose it, and 19 percent say they strongly oppose. The results are different when we ask about "gay men and lesbians." In this case, the number increases to 70 percent of Americans who say they support gay men and lesbians serving in the military, including 19 percent who are somewhat in favor. Seven percent oppose this group's participation in the military, and

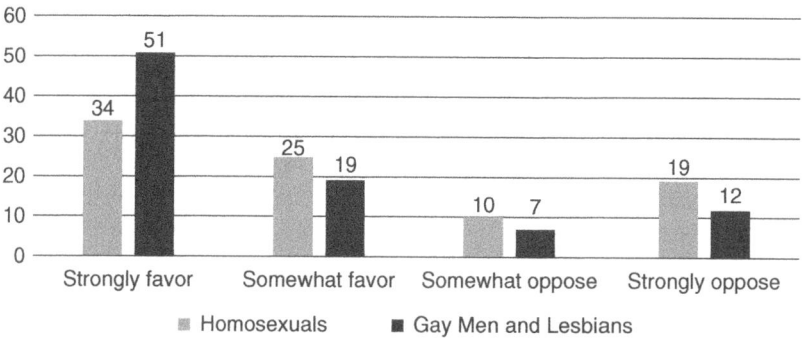

Figure 4.9 How language affects attitudes about military service (percentages)

Studying Sexuality

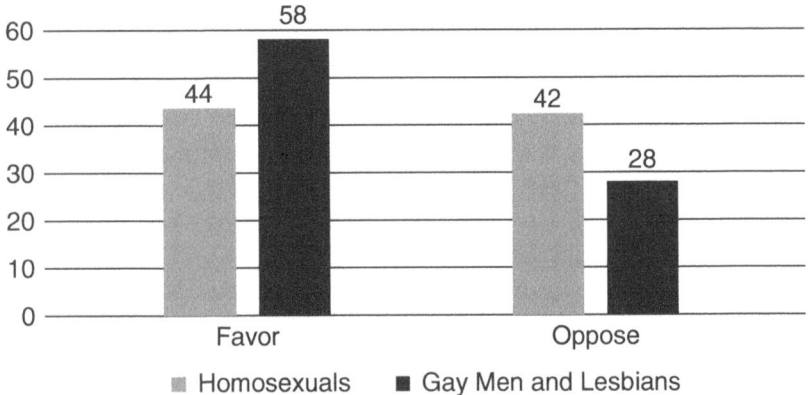

Figure 4.10 How language affects attitudes about open military service (percentages)

12 percent are strongly opposed to it. This pattern remains when we ask about serving *openly* in the military (figure 4.10).

Figure 4.10 shows that there is a similar effect when pollsters ask whether "homosexuals" or "gay men and lesbians" should be allowed to serve openly in the military. More people support allowing "gay men and lesbians" to serve openly (58 percent) than "homosexuals" (44 percent). An independent ABC/*Washington Post* poll found the same trend.[10] The words we use when we write survey questions (and even when we speak with our family and friends) change our perceptions of sex cultures by evoking certain emotions, attitudes, and opinions. We can generalize this lesson beyond the historical specificity of military debates. Now that "Don't Ask, Don't Tell" has been overturned, the precise numbers matter less, but the underlying point remains salient. Just as sexuality is shaped by an endless array of events, from the world-altering to the mundane, so too are our attitudes and beliefs about sexuality shaped by the words we use and hear. This is called the "Sapir–Whorf Hypothesis" (Sapir 1929; Whorf 1940): language molds our perception of reality. Sexuality is formed not merely by historical accidents and the mass shifts of culture but by the minutiae of words as well.

Studying the Transgender Population

In recent years, scholars have begun to explore a whole new challenge: studying the transgender population. The prefix "trans" comes from Latin, and it means "across from" or "on the other side of." "Transgender" is an umbrella term that refers to people whose gender identity is different from that implied by the sex organs they were born with or assigned at birth. The word also applies to those people who "live their lives in a social gender that is not the gender they were assigned at birth" (Schilt and Westbrook 2009: 441). Some people prefer the term "trans*" – with the asterisk – as a way to include all varieties of gender diversity, including terms such as transsexual, transvestite, gender queer, gender fluid, genderless, agender, non-gendered, third gender, two-spirit, and bigender, among others.[11] The common denominator is that a trans* person does not embrace the traditional categories of woman or man – what a growing number of scholars are calling "cisgender." The prefix "cis" also comes from Latin; it is the antonym of "trans," and it means "on this side of." Cisgender people are those who identify with the sex they were assigned at birth. Trans* people challenge the deeply held assumption that "gender identity is an immutable derivation of biology" (ibid.). Indeed, they literally embody a counterargument to the assumption.

Like sexual orientation, gender consists of three different dimensions: gender identity (how you think of yourself, for example, along a continuum between woman-ness and man-ness); gender expression (how you demonstrate your gender through actions, dress, behaviors, and interactions, for example, on a continuum from feminine to masculine, with androgynous in the middle); and biological sex (which includes the physical sex characteristics with which you are born – your organs, genitals, hormones, and chromosomes, whether biologically male, female or intersex).[12] Even these don't capture the full range of options. Consider a decision that Facebook made in 2015. Previously, the social media giant provided its users with a familiar binary: you could be

Studying Sexuality

either "male" or "female." Now, you can customize your gender. You can select from a long list of options, including transgender, bigender, cis, and gender questioning, or you can type your very own label into a blank field. The possibilities for specifying your gender are, truly, limitless.[13]

Similar challenges exist for measuring the transgender population as the ones that we considered for sexual orientation. What definition should we use when we construct our measure of the group: gender identity, gender expression, or biological sex? What about sex assignment at birth or sex reassignment later in life – or should we use both measures? How would you manage the terms that individuals use to describe themselves – something like gender queer, for instance? Then there are the knottier questions of perception: gender non-conformity or variance, which refers to the expression of gender by an individual that doesn't match the norms for their gender as mandated by society. And yet another quandary: Should you include sexual orientation when you measure gender? We should pause here to note that the reality of transgender lives is perhaps the greatest blow to our assumptions about sex. A person who is born into a biological body that does not match his or her sense of self and who then makes changes to honor that self – regardless of whether those changes are physiological, psychological, or performative – destroys the claims of biological determinism, privacy, and fixity.

As they do with sexuality (which we'll see in the next section), researchers recommend a set of best practices for studying trans* populations. For starters, they counsel separating questions about sex from those about gender. For the former, we can ask: What is your sex? Response categories would include male, female, and intersex. For the latter, we can ask: What is your gender? Those responses would likely be far more numerous and could include man, woman, transgender male-to-female (transwomen who socially transition from male to female), transgender female-to-male (transmen who socially transition from female to male), and transgender not identifying exclusively as a man or a woman (gender non-conforming or gender queer). A second option is to ask if people self-identify as transgender: "Are you

Studying Sexuality

transgender?" Or, perhaps a more slowly worded question: "Some people describe themselves as transgender when they experience a different gender identity from their sex at birth. For example, a person born into a male body, but who feels female or lives as a woman. Do you consider yourself to be transgender?"[14] A third option is to ask about gender appearance or gender mannerisms:

> Question 1. A person's appearance, style, or dress may affect the way people think of them. On average, how do you think people would describe your appearance, style, or dress? (Mark one answer)
>
> (a) Very feminine
> (b) Mostly feminine
> (c) Somewhat feminine
> (e) Equally feminine and masculine
> (d) Somewhat masculine
> (e) Mostly masculine
> (g) Very masculine
>
> Question 2. A person's mannerisms (such as the way they walk or talk) may affect the way people think of them. On average, how do you think people would describe your mannerisms? (Mark one answer)
>
> (a) Very feminine
> (b) Mostly feminine
> (c) Somewhat feminine
> (e) Equally feminine and masculine
> (d) Somewhat masculine
> (f) Mostly masculine
> (g) Very masculine

The final option is to ask about gender and sexual orientation in the same question but allow for multiple answers.

> Do you think of yourself as (please check all that apply):
>
> (a) Straight
> (b) Gay or lesbian
> (c) Bisexual
> (d) Transgender, male to female

Studying Sexuality

(e) Transgender, female to male
(f) Not listed above (please write in):

Clearly, there is not a "one size fits all" approach, according to the Gender Identity in US Surveillance Group (GenIUSS), a collaboration of scientists, scholars, and transgender community leaders.[15] There are many ways to incorporate gender into our surveys. Even the few options that we considered here would correct the problems that plague some of the largest, longest-running, and most highly regarded surveys in the United States. Consider the dramatic findings of Westbrook and Saperstein (2015), who examined 132 survey years of data from the American National Election Study (ANES), the Panel Study of Income Dynamics (PSID), the General Social Survey (GSS), and the 1979 National Longitudinal Survey of Youth (NLSY). These four surveys use national sampling frames, their findings are influential and widely shared, they provide models for newer surveys, and researchers use them when they train their students. For example, the National Opinion Research Center summarizes the impact of the GSS: "More than 22,000 journal articles, books, and PhD dissertations are based on the GSS; and about 400,000 students use the GSS in their classes each year" (Westbrook and Saperstein 2015: 539).

Westbrook and Saperstein analyzed all of the questionnaires, codebooks, interviewer instructions, and user's guides from each of the four surveys to see how they worded questions about sex and gender. They found that all the designers of these surveys operationalize sex and gender as binaries – males and females. "The answer options," the researchers note, "for direct determination of the respondent's sex or gender are always 'male' and 'female.' There are never additional sex options (such as 'intersex')" (2015: 542). The same applies to gender; there are no options like "transgender." Before you think to yourself, "I'm not surprised," recall the approach that Facebook took to enable people to express the diversity of their gender. In contrast, "by always providing the same two-answer options, surveys imply that the categories 'male' and 'female' cover all possible ways of being." In addition, all the surveys "conflate sex and gender, do not distinguish between self-identified and other-determined gender, treat sex and gender as obvious, and do not allow a person's gender to change over time" (ibid.). The authors characterized this position as "essentialist" – yet another manifestation of the assumptions that we have seen throughout our exploration (biological determinism and fixity, in this case). The consequences for how we write our questions and response categories are hefty. "Beliefs about the world shape how surveys are designed and data are collected," the authors of the study said in an interview about their work. "Survey research findings, in turn, shape beliefs about the world, and the cycle repeats."[16] Social change is entwined with methodological change; each influences the other. Thus, researchers must distinguish between sex and gender, rethink the use of binary categories, allow for granular self-identification, and acknowledge that gender can change over time.

Best Practices

The elaborateness of sexuality should compel us to seek out best practices for what to ask on a survey. As we know, researchers agree that sexual orientation consists conceptually of three dimensions: sexual attraction, sexual behavior, and self-identification. These components do not always line up. Not everyone who is attracted to a person of the same sex will engage in sexual contact with them or exclusively with same-sex partners. The same applies to self-identification. While conventional labels – gay, lesbian, bisexual, and straight – work for many of us, others select alternate labels, from same-gender loving, to queer, to polyamorous. Some people insist that what's most important is to not be labeled at all, while others shift their self-identification over time.

According to a report produced by the Williams Institute,[17] the discrepancy between these dimensions happens for a number of reasons: stigma, laws and legal risks, cross-cultural differences in the values and meanings assigned to sexual orientation,

Studying Sexuality

opportunities for selecting a partner, economic considerations, measurement error, and variation in the time periods during which researchers asked their questions. In addition, the sexual identities with which we are most familiar have all developed in what we might call "gay white contexts"; these identities don't have the same cultural resonance among non-whites. Research shows that Asian, black, and Latino men who have sex with men are less likely to identify as "gay" compared to their white counterparts. The same is true for foreign-born individuals, who are less likely to identify as gay compared to those who were born in the US. All of this is to say that there are significant "socio-demographic correlates of LGB identification, including ethnic ancestry or national origin, gender, and socioeconomic factors." Indeed, as I implied earlier when we talked about the pathways that produce sex cultures, the differences that emerge as a result of race mean that we can talk separately about black sex cultures, Latino/a sex cultures, and even immigrant sex cultures, among others.

Because of these conundrums, the Williams Institute recommends that we ask the following survey questions. To assess self-identification:

Do you consider yourself to be:

(a) Heterosexual or straight;
(b) Gay or lesbian; or
(c) Bisexual?

The National Center for Health Statistics (NCHS) developed this question to match the format they use when they ask about race and ethnicity. Most adults can understand the question, and it focuses on culturally dominant identity labels. In addition, gay/lesbian is separated from bisexual, which is more useful than the aggregate response category "Gay, lesbian, or bisexual" (prevalence rates for "gay/lesbian" are different than those for "bisexual," as we have seen). The risk in this question, however, is that it obscures the diversity of sexual identities. The limited number of answers conceals a larger variety, including queer,

Studying Sexuality

questioning, fluid, open, unlabeled. These are terms that women (Diamond 2003) and younger people (Savin-Williams 2005) are more likely to adopt. The Williams Institute acknowledges the possibility:

> Some people with same-sex attraction or behavior prefer to use less conventional labels (other than gay, lesbian, or bisexual) to describe their sexual orientation and would therefore choose an "other" category if it was offered. However, when sampling from the general population, this subpopulation is very small, and these people most likely would choose the terms gay, lesbian or bisexual if they were the only terms offered.

There may be statistical advantages to having limited categories, such as greater reliability and the power to detect an effect, although our turn to the cultural in this book has promoted plurality and validity.

To assess sexual behavior:

> In the past time period (e.g. year) who have you had sex with?
>
> (a) Men only,
> (b) Women only,
> (c) Both men and women,
> (d) I have not had sex

The institute recommends using the word "sex" or "sexual experience" in writing survey questions, since these terms imply a range of behaviors, including oral sex, kissing, and touching. Compare the words with "sexual intercourse." The latter is narrower, and it implies vaginal intercourse only. The word "sex" is not always clear either, but that's part of the point; it can mean many things. Researchers advise against defining the term and recommend allowing respondents to answer based on their own understanding. This can create problems of comparability, but specifying a definition in advance may confuse more than help if people don't accept the terms. An alternative would be to break our inquiry about sexual behavior into two questions:

Studying Sexuality

Have you ever (or in the past X time interval) had sex with a female?

(a) Yes
(b) No

Have you ever (or in the past X time interval) had sex with a male?

(a) Yes
(b) No

For some respondents, two questions may be easier to think about and answer, rather than one that combines the possibility of different sex partners into a single question.

To assess sexual attraction:

People are different in their sexual attraction to other people. Which best describes your feelings? Are you:

(a) Only attracted to females?
(b) Mostly attracted to females?
(c) Equally attracted to females and males?
(d) Mostly attracted to males?
(e) Only attracted to males?
(f) Not sure?

This question comes from the National Study of Family Growth. It can accommodate varying degrees of attraction to both sexes, similar to Kinsey's seven-point scale. It does not capture the absence of sexual attraction, however. If that is important in a study, the best practice is again to break the question into two parts:

Are you sexually attracted to men?

(a) Yes
(b) No

Are you sexually attracted to women?

(a) Yes
(b) No

Studying Sexuality

This structure allows researchers to identify the absence of attraction, an outcome that they have found among some teenagers who do not report feeling sexual attraction until their mid- to late adolescence (Saewyc et al. 2004).

One of the biggest concerns in writing survey questions is whether to include an "other" or "something else" response category. You may be tempted to do so if you think it's an easy way to capture diversity, but your results may be difficult to interpret. For example, a 2005 California Health Interview Survey (CHIS) found that 2.7 percent of men aged eighteen to seventy identified as "gay" or "homosexual" and 0.8 percent as "bisexual," while 0.8 percent were coded as "not sexual, celibate, none, or other." For women, the numbers were 1.2 percent "gay/lesbian/homosexual," 1.6 percent "bisexual," and 0.7 percent in the "other" category. Among women, more than a third of those who selected the "not sexual/celibate/none/other" category were currently married (compared to less than 3 percent of those who identified as lesbian or gay), and more than half had not completed high school. Based on these numbers, the Williams Institute concludes:

> Researchers should never assume that respondents who choose "I don't know" or "something else" as an option in a sexual orientation question are gay, lesbian, or bisexual. Most surveys demonstrate that these individuals appear to be primarily heterosexual in terms of attraction and behavior. They may be selecting the "something else" type of option because they don't understand the question, an outcome that is likely a product of other demographic characteristics including age, language ability, and education level.

Sexuality is a "sensitive topic" because it "raises concerns about disapproval or other consequences (such as legal sanctions) for reporting truthfully or if the question itself is seen as an invasion of privacy" (Tourangeau and Smith 1996) – hence the Williams Institute's strong caution against making assumptions about the sexuality of our respondents. By reflecting on best practices, we have deepened an insight that has emerged repeatedly in this chapter: how we measure sexual orientation, and

Studying Sexuality

the cultural knowledge that we bring to bear on our research protocols, will affect what we learn about the character and composition of sex cultures. The challenges associated with measuring attraction, behavior, and identity are compounded by questions of representation. Who do we define as belonging to the GLBT community? Who is excluded from those definitions? Who is in the closet? How should we handle sexual fluidity? What about misalignments between attraction, behavior, and identity? Do we need to devise new measurements for people of color and transgender individuals or adjust our existing ones to capture the effects of intersectionality? What about immigrant populations in an increasingly globalizing world? It's neither immediately nor intuitively clear how a list of best practices can answer all these questions. The persisting puzzles reveal a gap between demography (counting the GLBT and heterosexual populations) and culture (understanding the meanings that people create and negotiate about the sex cultures in which they participate).

Sociologists have a saying: "If people believe something is real, it is real in its consequences." Our cultural approach shows us that reality, as it is constructed by the science of sexuality that we have studied in this chapter, is never quite what it seems, even if we are armed with a list of best practices. Tiny changes in the format of a question can have vast effects, forcing researchers to be careful every step of the way. To measure sex cultures, we need to gauge with precision the extraordinary range of perspectives that are out there.

Conclusions

Policy debates about gender and sexuality require scientific data, and this is why we need to ensure that GLBT people and heterosexuals are accurately represented. Absent this knowledge, we will not be able to address our most pressing social issues – from health and economic disparities to discrimination in housing. We will not be able to make progress on entrenched problems: unemployment and homelessness, and insufficient services for youth and families.

Studying Sexuality

Our thinking about civil rights, our ability to evaluate social programs such as welfare or housing assistance, our assessment of public health, and our intervention into human services all require data and analysis that emerge from rigorous research.

Too often, however, these efforts ignore GLBT people by failing to include them or to identify them in our surveys. Why is it that we never wonder whether to ask about race and ethnicity yet we consider as optional questions about sexuality? The Williams Institute observes that "health, economic, and social surveys have always had to adapt to changing demands and changing times." The civil rights movement forced all of us, from academics to journalists to federal bureaucracies, to reckon with race in American life. Now we must do the same for sexuality. The institute continues, "Adding sexual orientation questions is simply one more adaptation to the changing world that surveys are designed to study, in this case a world with an increasingly visible LGB[T] population." The US is not as progressive as other countries in this regard. As we saw in our conversation about estimating the size of the gay, lesbian, and bisexual population, Canada, the United Kingdom, and other countries now routinely include questions about sexual orientation in several government surveys. The systematic study of sexuality will require international efforts and partnerships of this sort.[18]

Asking about sexuality should not threaten our respondents' willingness to participate in a survey and answer questions about it, the overall response rate of completion, or the likelihood that people will be honest. The key is to devise questions that demonstrate cultural sensitivity. The best practices we considered show that we can ask about sexual orientation with conceptual clarity by keeping in mind its different dimensions, and fine tuning our questions, to refer to identity, behavior, or attraction – or all three. The Williams Institute concludes: "Asking questions on sexual orientation is not only *necessary* for scientific, practical, and policy purposes, but is also *possible* to include such questions on surveys without sacrificing data integrity or respondent retention. Putting these two pieces together presents a compelling case for adding sexual orientation questions to many existing and future

Studying Sexuality

surveys."[19] I would urge that adding questions about gender is just as important.

Moving forward requires us to remedy our heteronormative and cisnormative biases and work hard to prevent the longstanding erasure of GLBT people. On his blog *Conditionally Accepted*, Eric Grollman notes, "In excluding measures that reflect or at least include LGBT people, we send the message that that population is unimportant to social science research. Or ... we signal the persistent taboo-ness of same-sex sexuality." The imperative to include GLBT people in our data-collection efforts applies not just to sexuality researchers from the humanities and the social sciences but also to those scholars for whom this is not a primary interest. Grollman says, "By treating sexual identity and gender identity as core elements of socio-demographics, we make clear the importance and normalness of these aspects of individuals' lives. Why not take the position of having a *positive* impact on the lives of LGBT people?"[20]

By studying the study of sexuality itself, we have seen the strengths of our current protocols and procedures as well as some frustrating limitations. Social scientists construct our understanding of reality, and they can drastically alter it based on the words they use – whether a question says "homosexual" instead of "gay," for example – or if an item is confusing or offers a "something else" option for an answer. All of these are conscious decisions that researchers make, and their choices affect the estimates we produce about the size of GLBT populations. Existing surveys still don't prioritize the culturally rich texture of sexuality (or gender). If they tried, they would stumble onto a paradox: the more we acknowledge fluidity and plurality, the more challenging it becomes to write questions that have just an "a) or b) or c)" answer. Our initial reaction might be to increase the number of categories, but, ironically, those increases make it harder for us to analyze the data we collect. Adding "other" isn't always helpful, as we've seen, and having too many categories, yet too few responses in each, diminishes the statistical power that we need to detect an effect. Absent those effects, we can't influence policy or public opinion.

Studying Sexuality

One possible conclusion from all this is that our perceptions of reality are so fragile! We rely on survey data and statistics to make claims about the world, and yet those claims frequently misalign with our lived experiences. So where does this lead us? The uncertainty we feel could push us toward cynicism, or to a pessimistic sense that social science is hopeless. After having taken the time to read this far, it's my hope that you don't feel this way. I think we can use the sense of fragility to remind ourselves of the pleasures and perils of knowledge. Data is wonderful and beguiling and perhaps revelatory, but it is not "the truth" in some absolute or singular sense. One of the goals of our cultural approach is to expose the limits of science by acknowledging the manifold influences that go into shaping each one of us – and thus the fantastic diversity of sex cultures. The more we seek to understand ourselves in all our complexities, however, the harder it becomes to name anything. Some among you might say that labels are ways to hold us back, that categories are hard boxes that confine us. I think a cultural approach succeeds when it finds a better balance: where we recognize our infinite variety as humans but still value the knowledge that comes from those boxes that have supple skins.

Case Study: Ex-Gays

During the late 1990s, Newsweek magazine ran a cover story with the headline "Gay for Life? Going Straight: The Uproar over Sexual 'Conversion.'" The story described the emergence of an "ex-gay movement," an international network of people who claimed that they had "cured" themselves of homosexuality – which they defined as a "biological error" – and successfully converted back to heterosexuality. These ex-gay activists vouched that they had transformed themselves from gay to straight. While some people achieved this outcome through their religion, many more turned to reparative, reorientation, or conversion therapy. These therapies include drugs, electroshock, lobotomies, radiation, testicular transplants and castration for men, and clitoridectomies and ovary removal for women to help reconfigure a homosexual orientation into a heterosexual one. Among behavioral interventions are sexual abstinence (which includes refraining from fantasizing and masturbation), reforming one's gender disposition through such activities as participating in sports for gay men or wearing dresses for women, and heterosexual marriage (Beckstead 2012).

Although reparative therapy can be traced to at least the early 1980s, the dialogue gained momentum in 1992 when the ex-gay movement consolidated into an institutional voice with the founding of the National Association for Research and Therapy of Homosexuality (NARTH), an organization whose goal is "to make effective psychological therapy available to all homosexual men and women who seek change." NARTH's website says: "[W]e want to clarify that homosexuality is not 'inborn,' and that gays are not 'a people,' in the same sense that an ethnic group is 'a people' . . . Most NARTH members consider homosexuality to represent a developmental disorder."

The ex-gay movement emerged amid an increasingly widespread debate about the origins of sexual orientation. A 1998 Princeton Survey Research Associates poll found that 33 percent of the American population felt homosexuality was a genetic trait present at birth, not the result of environmental or social factors. In contrast, 75 percent of gay respondents felt their sexuality was genetically predetermined. The poll also found that an astonishing 56 percent of the overall population believed that gay men and lesbians could change their sexual orientation through therapy, will power, or religious intervention, whereas only 11 percent of gay respondents felt similarly (Ghaziani 2008).

The American Psychological Association (APA), American Psychiatric Association, American Academy of Pediatrics, National Association of Social Workers, American Counseling Association, and American Psychoanalytic Association have all spoken out against these conversion programs. In 2007, the national organization Beyond Ex-Gay formed to provide a safe space for "survivors" of ex-gay therapies. These individuals cite a host of personal damages, including shame, emotional trauma, depression, suicidal tendencies, and excessive self-hate. Two years after this group formed, the APA concluded that there is "no evidence for the efficacy of sexual orientation change efforts, and such attempts are potentially harmful." Other opponents of reparative therapies note that such programs "devalue homosexuality" and "reify stereotypical notions of what it means to be a man or a woman," along with the stability of sexual orientation (Waidzunas 2015: 7). In his study, Tom Waidzunas (ibid.: 8) observes that the ex-gay movement generated an intense conversation in scientific communities about "the definition of 'sexual orientation,' how to measure this entity, and what exactly constitutes good 'evidence' of a person's sexual orientation." We might ask some questions based on his careful observations:

❖ *How does the proposition that a person can change his or her sexual orientation, especially through behavioral means, compare with the assumptions about sexuality that we considered in the Introduction?*
❖ *Do you think that the ex-gay movement essentializes sexuality when its members say that it's possible to "return" to heterosexuality? Or do they denaturalize sexuality by suggesting the possibility of change?*
❖ *What standards of "proof" would you require to conclude that someone is heterosexual or homosexual? How would you measure change in a person's sexual orientation?*
❖ *Compare the ex-gay logic of mutability with research on sexual fluidity. What do you think they have in common? What do you think they suggest about measuring sexuality?*
❖ *Analyze the ex-gay phenomenon, along with the APA's rejection of reparative therapies, from a cultural perspective. What new insights does our cultural approach offer to this conversation?*

Studying Sexuality

Questions to Consider

1 Why is it important to have scientific data on gender and sexual orientation?
2 Our ability to study gender and sexuality depends on the particular dimension that we isolate for observation. Explain what this means.
3 How accurately do people guess the size of the gay, lesbian, and bisexual population? What patterns have researchers found in the assessments that people offer? Why are we so prone to making mistakes in our estimates?
4 What challenges do researchers face in measuring the non-heterosexual and transgender populations?
5 What questions do researchers ask to learn about the expressions of sexual orientation?
6 How do demographers measure the closet? How would researchers who study heterosexuality – the ones we read about in chapter 3 – respond to their strategies?
7 Why does asking about "homosexuals" versus "gay men and lesbians" elicit different responses?
8 How do the best practices for studying sexuality challenge the conventional assumptions that we reviewed in the Introduction?
9 Using a cultural approach to sexuality, what advice would you offer to survey writers?
10 Find an article online that addresses any issue related to the scientific study of sexuality. What did you learn from reading it? How does it relate to the ideas we discussed in this chapter?

Conclusion: Culture Wars?

Case Study: Sexual Morality

Since 2001, Gallup, Inc., an American research consulting company, has conducted an annual public opinion poll called the Values and Beliefs Survey. Pollsters have routinely asked questions about Americans' views on sexual morality, including whether the following are acceptable: sex before marriage, extramarital affairs, having children outside of marriage, divorce, polygamy, abortion, and gay/lesbian relations (see table C.1).

The media have taken a keen interest in one particular question: How do Americans perceive the moral acceptability of gay and lesbian relations? In 2015, 63 percent of the public felt that these relationships were "morally acceptable." Compare this with how Americans felt about gays and lesbians in 2001, when Gallup first asked the question: only 40 percent felt the same. This is a 23 percentage point change in attitudes, and it is the largest shift among the items in table C.1. The reversal began in 2010 when, as Gallup observed, "Americans' support for the moral acceptability of gay and lesbian relations crossed the symbolic 50 percent threshold ... At the same time, the percentage calling these relations 'morally wrong' dropped to 43 percent, the lowest in Gallup's decade-long trend."[1] This trend has

Conclusion: Culture Wars?

Table C.1 Moral acceptability: changes over time

	2001 %	2015 %	Change (pct. pts.)
Gay or lesbian relations	40	63	23
Having a baby outside of marriage*	45	61	16
Sex between an unmarried man and women	53	68	15
Divorce	59	71	12
Medical research using stem cells obtaint from human embryos*	52	64	12
Polygamy (when a married person has more than one spouse at the same time)**	7	16	9
Cloning humans	7	15	8
Doctor-assisted suicide	49	56	7
Suicide	13	19	6
Gambling**	63	67	4
Abortion	42	45	3
Cloning animals	31	34	3
Buying and wearing clothing made of animal fur	60	61	1
Married men and women having an affair	7	8	1
The death penalty	63	60	–3
Medical testing on animals	65	56	–9

Notes: Sorted by change in the percentage saying each is "morally acceptable"; unless otherwise marked, issues first measured in 2001
*First measured in 2002
**First measured in 2003
Source: Copyright © 2015 Gallup, Inc.[2] All rights reserved. The content is used with permission; however, Gallop retains all rights of republication.

continued into the present day (figure C.1). Rapid transformations in public opinion are quite rare. In this case, the outcome is the result of generational changes (older, more conservative people die and are replaced by a younger, more liberal cohort) alongside broad shifts in which the entire population has changed its attitudes (Flores 2014). These developments in public opinion have affected a range of issues, including presidential elections, public policy, media visibility, Supreme Court decisions, and other matters related to civil rights

The upward tick in public opinion that we see in figure C.1 also corresponds to higher levels of acceptance for the other

Conclusion: Culture Wars?

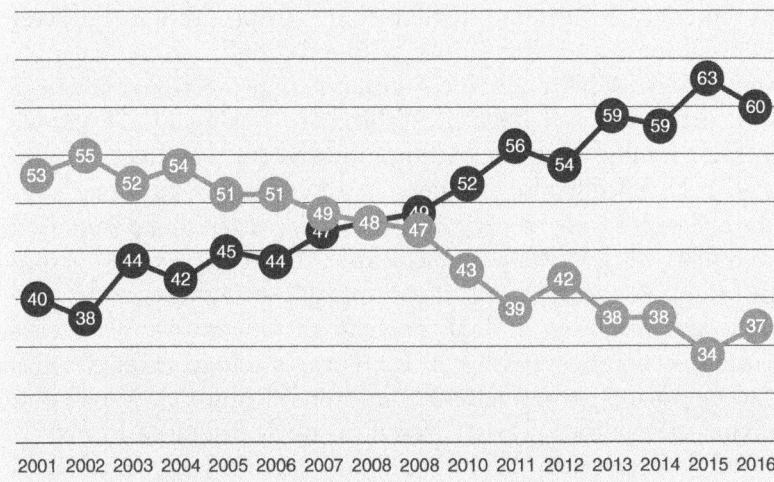

Figure C.1 Perceived moral acceptability of gay and lesbian relations (percentages). Created with data from Gallup, 2016.[3]

sexual behaviors in table C.1. Gallup notes: "More Americans now rate themselves as socially liberal than at any point in Gallup's 16-year trend, and for the first time, as many say they are liberal on social issues as say they are conservative ... This liberalization of attitudes toward moral issues is part of a complex set of factors affecting the social and cultural fabric of the U.S."[4] Still, there is something unique about how Americans perceive gay and lesbian relations. According to Patrick Egan, a scholar who specializes in public opinion, "The sharp rise in the share of the public viewing [gay and lesbian relations] as morally acceptable is unmatched by any of the other items on the Gallup survey."[5] The issue that has witnessed the greatest improvement in public acceptability after "gay and lesbian relations" is having a baby outside of marriage, which rose 16 points between 2001 and 2015.

Progress in public opinion does not signal the end of discrimination. In February 2015, the Gay and Lesbian Alliance Against Defamation (GLAAD) issued an "Accelerating Acceptance Report." The results of their nationally representative survey

Conclusion: Culture Wars?

of American adults found that "beneath progress lies a layer of uneasiness and discomfort. While the public is increasingly embracing LGBT civil rights and equal protection under the law, many are still uncomfortable with having LGBT people in their families and the communities where they live" (Stokes 2015: 2). Specifically, 56 percent of heterosexual Americans are uncomfortable or very uncomfortable attending a same-sex wedding (34 percent uncomfortable, 22 percent very uncomfortable); 43 percent are uncomfortable bringing a child to a same-sex wedding; and 36 percent are uncomfortable seeing same-sex couples hold hands. These findings suggest that "acceptance is tentative and conditional" (ibid.: 3) – and that sexual inequalities persist, even if in subtly disguised forms.

Public opinion in the United States is consistent with that in some countries and dissimilar from that in others. In a 2013 survey of 37,653 respondents from thirty-nine countries, the Pew Research Center finds broad acceptance of homosexuality in North America, the European Union, and much of Latin America. In contrast, in predominantly Muslim countries, African nations, parts of Asia, and Russia, we see widespread rejection of homosexuality. Finally, acceptance is uneven in countries such as Israel, Poland, and Bolivia. Figure C.2 shows considerable variation in global attitudes toward homosexuality. In general, the more secular, more affluent, and less religious a country is, the more likely its citizens are to accept gays and lesbians. People who live in countries that are poorer and with high levels of religiosity are less likely to believe that society should accept homosexuality. In addition, younger respondents and women are generally more tolerant than older respondents and men.

Most countries have become more accepting as time has gone by, but some countries, such as Ghana, the Czech Republic, Poland, Jordan, Russia, Turkey, the Palestinian Territories, and France have become less tolerant (table C.2).

❖ *Why do you think that 50 percent represents a "symbolic threshold" for public opinion about sexual morality?*

Conclusion: Culture Wars?

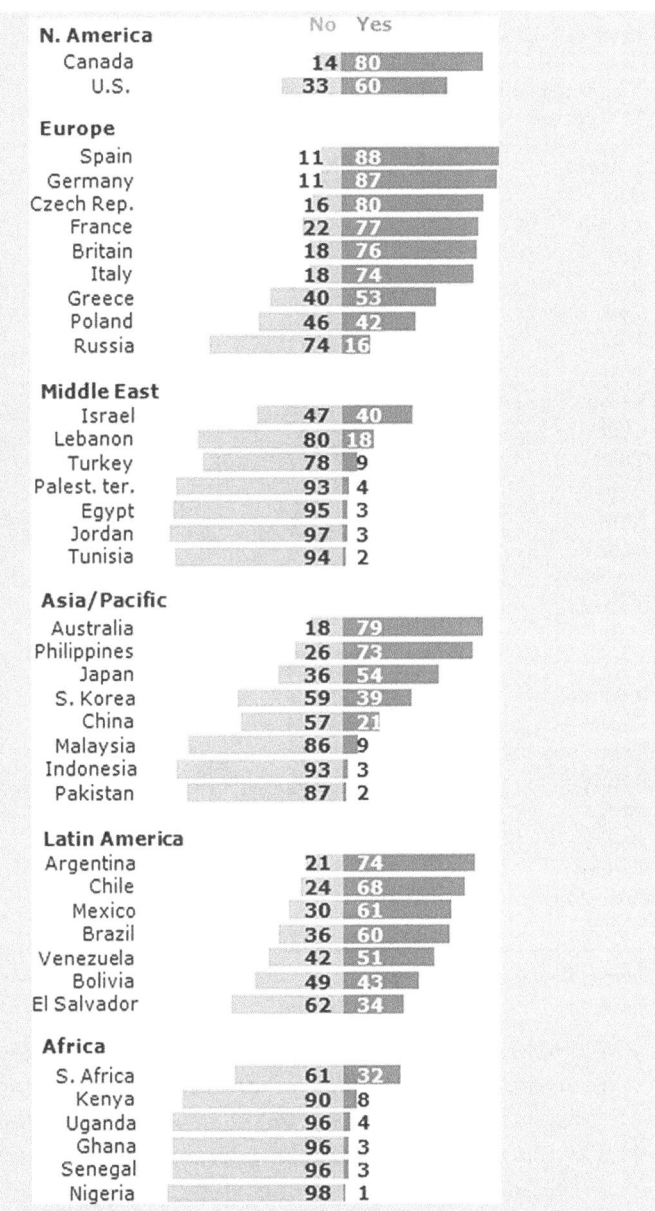

Figure C.2 Should society accept homosexuality? A global view
Source: Pew Research Center.[6]

Conclusion: Culture Wars?

Table C.2 Changing global views of homosexuality

% Homosexuality should be accepted	2007 %	2013 %	Change
S. Korea	18	39	+21
U.S.	49	60	+11
Canada	70	80	+10
Italy	65	74	+9
Spain	82	88	+6
Germany	81	87	+6
Britain	71	76	+5
Japan	49	54	+5
Kenya	3	8	+5
Chile	64	68	+4
China	17	21	+4
Argentina	72	74	+2
Israel	38	40	+2
Egypt	1	3	+2
Mexico	60	61	+1
Malaysia	8	9	+1
Uganda	3	4	+1
Lebanon	18	18	0
Indonesia	3	3	0
Ghana	4	3	–1
Czech Rep.	83	80	–3
Poland	45	42	–3
Jordan	6	3	–3
Russia	20	16	–4
Turkey	14	9	–5
Palest. ter.	9	4	–5
France	83	77	–6

Source: Pew Research Center.[6]

❖ *Compare how Americans feel about gay and lesbian relations with their attitudes toward other issues about sexuality. Which one surprises you the most? Which one the least?*
❖ *Compare attitudes about homosexuality in countries around the world. What, if anything, surprises you?*
❖ *Gallup notes that the liberalization in sexual attitudes is "part of a complex set of factors affecting the social and*

cultural fabric of the U.S." What factors might be causing this larger shift?
* What does it mean to say that acceptance is "tentative and conditional"?
* Go online and see if you can find updates to either the Gallup or the Pew survey. What patterns or trends do you notice?

Into the Crucible of Culture

Sex is without history, we heard in the Introduction, because it is a biological fact of the body. Fine – except that we never encounter a body that is unmediated by or completely unattached from meanings. This is why we have been thinking in terms of sexuality; it is a "cultural effect" (Halperin 1993: 416). In this book, we have followed a trail of breadcrumbs that scholars and journalists have left for us. Piece by piece, we have concerned ourselves with what I believe is an urgent task: moving beyond our habitual reliance on certain assumptions about sex – convenient, yes, and a satisfyingly simple means to explain a bewildering world. But these assumptions have done great harm. I have challenged us to embrace instead a cultural approach, one which can unpack that complex whole we call sexuality and celebrate the range of thought and awareness we have about it.

The lens with which we have been experimenting magnifies an intellectual sensitivity toward meanings. Sex cultures, the eponymous concept at the beating heart of this book, hones in on how the materiality of the body acquires meaning as it interacts with other bodies, institutions, symbols, societal norms, values, and worldviews. The formula for how this happens is by now familiar: culture shapes sex into sexuality as bodies encounter other bodies in a network of meanings that are located in specific times and places. Or, to put it more simply and as we have seen throughout the book: sex plus culture equals sexuality (figure C.3).

The radical shift in how we have understood homosexuality over time is one among a number of opportunities we have had

Conclusion: Culture Wars?

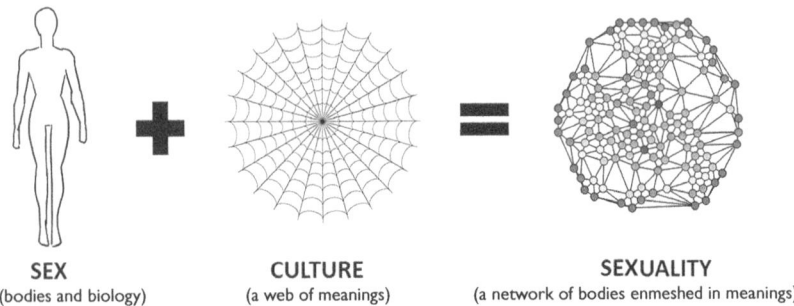

SEX　　　　　　　　CULTURE　　　　　　　　SEXUALITY
(bodies and biology)　　(a web of meanings)　　(a network of bodies enmeshed in meanings)

Figure C.3 Sex becomes sexuality

to see how sexuality is culturally created. Recall that the meaning of homosexuality changed from a behavior and an act in the nineteenth century (sodomy) to a deviant individual pathology in the early twentieth century (homosexuality) and to a positive identity today (gay and lesbian). Michel Foucault was one of the first scholars to chronicle this sequence. In *The History of Sexuality*, he asserts: "Homosexuality appeared as one of the forms of sexuality when it was transposed from the practice of sodomy onto a kind of interior androgyny." This created a distinction between the sodomite and the homosexual: "The sodomite had been a temporary aberration; the homosexual was now a species" (Foucault 1978: 43). There was nothing biological, universal, or private about this process. Today, being gay is a "cultural practice" that entails "a specific way of being," Halperin adds in his provocatively titled book *How to be Gay* (2012). We saw how the sex cultures of lesbians, gay men, bisexuals, and transgender individuals have shaped, and been shaped by, modern life, from politics and protest to city planning and survey design.

The same insights apply to heterosexuality, even if it's harder for us to see them (remaining unmarked and receding into the background is the conceit of privilege after all). Sure, heterosexuality is "as old as procreation, ancient as the lust of Eve and Adam" (Katz 1990: 7), but its cultural history is "surprisingly short" (Blank 2012). The elaborate set of acts, feelings, and identities that shape the many sex cultures of heterosexuality have changed at a breath-

178

Conclusion: Culture Wars?

taking pace: from gender-based standards of "true love" to "sex love" to "psychical hermaphroditism"; from a procreant urge linked inexorably with carnal lust to a "mystique," "cult," and "hegemonic standard"; and from the object of vociferous criticism by anti-establishment forces to an intensely intricate entanglement of contemporary meanings. Today, we live in a heteroflexible world, a place defined by bromances and bro-jobs, heterodykes on a lesbian continuum, and dudes who have sex with dudes and sexually fluid women. Indeed, heterosexualities show no sign of ceasing their remarkable inventions.

We learned sophisticated lessons as we absorbed these and many other fascinating findings: sexuality is neither ahistorical (it has a history), nor transhistorical (its meanings have changed over time), nor invariant (its expressions are diverse within and across countries). In fact, the words "homosexuality" and "heterosexuality" haven't always been around. German sodomy-law reformer Karl Maria Kertbeny coined both in 1868 (Katz 1995). Therefore, neither gay nor straight people, to use contemporary language, are "a fixed, natural, universal sort of being." Embracing a cultural approach showed us that the assumptions we make about sex can blind us from seeing the beautiful mutability of sexuality.

As these snippets show, I have insisted that we jump back and forth between various sexualities but also that we talk about them in concert with one another. I did this to encourage us to think about sex cultures and the cultural imagination as they pertain to all of us – gay and straight and everything in between and beyond. We challenged entrenched assumptions that pit sex against society, and, by thinking about sex cultures instead, we identified the collective contexts and customs that give meaning to what we do with our bodies. Your cultural imagination, I hope, has ripened with the turn of each page. Things should look different now – whether you're thinking about attending the pride parade, or if you're sexting your boyfriend or girlfriend, or if you're wondering about finding love online. Your sexuality is enmeshed in the wider world around you. It is within this networked cultural web that your sexuality lives and breathes.

Conclusion: Culture Wars?

Behind the Veil

Despite my best efforts, arguments about the social construction of sexuality may not resonate for every person who reads this book, especially if you feel like your sexuality has not changed very much or if you define it as a central and natural part of who you are (Epstein 1987). While reading, you may have found yourself getting frustrated – or even angry. You might have thought that I was making these arguments just because I'm gay myself. Or maybe you dismissed me as a politically correct, left-wing academic with an agenda. If any of this is true for you, I appreciate the candor. I'm not sure I can change your mind, but nevertheless I still want our time together to have been meaningful. What can you take away from this book?

The careful attention that we've paid to cultural meanings can explain why some of us experience our sexuality as fixed despite overwhelming evidence of its ongoing creation. First of all, you should know that a sense of continuity and stability is compatible with our cultural approach; acknowledging connections across time and place or over the course of your own life doesn't undermine an argument about why culture matters. To conflate the two is "to draw a deceptively simple and very old-fashioned division between representations, conceived as socially specific and historically variable products of human culture, and realities ... conceived as something static and unchanging" (Halperin 2002: 9). Sexuality has a history, and we human beings are its subjects. If you accept this premise, then the continuities you feel between the past and the present are not inconsistent with your cultural imagination about sexuality. In fact, the reason why I designed this book using case-study, debate-driven, and international approaches was precisely to inspire you to think about the relationship between your biography and society, between meanings and materiality. Each case that we considered contained a number of controversies which we used to illuminate the terrain of our journey. The debates that we have encountered brought tacit assumptions to light. I deliberately highlighted disputes in order to complicate the cases, not to clarify

Conclusion: Culture Wars?

them. The cases you have read, like life itself, do not provide simple "yes" or "no" answers. We must learn to delight in uncertainty.

The logic that I used in creating the cases is called "praxis." It was never our objective to "solve irresolvable contradictions" (Dello Buono 2015: 336), such as whether we are born pre-wired with our sexuality or if society shapes it. Praxis is a principle that allows contradictions to unfold in concrete situations. It allows us to appreciate the density of life. Now do you see with me behind the veil? Our goal in every chapter has been to apply what we have learned to actual scenarios, to think on our feet as we must in our own lives, and not to be artificially constrained by choosing one thing or another or forced to create simple consistencies.

There is another way to ease your hesitation about arguments that emphasize the cultural construction of sexuality. First, refresh your memory about something you learned in your introduction to sociology class. "If people believe something is real, then it is real in its consequences."[7] I mentioned the idea in passing in the previous chapter. It's called the "Thomas Theorem," and it was formulated in 1928 by William Isaac Thomas and his wife Dorothy Swaine Thomas. Their theorem reminds us that the meanings we bring to a situation direct how we act in response to it. The cultural approach that we've taken has shifted our questions away from never-ending debates about ontology and origins toward more profitable inquiries about effects and consequences. You know better than to ask if nature or nurture shapes our sexuality or whether we are born or bred as gay or straight. You know that these "either/or" inquiries are way too simple; the answer is always "both." Instead, we have focused on how sexuality affects urban planning and how it inspires people to become activists. We asked how our thoughts about sexuality inform the choices we make about whom to kiss, with whom to cuddle, or with whom to have sex. We used a similar style of thinking in each instance. We began with what people believe is real about sexuality, and from there we explored its cultural consequences.

Our thoughts about sexuality have massive institutional effects. Whether we think sexuality is natural or cultural shapes what we think is right and wrong, and our judgements direct how the

Conclusion: Culture Wars?

government regulates the morality and criminality of sex. If we define sexual feelings, desires, behaviors, interactions, and identities as natural, then we will also believe that some are "good, right, or normal" Seidman 2015: xi), while others are not. Okay, so what? Why does this matter? Seidman answers, "The authority of the government and other institutions is enlisted to support natural or normal sexualities." Heterosexuality, which still "reigns supreme" as "the building block of social life and social policy" (Stein 1989: 1), is an excellent example. "It expresses the natural fit between the bodies and the psyches of men and women," Seidman explains, and from this perspective is no less than "the basis of the survival of the species" (2015: xi). This cultural logic requires the condemnation and punishment of homosexuality on the basis that gays and lesbians cannot reproduce and thus cannot "ensure the survival of the species." The style of thinking also explains why some people believe that homosexuality is "perverse, abnormal, and perhaps a social threat." Once we divide the world into a set of oppositions and hierarchies – once we start seeing heterosexual sex as good, normal, and natural and gay sex, by default, as bad, immoral, and unnatural (Rubin 1993) – then the people around us suddenly become keen to promote heterosexuality through an intricate system of laws and social policies while repressing and punishing homosexuality. This is not the world I wish for you to inherit.

Along the Fault Lines

In the opening case study for this chapter, we saw that attitudes toward homosexuality have become liberal over time. This positive trend in public opinion obscures subtle yet persistent forms of prejudice. Recent research finds that heterosexuals are willing to extend "formal rights" to same-sex couples – things such as family leave, hospital visitation, inheritance rights, and insurance benefits – but they remain unwilling to grant them "informal privileges" (Doan et al. 2014: 1172) such as the freedom to express affection in public places by holding hands or sharing a kiss.

Conclusion: Culture Wars?

In my own work, I asked straight people who live in gay neighborhoods about their attitudes toward their gay and lesbian neighbors. I found a curious difference between their professed liberal positions on sexuality and their correspondingly conservative, if not outright hostile, behaviors on the ground. To explain this double standard, I introduced the concept of "performative progressiveness," which I define as "a blissful but non-malicious ignorance about sexual inequality" (Ghaziani 2014b: 255). Some straight people who live in gay neighborhoods proclaim to have supportive beliefs about their gay and lesbian neighbors yet behave in ways that contradict those sentiments. For me, the concept of performative progressiveness captures the primary paradox of our current era: the growth of liberal attitudes alongside sustained and persistent prejudice. We need to address this new form of sexual inequality.

In each chapter, we traveled along the fault lines of sexuality and saw that it is a source of chilling conflicts and controversies. The very nature of social movements suggests oppositions. Meanwhile, in the city, residents clash over sexual integration and its consequences for the viability of sex cultures. Sexual fluidity in women and dude sex or bro-jobs among men provoke anxieties in some people. Even in our discussion about the science of sexuality, we encountered disputes about how to measure gender and sexual orientation and how the decision that some researchers make can distort our perceptions of reality. Sexuality is clearly a contested object of expression and analytic inquiry. This is why scholars describe it as part of a "culture war" (Hunter 1991), "sex war" (Duggan and Hunter 1995), or "sex panic" (Lancaster 2011). According to James Hunter (1991), the United States and other Western nations are polarized by a series of hot-button topics: abortion, gun control, the separation of church and state, censorship, drug use, and sexuality. He uses the terms "cultural conflict" and "culture war" to describe the political and social hostilities that arise from ideas, beliefs, values, and moral commitments that seem irreconcilable – hence the "war." For Hunter, "the end to which these hostilities tend is the domination of one cultural and moral ethos over all others" (ibid.: 42). For us, the key insight is that culture wars are fought over sex cultures.

Conclusion: Culture Wars?

War-torn issues take on great symbolic importance for people – they "always have a character of ultimacy to them" (Hunter 1991: 42) – because we see them as defining everything from our national identity to our sense of self, from public policy to private morality. Thus, culture war issues such as abortion or gay rights "are not merely attitudes that can change on a whim but basic commitments and beliefs that provide a source of identity, purpose, and togetherness for the people who live by them" (ibid.). Culture is at once the object of struggle, the set of values and moral beliefs over which we fight, and the means by which we engage in political life (Williams 1997).

Journalists have taken a great liking to the term "culture war" because it provides them with an easy and "dramatic frame" for addressing social issues (DiMaggio 2003: 81). Calling something a "culture war" allows us to assemble some part of sexuality (from homosexuality to sex education) into "a coherent and navigable political terrain" (ibid.: 93). Patrick Buchanan brought the phrase into every American household when he used it in his address at the 1992 Republican National Convention to declare a "war for the nation's soul." Buchanan told the delegates that gay rights have no place "in a nation we still call God's country." In turn, delegates held signs that proclaimed, "Family Rights Forever! Gay Rights Never!" Later that year, Pat Robertson's Christian Coalition – an organization that had 2.2 million names on its roster of members at the time – convened to discuss "the homosexual-rights agenda and how to defeat it" (Ghaziani 2008). Buchanan's move was part of a long and sordid history of attacking gay people. In the 1980s, during the AIDS crisis (as we have seen), he declared, "The poor homosexuals – they have declared war upon nature and now nature is extracting an awful retribution." Buchanan's remarks exposed a cultural fault line. A 1989 *Newsweek* poll titled "Homosexuality and Politics" showed that 45 percent of Americans would vote against a public official who disclosed that he or she was homosexual. Fifty percent believed that homosexuals should not be school teachers (ibid.).

As these examples show us, culture war issues operate at the level of the "worldview." They "do more than just shape our

Conclusion: Culture Wars?

moral, social, and political ideas; they also mold our very perceptions of reality" (Williams 1997: 1). People like Buchanan gain energy, credibility, and money from screaming about culture wars. Others, such as the scholars who study sexuality and the activists who fight for our freedom to express it as we wish, argue that culture wars are a myth, a problem that people have manufactured to create conflict. Research shows that our position about a culture war depends on whether we define it as the polarizing of public attitudes (more likely a myth) or as a framing device that shapes how we think about current topics (more likely real) (DiMaggio 2003). What we believe is real is real in its consequences – again.

I don't think that the debate over culture wars is getting us anywhere. The imagery of a "war" captures only a small fraction of sex cultures, often the most explosive and violent parts like the ex-gays or hate crimes. These wars get all the headlines, but our deepest and most vital understanding of sexuality emerges not from wars but from the experiences we have on our own and with others as we explore our attractions, actions, and identities together – all those tiny moments that mold our minds and hearts. That's why I think we need a different perspective. Instead of trying to prove the other side wrong, we need to recognize that culture wars create a lot of noise while concealing the dynamism of sexuality.

So where does this leave us? What happens once you close this book, once you complete your assignments, once you take the test, once you move on to something else? My desire, as that of every author, is for these words to deepen the way that you think about the world around you – and the world inside you. And so I offer a quirky challenge as we part ways: embrace sapiosexuality! This lovely neologism combines "sapiens" or "sapience," which refers to the quality of being wise, sage, discerning, judicious, and knowledgeable, with "sexual" or "sexuality." A "sapiosexual" is a person who prioritizes the life of the mind,[8] a person who falls in love with ideas. You may do research in the future, or you may travel down a different path. Whatever happens, I hope more than anything else that you will awaken your passion for ideas – the inquisitive, insightful, and irreverent alike – and the pleasures of being aroused by the ideas of others.

Conclusion: Culture Wars?

Questions to Consider

1 What is distinct about a cultural approach to the study of sexuality?
2 Why do scholars resist describing sexuality as ahistorical, transhistorical, or invariant?
3 Why do some people feel uncomfortable with arguments about culture and cultural construction? How would you reply to them?
4 What are the institutional consequences associated with defining sexuality as natural?
5 What does it mean to say that sexuality is part of a cultural conflict? Why is the culture war frame so popular? How would you push beyond the terms of the culture wars?

Notes

Introduction

1 Deborah Netburn, "J. Crew and Jenna Lyons' pink toenail controversy," *Los Angeles Times*, April 13, 2011; see http://latimesblogs.latimes.com/alltherage/2011/04/j-crew-and-jenna-lyons-pink-toenail-controversy.html. "Toemageddon," *Daily Show* clip from April 13, 2011, which includes the Fox News interview with Ablow.
2 For more on Lawrence H. Summers and Caitlyn Jenner, see Elinor Burkett, "What makes a woman?," http://nytimes.com/2015/06/07/opinion/sunday/what-makes-a-woman.html, and Daniel J. Hemel, "Summers' comments on women and science draw ire," www.thecrimson.com/article/2005/1/14/summers-comments-on-women-and-science/.
3 See Katie Sola, "Ad agency DigitasLBi boycotts Dolce & Gabbana, drops 'D' and 'G' from their name," www.huffingtonpost.com/2015/03/18/dolce-and-gabbana-boycott_n_6894072.html, and Leigh Weingus, "Dolce & Gabbana face outrage after controversial comments about gay families," www.huffingtonpost.com/2015/03/15/dolce-and-gabbana-gay-families_n_6872710.html.
4 Philip Pullella, "Gay marriage a threat to humanity's future: pope," www.reuters.com/article/2012/01/09/us-pope-gay-idUSTRE8081RM20120109.

Chapter 1 The City

1 Patricia Leigh Brown, "Gay enclaves face prospect of being passé," www.nytimes.com/2007/10/30/us/30gay.html.
2 Nellie Bowles and Sam Levin, "San Francisco's tech bros told: quit changing the gayborhood," www.theguardian.com/world/2016/feb/02/san-francisco-gay-bars-shut-down-lgbt-tenderloin-castro-district.
3 www.glbthistory.org/news/1110_gayneighbors.html [no longer available];

Notes to pp. 23–43

Roger Brigham, "Panel to discuss gay neighborhoods," www.ebar.com/news/article.php?sec=news&article=1355.
4 Sarah Boesveld, "Gay neighbourhoods 'straightening' as LGBT community finds increased acceptance," http://news.nationalpost.com/news/canada/gay-neighbourhoods-straightening-as-lgbt-community-finds-increased-acceptance; Micah Toub, "There goes the gaybourhood," http://urbantoronto.ca/forum/threads/globe-there-goes-the-gaybourhood.3402/.
5 Alexander Dunphy, "A straight friendly guide to Montreal's gay village," www.tourisme-montreal.org/blog/a-straight-friendly-guide-to-montreals-gay-village/.
6 Yvonne Zacharias and Bethany Lindsay, "There goes the gaybourhood: study finds enclaves 'straightening,'" www.vancouversun.com/technology/there+goes+gaybourhood+study+finds+enclaves+straightening/10069109/story.html; Amin Ghaziani, "Dwindling gaybourhoods," www.dailyxtra.com/vancouver/news-and-ideas/news/dwindling-gaybourhoods-92662.
7 Philip Hensher, "Please keep out of gay bars and clubs," www.independent.co.uk/voices/commentators/philip-hensher/please-keep-out-of-gay-bars-and-clubs-646295.html.
8 Feargus O'Sullivan, "The 'gaytrification' effect: why gay neighbourhoods are being priced out," www.theguardian.com/cities/2016/jan/13/end-of-gaytrification-cities-lgbt-communities-gentrification-gay-villages.
9 Neal Broverman, "The party's over," www.advocate.com/arts-entertainment/2016/2/05/26-dead-or-dying-gay-bars-nyc-la-sf.
10 Figures from 1800, 1900, and 1950: www.prb.org/Publications/Lesson-Plans/HumanPopulation/Urbanization.aspx; World Health Organization: www.who.int/gho/urban_health/situation_trends/urban_population_growth_text/en/; World Bank: www.worldbank.org/en/topic/urbandevelopment/overview.
11 See www.stonewall.org.uk/.
12 Frank Newport, "Americans continue to shift left on key moral issues," www.gallup.com/poll/183413/americans-continue-shift-left-key-moral-issues.aspx; "A survey of LGBT Americans," www.pewsocialtrends.org/2013/06/13/a-survey-of-lgbt-americans/.
13 For the Supreme Court case, see www.supremecourt.gov/opinions/14pdf/14-556_3204.pdf; for Obama's address, see www.nytimes.com/live/supreme-court-rulings/president-obama-hails-decision-in-emotional-statement/.
14 For the PRRI report, entitled *A Shifting Landscape*, see: http://publicreligion.org/site/wp-content/uploads/2014/02/2014.LGBT_REPORT.pdf. The quotation may be found at: http://blogs.marketwatch.com/themargin/2014/02/26/support-for-gay-marriage-has-increased-over-past-decade-survey/. For the McClatchy-Marist survey, see: www.mcclatchydc.com/news/politics-government/article24771898.html.
15 For quotations from the US study, see: www.huffingtonpost.com/josh-a-

Notes to pp. 46–59

goodman/preparing-for-a-generation-that-comes-out-younger_b_2556346.html; for the study itself, see Savin-Williams and Diamond (2000). Quotes from the UK study: http://bicommunitynews.co.uk/719/coming-out-younger-or-are-we/.
16 Paul Aguirre-Livingston, "Dawn of a New Gay," *The Grid*, June 9, 2011. www.thegridto.com/city/sexuality/dawn-of-a-new-gay/ [no longer available].
17 For the quotation by Rosenfeld, see Adam Gorlick, "Forget Cupid: online connections have valentines falling in love, Stanford researcher says," *Stanford Report*, February 11, 2010, http://news.stanford.edu/news/2010/february8/rosenfeld-online-dating-02112010.html.
18 For the diaspora quote, see Keith Darc, "Adapting to the times," *San Diego Union-Tribune*, April 5, 2007, p. C1.
19 Charles M. Blow, "Gay? Whatever dude," *New York Times*, June 4, 2010, www.nytimes.com/2010/06/05/opinion/05blow.html.
20 Barbara Kantrowitz, "A town like no other," *Newsweek*, July 20, 1993, www.newsweek.com/town-no-other-193714.
21 For the report, see www.bls.gov/opub/reports/womens-earnings/archive/highlights-of-womens-earnings-in-2014.pdf; for a commentary about the report, see www.aei.org/publication/new-bls-report-on-womens-earnings-much-of-the-17-gender-pay-gap-in-2014-explained-by-age-marriage-hours-worked/.
22 Chris Matthews, "Gayborhoods: real estate's mysterious same-sex couple premium," http://fortune.com/2015/06/11/gayborhood-real-estate-expensive/.
23 Gary J. Gates, *Same-Sex and Different-Sex Couples in the American Community Survey: 2005–2011*, http://williamsinstitute.law.ucla.edu/wp-content/uploads/ACS-2013.pdf, and M. V. Lee Badgett, Laura E. Durso, and Alyssa Schneebaum, *New Patterns of Poverty in the Lesbian, Gay, and Bisexual Community*, http://williamsinstitute.law.ucla.edu/wp-content/uploads/LGB-Poverty-Update-Jun-2013.pdf. For a meta-analysis of the gay and bisexual wage gap, see http://williamsinstitute.law.ucla.edu/wp-content/uploads/Badgett-Sears-Lau-Ho-Bias-in-the-Workplace-Jun-2007.pdf. Lesbian and bisexual women earn about the same as straight women.
24 Brian W. Ward, James M. Dahlhamer, Adena M. Galinsky, and Sarah S. Joestl, *Sexual Orientation and Health among US Adults: National Health Interview Survey, 2013*, www.cdc.gov/nchs/data/nhsr/nhsr077.pdf.

Chapter 2 Politics and Protest

1 Peter Tatchell, "Our lost gay radicalism," www.theguardian.com/commentisfree/2009/jun/26/gay-lgbt-victimhood-stonewall.
2 Emine Saner, "Gay rights around the world: the best and worst countries for equality," www.theguardian.com/world/2013/jul/30/gay-rights-world-best-worst-countries.

3 Doug McAdam, "Occupy the future," www.bostonreview.net/forum/occupy-future/what-should-sustained-movement-look.
4 Guide to the National Gay and Lesbian Task Force Records, 1973–2008, http://rmc.library.cornell.edu/EAD/htmldocs/RMM07301.html.
5 Jodi Kantor, "Historic day for gays, but twinge of loss for an outsider culture," www.nytimes.com/2015/06/27/us/scotus-same-sex-marriage-gay-culture.html.
6 Paige Lavender, "Here are a few of the things the LGBT community is still fighting for," www.huffingtonpost.com/2015/06/26/employee-non-discrimination_n_7671726.html.
7 Timothy Stewart-Winter, "The price of gay marriage," www.nytimes.com/2015/06/28/opinion/sunday/the-price-of-gay-marriage.html.
8 Saner, "Gay rights around the world."

Chapter 3 Heterosexualities

1 Matthew Warren, "French kiss celebrates victory over Germany," *The Local*, March 1, 2012.
2 "1 in 2 young people say they are not 100% heterosexual," https://yougov.co.uk/news/2015/08/16/half-young-not-heterosexual/.
3 Rebecca Nicholson, "'I'm a bisexual homoromantic': why young Brits are rejecting old labels," *The Guardian*, August 18, 2015, www.theguardian.com/society/2015/aug/18/bisexual-british-adults-define-gay-straight-heterosexual.
4 Jocelyn Vena, "Blake Shelton admits 'man crush' on 'Voice' pal Adam Levine," *MTV News*, March 7, 2012, www.mtv.com/news/1680672/blake-shelton-adam-levine-the-voice/.
5 Lawrence K. Altman, "Rare cancer seen in 41 homosexual men," *New York Times*, July 3, 1981, p. A20, www.nytimes.com/1981/07/03/us/rare-cancer-seen-in-41-homosexuals.html.
6 Mark Joseph Stern, "Listen to Reagan's press secretary laugh about gay people dying of AIDS," www.slate.com/blogs/outward/2015/12/01/reagan_press_secretary_laughs_about_gay_people_dying_of_aids.html.
7 Patrick Buchanan, "Nature's retribution," *Washington Times*, May 27, 1983.
8 Buckley, W. F., "Crucial steps in combating the AIDS epidemic: identify all carriers," *New York Times*, March 18, 1986, p. A27.
9 "Homosexuality: born or bred?" *Newsweek*, February 24, 1992, pp. 46, 48.
10 National Gay and Lesbian Task Force, *Capital Gains and Losses: A State by State Review of Gay, Lesbian, Bisexual, Transgender, and HIV/AIDS-Related Legislation, 1996*. Washington, DC: National Gay and Lesbian Task Force.
11 David Colman, "Gay or straight? Hard to tell," *New York Times*, June 19, 2005, www.nytimes.com/2005/06/19/fashion/sundaystyles/gay-or-straight-hard-to-tell.html; Micah Toub, "Who's gay? And who's just gay-vague?,"

Notes to pp. 108–117

Globe and Mail, July 23, 2010, www.theglobeandmail.com/life/whos-gay-and-whos-just-gay-vague/article1389393/.
12 Johnny Diaz, "Tough love: metrosexuals are so last year: we're in the middle of a menaissance," *Boston Globe*, June 20, 2006, www.boston.com/yourlife/articles/2006/06/20/tough_love/; Paul Harris, "The menaissance," *The Observer*, July 9, 2006, www.theguardian.com/world/2006/jul/09/paulharris.theobserver.
13 For the articles in both the *Independent* and *Salon*, see www.marksimpson.com/here-come-the-mirror-men/.
14 Warren St John, "Metrosexuals come out," *New York Times*, June 22, 2003, www.nytimes.com/2003/06/22/style/metrosexuals-come-out.html.
15 Tim Elliott, "A grand bromance," *The Age*, August 23, 2007, www.theage.com.au/news/relationships/a-grand-bromance/2007/08/23/1187462423868.html.
16 Jennifer Lee, "The man date," New York Times, April 10, 2005, http://www.nytimes.com/2005/04/10/fashion/the-man-date.html.
17 Ann Oldenburg, "Comedy or drama, shows play it straight," *USA Today*, October 25, 2006,
18 Anthony Morrison, "Straight teen asks gay best friend to prom," May 1, 2015, www.cnn.com/2015/04/24/living/feat-straight-teen-asks-gay-best-friend-to-prom/index.html.
19 Carmen Cruz, "Straight men now feel the need to say 'no homo' when discussing emotions," *The Guardian*, February 23, 2014, www.theguardian.com/commentisfree/2014/feb/23/gay-rights-homophobia-michael-sam.
20 Nathan Siegel, "Straight men are kissing – here's why," *The Daily Dose*, January 22, 2015, www.ozy.com/acumen/straight-men-are-kissing-heres-why/38742.
21 As an example, consider the case of a Rutgers University undergraduate student, Tyler Clementi, who committed suicide after his roommate Dharun Ravi spied on him with a webcam. During Ravi's trial, his legal team used the ick factor and gay panic arguments. See Michelangelo Signorile, "Tyler Clementi and the Dharun Ravi trial: why the verdict is just," *Huffington Post*, March 19, 2012, www.huffingtonpost.com/michelangelo-signorile/tyler-clementi-dharun-ravi_b_1362562.html.
22 For the ick factor, see Winnie McCroy, "Girl-on-girl action becomes passé," *Village Voice*, June 22, 2011, www.villagevoice.com/news/girl-on-girl-action-becomes-pass-6431580. For Naussbaum's ideas of projective disgust, see Ben Smith, "Philosopher disclaims 'ick factor', demands Huckabee apology," June 25, 2010, www.politico.com/blogs/ben-smith/2010/06/philosopher-disclaims-ick-factor-demands-huckabee-apology-027753. In 2014, California became the first state to ban the "ick factor" or "gay panic" defense. See Parker Marie Molloy, "California becomes first state to ban gay, trans 'panic' defenses," *The Advocate*, September 29, 2014, www.advocate.com/crime/2014/09/29/california-becomes-first-state-ban-gay-trans-panic-defenses.

Notes to pp. 121–129

23 Graham Gremore, "More and more straight guys are giving each other 'bro-jobs,'" August 3, 2015, www.queerty.com/more-and-more-straight-guys-are-giving-each-other-bro-jobs-20150803.
24 Benjamin Lindsay, "Bro-ing out: straight guys, gay sex," *Next*, July 30, 2015, www.nextmagazine.com/content/bro-ing-out-whats-sex-between-straight-men.
25 J. K. Trotter, "Remember when Tom Hardy had sex with men?," May 27, 2015, http://defamer.gawker.com/remember-when-tom-hardy-had-sex-with-men-1707182772.
26 Thomas Rogers, "The invention of the heterosexual," *Salon*, January 22, 2012, www.salon.com/2012/01/22/the_invention_of_the_heterosexual/.
27 "Hot straight men take a stand against homophobia: Warwick Rowers," May 26, 2014, http://friendly.com.mx/news/2014/05/hot-straight-men-take-a-stand-against-homophobia-warwick-rowers/.
28 First quote: Cyd Zeigler, "Warwick Rowers explain why their gay fans are so important to them. Naked," October 28, 2015, www.outsports.com/2015/10/28/9631596/warwick-rowers-gay-fans-2016-calendar; second and third quotes: Curtis M. Wong, "The Warwick Rowers don't mind if gay men love their naked calendar," *Huffington Post*, October 23, 2015, www.huffingtonpost.com/entry/warwick-rowers-naked-calendar_562a59dde4b0443bb563b5b7.
29 At the time of writing, the page has been taken off Facebook. Two new groups called "Heterosexual PRIDE" (www.facebook.com/OfficialHeteroPride/) and "Heterosexual Parade" (www.facebook.com/events/426907587464714/) have since formed.
30 For coverage of the event, see Nick Duffy, "Man organises 'straight pride' parade, blames gays when no-one turns up," *Pink News*, July 26, 2015 (www.pinknews.co.uk/2015/07/26/man-organises-straight-pride-parade-blames-gays-when-no-one-turns-up/) and Brad Gilligan, "One is the loneliest number at Seattle's first ever 'Heterosexual Pride' parade," *Seattle Gay Scene*, July 25, 2015 (http://seattlegayscene.com/2015/07/one-is-the-loneliest-number-at-seattles-first-ever-heterosexual-pride-parade/).

Chapter 4 Studying Sexuality

1 Alex Gallafent, "Polari: a gay slang that flourished out of prejudice," August 15, 2012, www.pri.org/stories/2012-08-15/polari-gay-slang-flourished-out-prejudice; "Polari: the secret language of gay men," August 7, 2014, http://dangerousminds.net/comments/polari_the_secret_language_of_gay_men; Colin Richardson, "What brings you trolling back, then?," January 17, 2005, www.theguardian.com/world/2005/jan/17/gayrights.comment; J. Bryan Lowder, "Listen to Polari, the lost art of gay conversation," July 28, 2015, www.slate.com/blogs/outward/2015/07/28/polari_the_gay_dialect_can_be_heard_in_this_great_short_film_putting_on.html.

Notes to pp. 129–158

2 Mallory Ortberg, "Code words for 'gay' in classic films," May 22, 2015, http://the-toast.net/2015/05/22/code-words-for-gay-in-classic-films/.
3 Mallory Ortberg, "Code words for lesbianism in classic films," February 24, 2015, http://the-toast.net/2015/02/24/code-words-lesbianism-classic-films/.
4 Gallafent, "Potari: a gay slang that flourished out of prejudice."
5 American Psychological Association (2008), "Sexual orientation and homosexuality," https://web.archive.org/web/20130808032050/http://www.apa.org/helpcenter/sexual-orientation.aspx.
6 Frank Newport, "Americans greatly overestimate percent gay, lesbian, in U.S.," May 21, 2015, www.gallup.com/poll/183383/americans-greatly-overestimate-percent-gay-lesbian.aspx.
7 Ibid.
8 Arit John, "How many LGBT Americans are there? Depends on how you ask," *The Atlantic*, July 16, 2014, www.citylab.com/politics/2014/07/how-many-lgbt-americans-are-there-it-depends-on-what-you-ask/374529/.
9 Kevin Hechtkopf, "Support for gays in the military depends on the question," February 11, 2010, www.cbsnews.com/news/support-for-gays-in-the-military-depends-on-the-question/; Steve Williams, "Gay and lesbian or homosexual? What's in a word?," February 14, 2010, www.care2.com/causes/gay-and-lesbian-or-homosexual-does-it-matter.html; Lisa Wade, "Survey finds different levels of acceptance for 'gays' versus 'homosexuals,'" April 22, 2010, http://thesocietypages.org/socimages/2010/04/22/survey-finds-different-levels-of-acceptance-for-gays-versus-homosexuals/.
10 *Washington Post*–ABC News Poll, February 4–10, 2010, questions 29–30, www.washingtonpost.com/wp-srv/politics/polls/postpoll_021010.html.
11 Sam Killermann, "What does the asterisk in 'trans*' stand for?," http://itspronouncedmetrosexual.com/2012/05/what-does-the-asterisk-in-trans-stand-for/.
12 Sam Killermann, "The genderbread person," http://itspronouncedmetrosexual.com/2012/01/the-genderbread-person/ and http://itspronouncedmetrosexual.com/2015/03/the-genderbread-person-v3/.
13 For new options, see Kurt Wagner, "Facebook adds new gender identity options for users," February 13, 2014, http://mashable.com/2014/02/13/facebook-gender-options/. For limitless options, see Karissa Bell, "Facebook's new gender options let you choose anything you want," February 26, 2015, http://mashable.com/2015/02/26/facebooks-new-custom-gender-options/.
14 Williams Institute, *Best Practices for Asking Questions about Sexual Orientation on Surveys*, http://williamsinstitute.law.ucla.edu/wp-content/uploads/SMART-FINAL-Nov-2009.pdf.
15 The GenIUSS Group, "Gender-related measures overview," http://williamsinstitute.law.ucla.edu/research/census-lgbt-demographics-studies/geniuss-group-overview-feb-2013/.

Notes to pp. 159–185

16 Christina Dong, "Stanford sociologist urges rethinking of sex and gender in surveys," August 19, 2015, http://news.stanford.edu/news/2015/august/gender-sex-surveys-081915.html.
17 All quotes in this section not specifically referenced come from this same report by the Williams Institute: *Best Practices for Asking Questions about Sexual Orientation on Surveys*, http://williamsinstitute.law.ucla.edu/wp-content/uploads/SMART-FINAL-Nov-2009.pdf.
18 Ibid.
19 Ibid.
20 Eric Anthony Grollman, "Representing LGBT people in survey research," April 30, 2013, http://conditionallyaccepted.com/2013/04/30/representing-lgbt/.

Conclusion

1 Lydia Saad, "Americans' acceptance of gay relations crosses 50% threshold," May 25, 2010, www.gallup.com/poll/135764/americans-acceptance-gay-relations-crosses-threshold.aspx.
2 Frank Newport, "Americans continue to shift left on key moral issues," May 26, 2015, www.gallup.com/poll/183413/americans-continue-shift-left-key-moral-issues.aspx.
3 Jeff Jones and Lydia Saad "Gallup Poll Social Series: values and beliefs" www.gallup.com/file/poll/192407/Moral_Issues_II_16068.pdf.
4 Newport, "Americans continue to shift left on key moral issues."
5 Lisa Keen, "Are gay relations morally acceptable? Gallup data shows huge swing in public opinion," June 2, 2014, www.towleroad.com/2014/06/gallup-data/.
6 Pew Research Center, "The global divide on homosexuality," June 4, 2013, www.pewglobal.org/2013/06/04/the-global-divide-on-homosexuality/.
7 I've modified the original formulation, which states: "If men define situations as real, they are real in their consequences."
8 For more on sapiosexuality, see Diana Raab, "Sapiosexuality: what attracts you to the opposite sex," August 25, 2014, www.psychologytoday.com/blog/the-empowerment-diary/201408/sapiosexuality-what-attracts-you-the-opposite-sex; Neda Ulaby, "Sapiosexual seeks same: a new lexicon enters online dating mainstream," December 4, 2014, www.npr.org/sections/alltechconsidered/2014/12/04/368441691/sapiosexual-seeks-same-a-new-lexicon-enters-online-dating-mainstream. The term was coined in 1998 by LiveJournal writer Wolfieboy, who said: "Me? I don't care too much about the plumbing. I want an incisive, inquisitive, insightful, irreverent mind. I want someone for whom philosophical discussion is foreplay. I want someone who sometimes makes me go ouch due to their wit and evil sense of humor ... I decided all that means that I am sapiosexual." See "Stoked on sapiosexuality," http://wolfieboy.livejournal.com/2262.html.

References

Adam, Barry D. (1995) *The Rise of the Gay and Lesbian Movement*. New York: Twayne.
Adler, Sy, and Johanna Brenner (1992) "Gender and Space: Lesbians and Gay Men in the City," *International Journal of Urban and Regional Research* 16: 24–34.
Aguirre-Livingston, Paul (2011) "Dawn of a New Gay," *The Grid* [Toronto]; http://ontd-political.livejournal.com/8259206.html.
Aldrich, Robert (2004) "Homosexuality and the City: An Historical Overview," *Urban Studies* 41: 1719–37.
Almaguer, Tomás (1993) "Chicano Men: A Cartography of Homosexual Identity and Behavior," pp. 255–73 in *The Lesbian and Gay Studies Reader*, ed. H. Abelove, M. A. Barale, and D. M. Halperin. New York: Routledge.
Anacker, Katrin B., and Hazel A. Morrow-Jones (2005) "Neighborhood Factors Associated with Same-Sex Households in U.S. Cities," *Urban Geography* 26: 385–409.
Anderson, Eric (2008) "'Being Masculine Is Not about Who You Sleep With': Heterosexual Athletes Contesting Masculinity and the One-Time Rule of Homosexuality," *Sex Roles* 58: 104–15.
— (2011) "The Rise and Fall of Western Homohysteria," *Journal of Feminist Scholarship* 1: 80–94.
Anderson, Eric, and Mark McCormack (2015) "Cuddling and Spooning: Heteromasculinity and Homosocial Tactility among Student-Athletes," *Men and Masculinities* 18: 214–30.
Anderson, Eric, Adi Adams, and Ian Rivers (2012) "'I Kiss Them Because I Love Them': The Emergence of Heterosexual Men Kissing in British Institutes of Education," *Archives of Sexual Behavior* 41: 421–30.
Armstrong, Elizabeth A. (2002) *Forging Gay Identities: Organizing Sexuality in San Francisco, 1950–1994*. Chicago: University of Chicago Press.
Arnold, Matthew ([1869] 1949) "Culture and Anarchy," in *The Portable Matthew Arnold*, ed. L. Trilling. New York: Viking.

References

Babbie, Earl (2012) *The Practice of Social Research*. Belmont, CA: Wadsworth.
Bawer, Bruce (1993) *A Place at the Table: The Gay Individual in American Society*. New York: Simon & Schuster.
Becker, Howard S. (1998) *Tricks of the Trade: How to Think about Your Research while You're Doing It*. Chicago: University of Chicago Press.
Beckstead, A. Lee (2012) "Can We Change Sexual Orientation?," *Archives of Sexual Behavior* 41: 121–34.
Berger, Peter L., and Thomas Luckmann (1966) *The Social Construction of Reality*. Garden City, NY: Doubleday.
Berlant, Lauren, and Elizabeth Freeman (1993) "Queer Nationality," pp. 193–229 in *Fear of a Queer Planet*, ed. M. Warner. Minneapolis: University of Minnesota Press.
Bernstein, Mary (1997) "Celebration and Suppression: The Strategic Uses of Identity by the Lesbian and Gay Movement," *American Journal of Sociology* 103(3): 531–65.
Bernstein, Mary, and Mary C. Burke (2013) "Normalization, Queer Discourse, and the Marriage-Equality Movement in Vermont," pp. 319–44 in *The Marrying Kind? Debating Same-Sex Marriage within the Lesbian and Gay Movement*, ed. M. Bernstein and V. Taylor. Minneapolis: University of Minnesota Press.
Bernstein, Mary, and Verta Taylor (eds) (2013) *The Marrying Kind? Debating Same-Sex Marriage within the Lesbian and Gay Movement*. Minneapolis: University of Minnesota Press.
Berry, Brian J. L. (1985) "Islands of Renewal in Seas of Decay," pp. 69–96 in *The New Urban Reality*, ed. P. E. Peterson. Washington, DC: Brookings Institution.
Bérubé, Allan (1990) *Coming Out Under Fire: The History of Gay Men and Women in World War Two*. New York: Plume.
Bérubé, Allan, and Jeffrey Escoffier (1991) "Queer/Nation," *Out/Look: National Lesbian and Gay Quarterly* 11: 12–23.
Binder, Amy, Mary Blair-Loy, John Evans, Kwai Ng, and Michael Schudson (2008) "The Diversity of Culture," *Annals of the American Academy of Political and Social Science* 619: 6–14.
Binnie, Jon, and Gill Valentine (1999) "Geographies of Sexualities: A Review of Progress," *Progress in Human Geography* 23: 175–87.
Black, Dan, Gary Gates, Seth Sanders, and Lowell Taylor (2002) "Why Do Gay Men Live in San Francisco?," *Journal of Urban Economics* 51: 54–76.
Blank, Hanne (2012) *Straight: The Surprisingly Short History of Heterosexuality*. Boston: Beacon Press.
Blee, Kathleen M. (2012) *Democracy in the Making: How Activist Groups Form*. New York: Oxford University Press.
Boutcher, Steven A. (2010) "Mobilizing in the Shadow of the Law: Lesbian and Gay Rights in the Aftermath of Bowers v. Hardwick," *Research in Social Movements Conflict and Change* 31: 175–205.

References

Bouthillette, Anne-Marie (1997) "Queer and Gendered Housing: A Tale of Two Neighborhoods in Vancouver," pp. 213–32 in *Queers in Space: Communities, Public Places, Sites of Resistance*, ed. G. B. Ingram, A.-M. Bouthillette, and Y. Retter. Seattle: Bay Press.

Breines, Wini (1989) *Community and Organization in the New Left, 1962–1968: The Great Refusal*. New Brunswick, NJ: Rutgers University Press.

Brown, Gavin (2006) "Cosmopolitan Camouflage: (Post-)Gay Space in Spitalfields, East London," pp. 130–45 in *Cosmopolitan Urbanism*, ed. J. Binnie, J. Holloway, S. Millington, and C. Young. New York: Routledge.

Brown-Saracino, Japonica (2011) "From the Lesbian Ghetto to Ambient Community: The Perceived Costs and Benefits of Integration for Community," *Social Problems* 58: 361–88.

Brownstein, Ronald (2015) "Virtually Every Demographic Group Now Supports Gay Marriage," *The Atlantic*, May 27, www.nationaljournal.com/nextamerica/newsdesk/virtually-every-demographic-group-now-supports-gay-marriage.

Bruce, Katherine MacFarland (2013) "LGBT Pride as a Cultural Protest Tactic in a Southern City," *Journal of Contemporary Ethnography* 42: 608–35.

Butler, Judith (1990) "Performative Acts and Gender Constitution," pp. 270–82 in *Performing Feminism*, ed. S.-E. Case. Baltimore: Johns Hopkins University Press.

Carrillo, Héctor, and Amanda Hoffman (2016) "From MSM to Heteroflexibilities: Non-Exclusive Straight Male Identities and their Implications for HIV Prevention and Health Promotion," *Global Public Health*, DOI:10.1080/17441692.2015.1134272.

Casey, Mark (2004) "De-Dyking Queer Spaces: Heterosexual Female Visibility in Gay and Lesbian Spaces," *Sexualities* 7(4): 446–61.

Castells, Manuel (1983) *The City and the Grassroots: A Cross-Cultural Theory of Urban Social Movements*. Berkeley: University of California Press.

Chauncey, George (1994) *Gay New York: Gender, Urban Culture, and the Making of the Gay Male World, 1890–1940*. New York: Basic Books.

— (2004) *Why Marriage? The History Shaping Today's Debate over Gay Equality*. New York: Basic Books.

Clausen, Jan (1990) "My Interesting Condition," *Journal of Sex Research* 27: 445–59.

Collard, James (1998a) "Leaving the Gay Ghetto," *Newsweek*, August 17, p. 53.

— (1998b) "New Way of Being," *New York Times*, June 21.

Collins, Alan (2004) "Sexual Dissidence, Enterprise and Assimilation: Bedfellows in Urban Regeneration," *Urban Studies* 41: 1789–806.

Collins, Patricia Hill (2000) *Black Feminist Thought: Knowledge, Consciousness, and the Politics of Empowerment*. New York: Routledge.

References

Cox, William T. L., Patricia G. Devine, Alyssa A. Bischmann, and Janet S. Hyde (2016) "Inferences about Sexual Orientation: The Roles of Stereotypes, Faces, and the Gaydar Myth," *Journal of Sex Research* 53: 157–71.

Crenshaw, Kimberle (1991) "Mapping the Margins: Intersectionality, Identity Politics, and Violence against Women of Color," *Stanford Law Review* 43: 1241–99.

D'Augelli, Anthony R., Scott L. Hershberger, and Neil W. Pilkington (2001) "Suicidality Patterns and Sexual Orientation-Related Factors among Lesbian, Gay, and Bisexual Youths," *Suicide and Life-Threatening Behavior* 31: 250–64.

Dean, James Joseph (2014) *Straights: Heterosexuality in a Post-Closeted Culture*. New York: New York University Press.

Dello Buono, R. A. (2015) "Reimagining Social Problems: Moving Beyond Social Constructionism," *Social Problems* 62: 331–42.

D'Emilio, John (1983) *Sexual Politics, Sexual Communities: The Making of a Homosexual Minority in the United States, 1940–1970*. Chicago: University of Chicago Press.

— (1989) "Gay Politics and Community in San Francisco since World War II," pp. 456–73 in *Hidden from History: Reclaiming the Gay and Lesbian Past*, ed. M. Duberman, M. Vicinus, and G. Chauncey. New York: New American Library Books.

— (1993) "Capitalism and Gay Identity," pp. 467–76 in *The Lesbian and Gay Studies Reader*, ed. H. Abelove, M. A. Barale, and D. M. Halperin. New York: Routledge.

— (2002) *The World Turned: Essays on Gay History, Politics, and Culture*. Durham, NC: Duke University Press.

— (2006) "The Marriage Fight is Setting Us Back," *Gay and Lesbian Review* 13: 10–11.

D'Emilio, John, and Estelle B. Freedman (1997) *Intimate Matters: A History of Sexuality in America*. Chicago: University of Chicago Press.

Diamond, Lisa (2003) "Was it a Phase? Young Women's Relinquishment of Lesbian/Bisexual Identities over a 5-Year Period," *Journal of Personality and Social Psychology* 84: 352–64.

— (2008) *Sexual Fluidity: Understanding Women's Love and Desire*. Cambridge, MA: Harvard University Press.

DiMaggio, Paul (2003) "The Myth of the Culture War," pp. 79–97 in *The Fractious Nation? Unity and Division in Contemporary American Life*, ed. J. Rieder and S. Steinlight. Berkeley: University of California Press.

Doan, Long, Annalise Loehr, and Lisa R. Miller (2014) "Formal Rights and Informal Privileges for Same-Sex Couples: Evidence from a National Survey Experiment," *American Sociological Review* 79: 1172–95.

Doan, Petra L., and Harrison Higgins (2011) "The Demise of Queer Space? Resurgent Gentrification and the Assimilation of LGBT Neighborhoods," *Journal of Planning Education and Research* 31: 6–25.

References

Duberman, Martin (1993) *Stonewall*. New York: Penguin.
Duggan, Lisa (2002) "The New Homonormativity: The Sexual Politics of Neoliberalism," pp. 175–94 in *Materializing Democracy: Toward a Revitalized Cultural Politics*, ed. R. Castronovo and D. D. Nelson. Durham, NC: Duke University Press.
— (2003) *The Twilight of Equality? Neoliberalism, Cultural Politics, and the Attack on Democracy*. Boston: Beacon Press.
Duggan, Lisa, and Nan D. Hunter (1995) *Sex Wars: Sexual Dissent and Political Culture*. New York: Routledge.
Echols, Alice (1989) *Daring to Be Bad: Radical Feminism in America, 1967–1975*. Minneapolis: University of Minnesota Press.
Edozien, Frankie (2006) "Seeking 'Straight,'" *The Advocate*, August 15, pp. 64–5.
Engel, Stephen M. (2001) *The Unfinished Revolution: Social Movement Theory and the Gay and Lesbian Movement*. Cambridge: Cambridge University Press.
England, Paula (2013) "Sexualities in the Social World," *ASA Footnotes* 41: 5.
Epstein, Steven (1987) "Gay Politics, Ethnic Identity: The Limits of Social Constructionism," *Socialist Review* 17: 9–54.
— (1994) "A Queer Encounter: Sociology and the Study of Sexuality," *Sociological Theory* 12: 188–201.
— (1996) *Impure Science: AIDS, Activism, and the Politics of Knowledge*. Berkeley: University of California Press.
— (1999) "Gay and Lesbian Movements in the United States: Dilemmas of Identity, Diversity, and Political Strategy," pp. 30–90 in *The Global Emergence of Gay and Lesbian Politics*, ed. B. D. Adam, J. W. Duyvendak, and A. Krouwel. Philadelphia: Temple University Press.
Escoffier, Jeffrey (1998) *American Homo: Community and Perversity*. Berkeley: University of California Press.
Eskin, Mehmet, Hadiye Kaynak-Demir, and Sinem Demir (2005) "Same-Sex Sexual Orientation, Childhood Sexual Abuse, and Suicidal Behavior in University Students in Turkey," *Archives of Sexual Behavior* 34: 185–95.
Evans, Sara M., and Harry C. Boyte (1986) *Free Spaces: The Sources of Democratic Change in America*. Chicago: University of Chicago Press.
Faderman, Lillian (1999a) "Who Hid Lesbian History," pp. 241–5 in *Columbia Reader on Lesbians and Gay Men in Media, Society, and Politics*, ed. L. Gross and J. D. Woods. New York: Columbia University Press.
— (1999b) "A Worm in the Bud: The Early Sexologists and Love Between Women," pp. 56–67 in *The Columbia Reader on Lesbians and Gay Men in Media, Society, and Politics*, ed. L. Gross and J. D. Woods. New York: Columbia University Press.
Fausto-Sterling, Anne (2000) *Sexing the Body: Gender Politics and the Construction of Sexuality*. New York: Basic Books.
Fetner, Tina (2008) *How the Religious Right Shaped Lesbian and Gay Activism*. Minneapolis: University of Minnesota Press.

References

Fetner, Tina, and Athena Elafros (2015) "The GSA Difference: LGBTQ and Ally Experiences in High Schools with and without Gay–Straight Alliances," *Social Sciences* 4: 563–81.

Fine, Gary Alan (1979) "Small Groups and Cultural Creation: The Idioculture of Little League Baseball Teams," *American Sociological Review* 44: 733–45.

Fischer, Nancy L. (2013) "Seeing 'Straight,' Contemporary Critical Heterosexuality Studies and Sociology: An Introduction," *Sociological Quarterly* 54: 501–10.

Flores, Andrew R. (2014) *National Trends in Public Opinion on LGBT Rights in the United States*. Los Angeles: Williams Institute.

Flores, Andrew R., and Scott Barclay (2013) *Public Support for Marriage for Same-Sex Couples by State*. Los Angeles: Williams Institute.

Florida, Richard (2002) *The Rise of the Creative Class*. New York: Basic Books.

Forest, Benjamin (1995) "West Hollywood as Symbol: The Significance of Place in the Construction of a Gay Identity," *Environment and Planning D: Society and Space* 13: 133–57.

Forsyth, Ann (2001) "Sexuality and Space: Nonconformist Populations and Planning Practice," *Journal of Planning Literature* 15: 339–58.

Foucault, Michel (1978) *The History of Sexuality*, vol. 1. New York: Vintage Books.

Freud, Sigmund (1905) *Three Essays on the Theory of Sexuality*. New York: Basic Books.

— (1910) *Three Contributions to the Theory of Sex*. New York: Journal of Nervous and Mental Disease Pub. Co.

Friedan, Betty (1963) *The Feminine Mystique*. New York: Dell.

Gagnon, John, and William Simon (1973) *Sexual Conduct: The Social Sources of Human Sexuality*. Chicago: Aldine.

Gamson, Joshua (1989) "Silence, Death, and the Invisible Enemy: AIDS Activism and Social Movement 'Newness,'" *Social Problems* 36: 351–67.

— (1995) "Must Identity Movements Self-Destruct? A Queer Dilemma," *Social Problems* 42(3): 390–407.

— (1997) "Messages of Exclusion: Gender, Movements, and Symbolic Boundaries," *Gender & Society* 11: 178–99.

— (2010) "Representing Sex: An Interview with Joshua Gamson," pp. 93–6 in *Sex Matters: The Sexuality and Society Reader*, ed. M. Stombler, D. M. Baunach, E. O. Burgess, D. Donnelly, W. Simonds, and E. J. Windsor. Boston: Allyn & Bacon.

— (2013) "The Normal Science of Queerness: LGBT Books in the Twenty-First Century," *Contemporary Sociology* 42: 801–8.

Gamson, Joshua, and Dawne Moon (2004) "The Sociology of Sexualities: Queer and Beyond," *Annual Review of Sociology* 30: 47–64.

Gates, Gary J. (2011) *How Many People Are Lesbian, Gay, Bisexual, and Transgender?* Los Angeles: Williams Institute.

References

— (2012) "LGBT Identity: A Demographer's Perspective," *Loyola of Los Angeles Law Review* 45: 693–714.
Gates, Gary J., and Abigail M. Cooke (2011) United States Census Snapshot: 2010. Los Angeles: Williams Institute.
Geertz, Clifford (1973) *The Interpretation of Cultures*. New York: Basic Books.
Ghaziani, Amin (2008) *The Dividends of Dissent: How Conflict and Culture Work in Lesbian and Gay Marches on Washington*. Chicago: University of Chicago Press.
— (2009) "An 'Amorphous Mist'? The Problem of Measurement in the Study of Culture," *Theory and Society* 38: 581–612.
— (2011) "Post-Gay Collective Identity Construction," *Social Problems* 58: 99–125.
— (2014a) "Measuring Urban Sexual Cultures," *Theory and Society* 43: 371–93.
— (2014b) *There Goes the Gayborhood?* Princeton, NJ: Princeton University Press.
Gitlin, Todd (1995) *The Twilight of Common Dreams: Why America is Wracked by Culture Wars*. New York: Metropolitan Books.
Gould, Deborah B. (2009) *Moving Politics: Emotion and ACT UP's Fight Against AIDS*. Chicago: University of Chicago Press.
Gramsci, Antonio (1971) *Prison Notebooks*. New York: International.
Green, Adam Isaiah (2007) "Queer Theory and Sociology: Locating the Subject and the Self in Sexuality Studies," *Sociological Theory* 25: 26–5.
— (2008) "The Social Organization of Desire: The Sexual Fields Approach," *Sociological Theory* 26: 25–50.
Griswold, Wendy (2008) *Cultures and Societies in a Changing World*. Thousand Oaks, CA: Pine Forge Press.
Grzanka, Patrick R., Jake Adler, and Jennifer Blazer (2015) "Making Up Allies: The Identity Choreography of Straight LGBT Activism," *Sexuality Research and Social Policy* 12: 165–81.
Halberstam, Judith (1998) *Female Masculinity*. Durham, NC: Duke University Press.
Hall, Stuart (1990) "Cultural Identity and Diaspora," pp. 222–37 in *Identity: Community, Culture, Difference*, ed. J. Rutherford. London: Lawrence & Wishart.
Halley, Janet (1993) "The Construction of Heterosexuality," pp. 82–102 in *Fear of a Queer Planet: Queer Politics and Social Theory*, ed. M. Warner. Minneapolis: University of Minnesota Press.
Halperin, David M. (1993) "Is There a History of Sexuality?," pp. 416–31 in *The Lesbian and Gay Studies Reader*, ed. H. Abelove, M. A. Barale, and D. M. Halperin. New York: Routledge.
— (2002) *How to Do the History of Homosexuality*. Chicago: University of Chicago Press.
— (2012) *How to Be Gay*. Cambridge, MA: Harvard University Press.

References

Hanhardt, Christina B. (2008) "Butterflies, Whistles, and Fists: Gay Safe Street Patrols and the New Gay Ghetto, 1976–1981," *Radical History Review*, winter, pp. 60–85.

Heap, Chad (2003) "The City as a Sexual Laboratory: The Queer Heritage of the Chicago School," *Qualitative Sociology* 26: 457–87.

Hennen, Peter (2008) *Faeries, Bears, and Leathermen: Men in the Community Queering the Maculine*. Chicago: University of Chicago Press.

Hull, Kathleen E. (2001) "The Political Limits of the Rights Frame: The Case of Same-Sex Marriage in Hawaii," *Sociological Perspectives* 44: 207–32.

Hull, Kathleen E., and Timothy A. Ortyl (2013) "Same-Sex Marriage and Constitutent Perceptions of the LGBT Rights Movement," in *The Marrying Kind? Debating Same-Sex Marriage within the Lesbian and Gay Movement*, ed. M. Bernstein and V. Taylor. Minneapolis: University of Minnesota Press.

Humphreys, Laud (1972) *Out of the Closets: The Sociology of Homosexual Liberation*. Englewood Cliffs, NJ: Prentice Hall.

Hunt, Sally (2014) "Chasing the Rainbow Roads," *Times Higher Education Supplement*, November 6.

Hunter, James Davison (1991) *Culture Wars: The Struggle to Define America*. New York: Basic Books.

Ingraham, Chrys (2006) "Ritualizing Heterosexuality: Weddings as Performance," pp. 235–345 in *Sexual Lives*, ed. R. Heasley and B. Crane. New York: McGraw-Hill.

Isherwood, Christopher (1997) *Diaries, Vol. 1: 1939–1960*, ed. K. Bucknell. London: HarperCollins.

Jay, Karla (1999) *Tales of the Lavender Menace*. New York: Basic Books.

Johnson, David K. (2004) *The Lavender Scare: The Cold War Prosecution of Gays and Lesbians in the Federal Government*. Chicago: University of Chicago Press.

Kaiser, Charles (1997) *The Gay Metropolis: The Landmark History of Gay Life in America Since World War II*. New York: Harcourt, Brace.

Kastanis, Angeliki, and Gary J. Gates (2013a) *LGBT African-Americans and African-American Same-Sex Couples*. Los Angeles: Williams Institute.

— (2013b) *LGBT Latino/a Individuals and Latino/a Same-Sex Couples*. Los Angeles: Williams Institute.

Katz, Jonathan Ned (1990) "The Invention of Heterosexuality," *Socialist Review* 20: 7–33.

— (1995) *The Invention of Heterosexuality*. Chicago: University of Chicago Press.

Kazyak, Emily (2012) "Midwest or Lesbian? Gender, Rurality, and Sexuality," *Gender & Society* 26: 825–48.

Keen, Lisa, and Suzanne. B. Goldberg (2000) *Strangers to the Law: Gay People on Trial*. Ann Arbor: University of Michigan Press.

References

Kennedy, Elizabeth Lapovsky, and Madeline D. Davis (1993) *Boots of Leather, Slippers of Gold: The History of a Lesbian Community*. New York: Routledge.

Kimport, Katrina (2014) *Queering Marriage: Challenging Family Formation in the United States*. New Brunswick, NJ: Rutgers University Press.

Kinsey, Alfred Charles, Wardell Baxter Pomeroy, and Clyde E. Martin (1948) *Sexual Behavior in the Human Male*. Bloomington: Indiana University Press.

Knopp, Lawrence (1992) "Sexuality and the Spatial Dynamics of Capitalism," *Environment and Planning D: Society and Space* 10: 651–69.

Kort, Joe (2008) "Gay Guise: When Straight Men Have Sex With Other Men," *Psychology Today*, October 15.

Lancaster, Roger N. (2011) *Sex Panic and the Punitive State*. Berkeley: University of California Press.

Laumann, Edward O., John H. Gagnon, Robert T. Michael, and Stuart Michaels (1994) *The Social Organization of Sexuality: Sexual Practices in the United States*. Chicago: University of Chicago Press.

Lauria, Mickey, and Lawrence Knopp (1985) "Toward an Analysis of the Role of Gay Communities in the Urban Renaissance," *Urban Geography* 6: 152–69.

Lauster, Nathanael, and Adam Easterbrook (2011) "No Room for New Families? A Field Experiment Measuring Rental Discrimination against Same-Sex Couples and Single Parents," *Social Problems* 58: 389–409.

McCormack, Mark (2012) *The Declining Significance of Homophobia*. New York: Oxford University Press.

McIntosh, Mary (1968) "The Homosexual Role," *Social Problems* 16: 182–92.

Meeker, Martin (2006) *Contacts Desired: Gay and Lesbian Communications and Community, 1940s–1970s*. Chicago: University of Chicago Press.

Mendelsohn, Daniel (1996) "When Did Gays Get So Straight," *New York*, September 30, pp. 24–31.

Meyers, Daniel J. (2008) "Ally Identity: The Politically Gay," pp. 167–87 in *Identity Work in Social Movements*, ed. J. Reger, D. J. Myers, and R. L. Einwohner. Minneapolis: University of Minnesota Press.

Michael, Robert T. (1994) *Sex in America: A Definitive Survey*. Boston: Little, Brown.

Mills, C. Wright (1959) *The Sociological Imagination*. London: Oxford University Press.

Mohr, John W., and Amin Ghaziani (2014) "Problems and Prospects of Measurement in the Study of Culture," *Theory and Society* 43: 225–46.

Moon, Dawne (2008) "Culture and the Sociology of Sexuality: It's Only Natural?" *Annual Review of Sociology* 619: 183–205.

— (2012) "Who Am I and Who Are We? Conflicting Narratives of Collective Selfhood in Stigmatized Groups," *American Journal of Sociology* 117: 1336–79.

Moscowitz, Leigh (2013) *The Battle Over Marriage: Gay Rights Activism through the Media*. Urbana: University of Illinois Press.

Murray, Stephen O. (1979) "Institutional Elaboration of a Quasi-Ethnic Community," *International Review of Modern Sociology* 9: 165–78.

References

— (1992) "Components of Gay Community in San Francisco," pp. 107–46 in *Gay Culture in America*, ed. G. Herdt. Boston: Beacon Press.

Myslik, Wayne (1996) "Renegotiating the Social/Sexual Identities of Places: Gay Communities as Safe Havens or Sites of Resistance?," pp. 156–69 in *Bodyspace: Destabilizing Geographies of Gender and Sexuality*, ed. N. Duncan. New York: Routledge.

NeJaime, Douglas (2015) "Griswold's Progeny: Assisted Reproduction, Procreative Liberty, and Sexual Orientation Equality," *Yale Law Journal Forum* 340: 1–10.

Newton, Esther (1993) "The Mythic Mannish Lesbian: Radclyffe Hall and the New Woman," pp. 281–93 in *Hidden from History*, ed. M. Duberman, M. Vicinus, and G. Chauncey. New York: Meridian.

Oliviero, Kate (2013) "Yes on Proposition 8: The Conservative Opposition to Same-Sex Marriage," pp. 167–218 in *The Marrying Kind? Debating Same-Sex Marriage within the Lesbian and Gay Movement*, ed. M. Bernstein and V. Taylor. Minneapolis: University of Minnesota Press.

Park, Robert E., and Ernest W. Burgess (1925) *The City: Suggestions for Investigation of Human Behavior in the Urban Environment*. Chicago: University of Chicago Press.

Peterson, Richard A. (1979) "Revitalizing the Culture Concept," *Annual Review of Sociology* 5: 137–66.

Phillips, Layli (2005) "Deconstructing 'Down Low' Discourse: The Politics of Sexuality, Gender, Race, AIDS, and Anxiety," *Journal of African American Studies* 9: 3–15.

Plummer, Ken (1975) *Sexual Stigma: An Interactionist Account*. London: Routledge & Kegan Paul.

Powell, Brian, Catherine Blozendahl, Claudia Geist, and Lala Carr Steelman (2010) *Counted Out: Same-Sex Relations and Americans' Definitions of Family*. New York: Russell Sage Foundation.

Pritchard, Annette, Nigel Morgan, and Diane Sedgley (2002) "In Search of Lesbian Space? The Experience of Manchester's Gay Village," *Leisure Studies* 21: 105–23.

Reiss, Samuel (2002) "Standing Straight," *Instinct* 5: 49–50.

Rich, Adrienne (1980) "Compulsory Heterosexuality and Lesbian Existence," *Signs* 5: 631–60.

Rimmerman, Craig A. (1996) *Gay Rights, Military Wrongs: Political Perspectives on Lesbians and Gays in the Military*. New York: Garland.

— (2008) *The Lesbian and Gay Movements: Assimilation or Liberation?* Boulder, CO: Westview Press.

Rosenfeld, Michael J., and Reuben J. Thomas (2012) "Searching for a Mate: The Rise of the Internet as a Social Intermediary," *American Sociological Review* 77: 523–47.

Rosser, Simon B. R., William West, and Richard Weinmeyer (2008) "Are Gay

References

Communities Dying or Just in Transition? Results from an International Consultation Examining Possible Structural Change in Gay Communities," *AIDS Care* 20: 588–95.
Rothenberg, Tamar (1995) "'And She Told Two Friends': Lesbians Creating Urban Social Space," pp. 165–81 in *Mapping Desire: Geographies of Sexualities*, ed. D. Bell and G. Valentine. London: Routledge.
Rubin, Gayle S. (1975) "The Traffic in Women: Notes on the 'Political Economy' of Sex," pp. 157–210 in *Toward an Anthropology of Women*, ed. R. R. Reiter. New York: Monthly Review Press.
— (1993) "Thinking Sex: Notes for a Radical Theory of the Politics of Sexuality," pp. 3–44 in *The Lesbian and Gay Studies Reader*, ed. H. Abelove, A. Barale, and D. M. Halperin. New York: Routledge.
Rule, Nicholas O., and Nalini Ambady (2008) "Brief Exposures: Male Sexual Orientation is Accurately Perceived at 50ms," *Journal of Experimental Social Psychology* 44: 1100–05.
Rupp, Leila J. (2001) "Romantic Friendship," pp. 13–23 in *Modern American Queer History*, ed. A. M. Black. Philadelphia: Temple University Press.
Rupp, Leila J., and Verta Taylor (2010) "Straight Girls Kissing," *Contexts* 9: 28–32.
Rushbrook, Dereka (2002) "Cities, Queer Space, and the Cosmopolitan Tourist," *GLQ: A Journal of Lesbian and Gay Studies* 8: 183–206.
Russell, Stephen T., Thomas J. Clarke, and Justin Clary (2009) "Are Teens 'Post-Gay'? Contemporary Adolescents' Sexual Identity Labels," *Journal of Youth and Adolescence* 38: 884–90.
Saewyc, Elizabeth M., Greta R. Bauer, Carol L. Skay, Linda H. Bearinger, Michael D. Resnick, Elizabeth Reis, and Aileen Murphy (2004) "Measuring Sexual Orientation in Adolescent Health Surveys: Evaluation of Eight School-Based Surveys," *Journal of Adolescent Health* 35: 345.e1–e15.
Sapir, Edward (1929) "The Status of Linguistics as a Science," *Language* 5: 207–14.
Sassen, Saskia (2001) *The Global City*. Princeton, NJ: Princeton University Press.
Savin-Williams, Ritch C. (2005) *The New Gay Teenager*. Cambridge, MA: Harvard University Press.
— (2006) "Who's Gay? Does It Matter?," *Current Directions in Psychological Science* 15: 40–44.
Savin-Williams, Ritch C., and Lisa Diamond (2000) "Sexual Identity Trajectories among Sexual-Minority Youths: Gender Comparisons," *Archives of Sexual Behavior* 29: 607–27.
Schilt, Kristen, and Laurel Westbrook (2009) "Doing Gender, Doing Heteronormativity: 'Gender Normals,' Transgender People, and the Social Maintenance of Heterosexuality," *Gender & Society* 23: 440–64.
Schneider, Beth E., and Nancy E. Stoller (1995) *Women Resisting AIDS: Feminist Strategies of Empowerment*. Philadelphia: Temple University Press.

References

Sedgwick, Eve Kosofsky (1990) *Epistemology of the Closet*. Berkeley: University of California Press.
Seidman, Steven (1993) "Identity and Politics in a 'Postmodern' Gay Culture: Some Historical and Conceptual Notes," pp. 105–42 in *Fear of a Queer Planet: Queer Politics and Social Theory*, ed. M. Warner. Minneapolis: University of Minnesota Press.
— (1996) *Queer Theory/Sociology*. Oxford: Blackwell.
— (1997) *Difference Troubles*. Cambridge: Cambridge University Press.
— (2002) *Beyond the Closet: The Transformation of Gay and Lesbian Life*. New York: Routledge.
— (2011) "Theoretical Perspectives," pp. 3–12 in *Introducing the New Sexuality Studies*, ed. S. Seidman, N. Fischer, and C. Meeks. New York: Routledge.
— (2015) *The Social Construction of Sexuality*. New York, W. W. Norton.
Shenk, David, and Stephen L. Silberman (1994) *Skeleton Key*. New York: Doubleday.
Shilts, Randy (1987) *And the Band Played On*. New York: St Martin's Press.
Sibalis, Michael (2004) "Urban Space and Homosexuality: The Example of the Marais, Paris' 'Gay Ghetto'," *Urban Studies* 41(9): 1739–58.
Spring, Amy L. (2013) "Declining Segregation of Same-Sex Partners: Evidence from Census 2000 and 2010," *Population Research and Policy Review* 32: 687–716.
Staggenborg, Suzanne (2011) *Social Movements*. New York: Oxford University Press.
Stein, Arlene (1989) "Three Models of Sexuality: Drives, Identities and Practices," *Sociological Theory* 7: 1–13.
— (1997) *Sex and Sensibility: Stories of a Lesbian Generation*. Berkeley: University of California Press.
Stein, Arlene, and Ken Plummer (1994) "'I Can't Even Think Straight': 'Queer' Theory and the Missing Sexual Revolution in Sociology," *Sociological Theory* 12: 178–87.
Stein, Marc (2000) *City of Brotherly and Sisterly Loves: Lesbian and Gay Philadelphia, 1945–1972*. Chicago: University of Chicago Press.
— (2012) *Rethinking the Gay and Lesbian Movement*. New York: Routledge.
Stokes, Zeke (2015) *Accelerating Acceptance*. New York: GLAAD.
Stoller, Robert J., Judd Marmor, Irving Bieber, Ronald Gold, Charles W. Socarides, Richard Green, and Robert Spitzer (1973) "A Symposium: Should Homosexuality be in the APA Nomenclature," *American Journal of Psychiatry* 130: 1207–16.
Stone, Amy L. (2012) *Gay Rights at the Ballot Box*. Minneapolis: University of Minnesota Press.
Sullivan, Andrew (1997) *Same-Sex Marriage: Pro and Con*. New York: Vintage.
Tabak, Joshua A., and Vivian Zayas (2012) "The Roles of Featural and

References

Configural Face Processing in Snap Judgments of Sexual Orientation," *PLoS ONE* 7:e36671.

Tarrow, Sidney (1998) *Power in Movement*. Cambridge: Cambridge University Press.

Taylor, Verta, and Nancy E. Whittier (1992) "Collective Identity in Social Movement Communities," pp. 104–29 in *Frontiers in Social Movement Theory*, ed. A. D. Morris and C. McClurg. New Haven, CT: Yale University Press.

Taylor, Verta, Katrina Kimport, Nella Van Dyke, and Ellen Ann Andersen (2009) "Culture and Mobilization: Tactical Repertoires, Same-Sex Weddings, and the Impact on Gay Activism," *American Sociological Review* 74: 865–90.

Tourangeau, R., and T. W. Smith (1996) "Asking Sensitive Questions: The Impact of Data Collection Mode, Question Format, and Question Context," *Public Opinion Quarterly* 60: 275–304.

Tylor, Edward Barrett ([1871] 1958) *Primitive Culture: Researches into the Development of Mythology, Philosophy, Religion, Art, and Custom*. Gloucester, MA: Smith.

Udry, J. Richards, and Kim Chantala (2005) "Risk Factors Differ according to Same-Sex and Opposite-Sex Interest," *Journal of Biosocial Science* 37: 481–97.

Usher, Nikki, and Eleanor Morrison (2010) "The Demise of the Gay Enclave, Communication Infrastructure Theory, and the Transformation of Gay Public Space," pp. 271–8 in *LGBT Identity and Online New Media*, ed. C. Pullen and M. Cooper. New York: Routledge.

Vaid, Urvashi (1995) *Virtual Equality: The Mainstreaming of Gay and Lesbian Liberation*. New York: Anchor Books.

Valocchi, Steve (1999) "Riding the Crest of a Protest Wave? Collective Action Frames in the Gay Liberation Movement, 1969–1973," *Mobilization* 4: 59–73.

Valocchi, Stephen (2005) "Not Yet Queer Enough: The Lessons of Queer Theory for the Sociology of Gender and Sexuality," *Gender & Society* 19: 750–70.

Waidzunas, Tom (2015) *The Straight Line: How the Fringe Science of Ex-Gay Therapy Reoriented Sexuality*. Minneapolis: University of Minnesota Press.

Walker, Brian (1997) "Social Movements as Nationalisms or, On the Very Idea of a Queer Nation," *Canadian Journal of Philosophy* 26: 505–47.

Ward, Jane (2008a) "Dude-Sex: White Masculinities and 'Authentic' Heterosexuality among Dudes who Have Sex with Dudes," *Sexualities* 11: 414–34.

— (2008b) *Respectably Queer: Diversity Culture in LGBT Activist Organizations*. Nashville: Vanderbilt University Press.

— (2015) *Not Gay: Sex between Straight White Men*. New York: New York University Press.

Warner, Michael (1993a) *Fear of a Queer Planet: Queer Politics and Social Theory*. Minneapolis: University of Minnesota Press.

References

— (1993b) "Introduction," pp. vii–xxxi in *Fear of a Queer Planet*, ed. M. Warner. Minneapolis: University of Minnesota Press.
— (1999) *The Trouble with Normal: Sex, Politics, and the Ethnics of Queer Life*. New York: Free Press.
— (2002) "Publics and Counterpublics," *Public Culture* 14: 49–90.
Weeks, Jeffrey (2010) *Sexuality*. New York: Routledge.
West, Candace, and Don H. Zimmerman (1987) "Doing Gender," *Gender & Society* 1: 125–51.
Westbrook, Laurel, and Aliya Saperstein (2015) "New Categories Are Not Enough: Rethinking the Measurement of Sex and Gender in Social Surveys," *Gender & Society* 29: 534–60.
Weston, Kath (1995) "Get Thee to a Big City: Sexual Imaginary and the Great Gay Migration," *GLQ: A Journal of Lesbian and Gay Studies* 2: 253–77.
Whorf, Benjamin Lee (1940) "Science and Linguistics," *Technology Review* 42: 229–31.
Williams, Raymond (1976) *Keywords: A Vocabulary of Culture and Society*. New York: Oxford University Press.
Williams, Rhys H. (1997) "Introduction," pp. 1–14 in *Cultural Wars in American Politics*, ed. R. H. Williams. New York: Aldine de Gruyter.
Wilson, William Julius (1987) *The Truly Disadvantaged: The Inner City, the Underclass, and Public Policy*. Chicago: University of Chicago Press.
Wittman, Carl (1970) *A Gay Manifesto*. New York: Red Butterfly.
Wright, Les (1999) "San Francisco," pp. 164–89 in *Queer Sites: Gay Urban Histories since 1600*, ed. D. Higgs. New York: Routledge.

Index

Ablow, Keith 1–2, 7, 14–15
abortion 6, 183, 184
ACT UP (AIDS Coalition to Unleash Power) 69
activism *see* political sex cultures
Adams, Adi 116
Adler, Jake 111
adoption rights 58, 82
advertising
   J. Crew and Toemaggedon 1–2, 3, 5, 7
Advocate magazine
   "Seeking Straight" story 109
African countries
   attitudes to homosexuality 174, 175
African-Americans *see* black sex cultures
age
   of experiencing same-sex attractions 43
   responses to sexuality surveys 136, 137
   and sexual identity 86–7
Aguirre-Livingston, Paul 46, 49–50
AIDS/HIV 97–9, 102, 184
   activism 69, 70
   identification and naming of 97–8

   and marriage equality 73
   rates of infection 83
allies, straight 111–13
Almaguer, Tomás 17
American Psychological Association (APA)
   on reparative therapies 168–9
   on sexual orientation 131
Anderson, Eric 86, 108, 114, 115, 116, 117, 118–19
animals
   and human culture 11, 14
antiquity, sexuality in 17, 89
APA *see* American Psychological Association (APA)
Armstrong, Elizabeth A. 64, 99
Arnold, Matthew 133
ASA (American Sociological Association) 17
   conference on "Sexualities in the Social World" 11–12
Asian/Pacific countries
   attitudes to homosexuality 174, 175
assimilation
   and gay politics 61
   in gayborhoods 49, 50
   and marriage equality 77

209

Index

assumptions about sex 3–8, 97
essentialist 3–5, 8, 130, 159
fixity 6–8, 156
privacy and individuality 5–6
see also privacy, sexual
The Atlantic
article on sexuality surveys 139, 141
Australia
survey on GLB-identified adults 142, 143, 144, 146

backlash
and LGBT rights 58–9
Baker, Gilbert 68
bars in gayborhoods 32
closing of 24–5, 46
and lesbian sex cultures 30
police raids 32–3
and urban sex cultures 26
Bartell, Dr Susan
on Toemaggedon/J. Crew controversy 2, 4
Bawer, Bruce 103
Beckham, David 109
behavior *see* sexual behavior
Benedict, Pope
on same-sex marriage 7, 8
Berger, Peter 11
Bernstein, Mary 77
Beyond Ex-Gay 169
Billings, Robert J. 99
biological determinism 5
biological sex 8–9, 16
and the transsexual population 155, 156
biology and sexuality 9–10
early Victorian era 91
heterosexuality 89
and homosexuality 105–6
and LGBT activism 60
bisexuals
GLB-identified adults 142–7

and lesbian feminists 66
and marriage equality 77
and political sex cultures 79
in the population 55
and sexual identity 87, 132
and survey questions 160
Black Lives Matter 80
black sex cultures
GLB-identified adults 147–8
and sexual identification 160
see also people of color
Blank, Hannah
Straight: The Surprisingly Short History of Heterosexuality 123
Blazer, Jennifer 111
Blow, Charles 48–9
bodies
and queer activism 71–2
and sex cultures 26–7
Britain *see* United Kingdom
bromances 110, 124, 131
Brown, Patricia Leigh 22, 23
Brussels Tribunal on Crimes Against Women 96
Buchanan, Patrick 98, 184, 185
Buckley, William 98
Burgess, Ernest W. 25
Burston, Paul 40
Butler, Judith 8

California Health Interview Survey (CHIS) 163
Californian Supreme Court
and marriage equality 75
ruling on gay bars 32, 53
Call Her Savage (movie) 31
Canada
survey on GLB-identified adults 142, 143, 144, 146
urban sex cultures 23–4
capitalism
and urban sex cultures 27–8
Carmichael, Stokely 51

210

Index

Carnie, Dave 110
Carrillo, Héctor 151–2
case studies 18–19
  ex-gays 167–9
  gayborhoods 22–5, 54–5
  gaydar 128–31
  how to define straight 124–5
  sexual morality 171–7
  straight gays 57–9
  straight men kissing 86–8
  Toemaggedon (J. Crew ad) 1–2, 3, 5, 7, 10, 14–15
  What Does Victory Mean? 81–4
Castells, Manuel 32, 38, 51–2
Chauncey, George 17, 28, 29, 30, 89
Chicago
  urban sex cultures 26
Chicago School of Urban Sociology 25
Christian Coalition 99, 184
cisgender people 155
cities
  increase in urban populations 25–6
  same-sex couples in 22–3
  see also urban sex cultures
civil rights movement 61–2, 165
Clinton, Bill 104
the closet
  logic of 118
  and studies of sexuality 149–52
  urban sex cultures in the closet era 27–31, 50
Coleman, David 107–8
Collard, James
  on the post-gay era 40–1, 43
Collins, Patricia Hill 20
Colorado Supreme Court Amendment 2 104–5
coming out acts 68
  and marriage equality 75
coming out era
  and urban sex cultures 27, 31–40, 50, 51

commemorations
  and urban sex cultures 26
communities
  and political sex cultures 66–7
  and urban sex cultures 34–5, 46
continuum
  of heterosexuality 96
  Rich's "lesbian continuum" 89, 113, 124
contraception
  US Supreme Court rulings on 6
conversion therapy 82, 167–9
Couples Inc.
  The Wedding 73
critical heterosexuality studies 123–4
cultural construction of sexuality 180–2
cultural feminism 67
cultural imagination 12–15, 16, 179, 180
  and gaydar 130
  of heterosexuality 86–7, 88, 94, 95, 96, 111, 122, 123
  of LGTB people 59
  and marriage equality 73, 75, 76, 78, 82
  and political sex cultures 62, 65–6, 79–80
  in the post-gay era 41–3
  and queer activists 70, 71–2
  and same-sex kissing 116–17
  and sexual identity 132, 133
  and studies of sexuality 133–4
  and urban sex cultures 32, 33, 35, 49
  and Victorian heterosexuality 91–2
cultural provocation
  and queer activism 69–70
cultural sameness
  and sexual difference 49

Index

culture
  defining as a concept 133
  and gaydar 129
  and heterosexuality 89
  and homosexuality 104
  learning about culture and sexuality 15–17
  sex and sexuality 8–12, 17, 18–21, 44, 133, 177–82
  and sexual identity 17, 121, 133
culture wars 15, 182–5
customs
  and urban sex cultures 26
cycles of contention 61

Davis, M. D. 30
Dean, James Joseph 6, 111
death penalty for homosexuality 84
debate-driven approach 19
Debuchy, Mathieu 86
D'Emilio, John 103
  "The Marriage Fight Is Setting Us Back" 107
Diamond, Lisa 113–14
discrimination
  and gay culture 58
  and gayborhoods 53
  housing 82
  and marriage equality 106–7
  and public opinion 173–4
  and the religious right 72–3
  and same-sex kissing 117
  workplace 82
Dolce & Gabbana 4, 8
DOMA (Defense of Marriage Act) 73–4, 76, 106–7
dude sex 119–23, 149
Duggan, Lisa 77
Dunphy, Alexander 24
Duran, John 23
dyke marches 35

economics
  and urban sex cultures 36–7, 47–8, 52, 54–5
effeminacy effect 114–15
Egan, Patrick 173
essentialist assumptions about
  sex 3–5, 8
  and gaydar 130
  in surveys 159
ex-gays 167–9

Facebook
  gender customization 155–6, 158
facial photographs
  and gaydar 130
Faderman, Lillian 96
Falwell, Jerry 99
families
  and gay neighborhoods 22
feminism
  and AIDS activism 69
  cultural 67
  and Katz's history of heterosexuality 94
  and marriage equality activism 73
  psychoanalytic 12
  and urban sex cultures 52
  see also lesbian feminism
Fine, Gary Alan 133
fixity of sex 6–8
  and transgender people 156
  see also sexual fluidity
Florida, Richard 48
football, homosocial bonding in 86
Forest, Benjamin 38
Forsyth, Ann 28
Foucault, Michel 9, 26
  on the birth of the homosexual 27, 89, 178
France 24, 174
Freud, Sigmund
  theory of sexual development 5–6

Index

Three Contributions to the Theory of Sex 94
Fun Home (musical) 82

Gagnon, John H. 131
Gallup public opinion polls
 on estimates of the non-heterosexual population 134–7, 138
 Values and Beliefs survey 171–3, 176–7
Gamson, Joshua 11, 59, 71
Gates, Gary J. 23, 142, 143, 144, 145, 146, 149, 150
Gay, Lesbian, Bisexual and Transgender Historical Society of Northern California 23
gay liberation
 and marriage equality 77
 as a political sex culture 60, 62, 63–7, 78–9
 and urban sex cultures 33, 37
gay neighborhoods (gayborhoods) 31–65
 case studies 22–5, 54–5
 economics of 36–7
 emergence of 31–40
 history as a trigger of 45
 politics of 37–40, 48–50, 67
 in the post-gay era 40–50
 straight people in 22, 23–4, 25, 183
gay pride *see* pride parades
gay vague 20, 107–8, 115, 124, 131
Gay–Straight Alliance (GSA) 112
gaydar 108, 128–31
gender
 assumptions about 4, 7
 customization 155–6
 sexuality and culture 10–11
 and urban sex cultures 28, 51–3
 see also transgender people

gender differences
 and Katz's history of heterosexuality 94
 responses to sexuality surveys 136, 137
 and self-identification as bisexual 146–7
gender expression 155
 and the transsexual population 155, 156
gender identity
 and the transsexual population 155, 156–8
gender inversion 31
generational shifts
 and urban sex cultures 46
GenIUSS (Gender Identity in US Surveillance Group) 158
gentrification
 and gayborhoods 37, 47–8
Germany 24, 92, 93, 179
Gide, André
 The Immoralist 94–5
Giroud, Oliver 86
GLAAD (Gay and Lesbian Alliance Against Defamation) 173–4
GLB population studies 134–67
 and the closet 149–52
 estimating GBL population size 134–9, 166
 and gaydar 128–31
 GLB-identified adults 142–9
 language of 152–4, 166
 and social problems 164–5
 see also sexuality studies; transgender people
Goldberg, Suzanne B. 105
"good cause argument"
 straight men and homosexual behavior 119
Griswold, Wendy 14
Grollman, Eric
 Conditionally Accepted (blog) 166

213

Index

GSA (Gay–Straight Alliance) 112
The Guardian (newspaper)
  on gay neighborhoods 24
  on gay politics 58
  on sexual identity 87
Gzranka, Patrick R. 111

Hall, Stuart 11
Halley, Janet 102
Halperin, David 9, 17, 89
  How to be Gay 178
Hardwick, Michael 99–100
Hardy, Tom 122
hate crimes 53, 59, 82
Hawaii Supreme Court
  and marriage equality 73–4, 106–7
hegemony
  heterosexual 90, 95–6
Hennen, Peter 70
heterocentric, Faderman's concept of 96
heteroflexibility 120–1, 179
heteronormativity
  and marriage equality 77
heterosexual sex cultures 17, 86–127
  anxieties 103–7
  critical heterosexuality studies 123–4
  and gaydar 131
  homosocial bonding/intimacy 86, 110, 114–15, 116
  Katz on the history of 88, 89–97, 123
  men who have sex with men 151–2
  pluralization of 107–23
  "politically gay" heterosexuals 42
  revitalization of 97–103
  same-sex kissing 86–8, 87, 115–17
  and sexual identity 86–7, 88
heterosexuality 19
  assumptions about 7
  cultural history of 178–9, 182
  cultural imagination of 86–7, 88, 94, 95, 96, 111, 122, 123
  early uses of the term 92, 93, 179
  the hetero/homo binary 95–6
  heterosexualization of gay culture 58
  heterosexuals in gay neighborhoods 22, 23–4, 43, 48
  history of 90–6, 123
  and the Toemaggedon case study 2
  unending invention of 96–123
history
  cultural history of sexuality 177–9
  of heterosexuality 90–6, 123, 178–9
  and the post-gay era 45
  sex existing independently of 9, 177
  and urban sex cultures 26, 34
HIV *see* AIDS/HIV
Hoffman, Amanda 151–2
Hollywood films
  and homosocial bonding 110
homelessness 82, 83
homoflexibility 108–9
homohysteria 115, 122
homophile movement 63, 65, 66
homophobia
  and activism 59
  and AIDS 99
  and gay people of color 65
  and heterosexual sex cultures 110–11, 112
  and race 122
  and the Warwick Rowers 125
homosexual population *see* GLB population studies
homosexuality
  born or bred debate 103, 105–6, 168, 181
  in the closet era 30
  cultural history of 177–8
  death penalty for 84

214

Index

declassification of as a mental illness 39
decriminalization of in the UK 34
defined by same-sex behavior 132
early uses of the term 92, 93, 179
Foucault on the birth of 27, 89, 178
global views on 175–7
the hetero/homo binary 95–6
and Katz's history of heterosexuality 92, 95
"logic of the closet" 118
one-time rule of 118–19, 149
as a pathology 104
public attitudes to conversion therapy 168
public opinion on 41–2, 44, 171–4
seen as sickness or sin 63
social construction of 88–9
and urban sex cultures 33
see also sodomy
homosocial bonding/intimacy 86, 110, 114–15, 116
housing discrimination 82
HuffPost Gay Voices 82
hunger metaphor
and sex cultures 16–17
Hunt, Sally 44
Hunter, James 183

ick factor 117
ideas
and sapiosexuality 185
identity *see* sexual identity
The Independent newspaper
on gay neighborhoods 24
on metrosexuals 109
individuality, sexual 5–6
industrial capitalism
and urban sex cultures 27–8
Internet
and urban sex cultures 46–7
intersectionality 147–8, 152–3, 164

intersex individuals 9, 156
invert, concept of 91
invisibility, myth of 30
Isherwood, Christopher 96
IVF (in-vitro fertilization) 4

Jenner, Caitlin 4
John, Arit 139

Kameny, Franklin 51
Kantor, Jodi 81
Katz, Jonathan Ned 7
"The Invention of Heterosexuality" 88–97, 123
Keen, Lisa 105
Kennedy, Anthony 42, 81
Kennedy, E. L. 30
Kertbeny, Karl Maria 92, 179
Kiernan, James 90
Kimmel, Michael 49
Kimport, Katrina 78
King, Martin Luther 80
Kinsey, Alfred
Sexual Behavior in the Human Male 5, 70, 95–6, 162
Kinsolving, Larry 98
kissing, same-sex 86–8, 87, 115–17
Knopp, Lawrence 28
Kort, Joe 118
Krafft-Ebing, Richard Freiherr von
Psychopathia Sexualis 5, 93
Kron, Lisa 82

Lady Gaga 4
language
and gaydar 129, 131
of sexuality surveys 152–4, 166
Latin America
attitudes to homosexuality 175
Latino sex cultures 17, 147–8, 160
Laumann, Edward O. 130, 131
Lavender Scare 63, 79
the Lesbian Avengers 69

215

Index

lesbian feminism
  and marriage equality 7, 77
  as a political sex culture 60, 62, 65–7, 78–9, 148
lesbians
  and gay liberation 64
  and gaydar 129
  and marriage equality activism 73, 78
  privacy rights for lesbian couples 6
  public opinion on lesbian relations 171–4
  Rich's "lesbian continuum" 89, 113, 124
  and urban sex cultures 29–30, 51–3
Lescenski, Jacob 112–13
LeVay, Simon 105
Levine, Adam 87, 110
LGBT people
  activism *see* political sex cultures
  American public opinion on 174
  cultural imagination of 59
  see also GLB population studies; homosexuality
liberals
  and heterosexual hegemony 95
Lorde, Audre 65
Luckmann, Thomas 11
Lyons, Jenna 1, 5, 14–15

March on Washington for Lesbian and Gay Rights 73
Marcus, Eric 82
marriage equality 58, 60, 62, 72–8, 79
  accumulation of support for 76
  and assimilation 77
  legalization of 41–2
  Pope Benedict on same-sex marriage 7, 8
  and Proposition 8 (Prop 8) 75
  public opinion on 137, 138, 174

San Francisco protest (2004) 74–5
  US legislation on 41–2, 76–7, 81
  US state rulings on 73–4, 106–7
  and the US Supreme Court 76–7, 82
Martinez, Anthony 112–13
Mattachine Society 63
Matthews, Chris 54
McAdam, Doug 61–2
McCormack, Mark 114, 115
McLauglin, Ralph 54
medical profession
  and the history of heterosexuality 91, 92, 93–4
men
  characterization of gay men in movies 128–31
  and early Victorian true love 91
  male breadwinner model 95
  sexual experiences and sexual identity 131–2
  straight men in gayborhoods 48–9
  support for same-sex marriage 137
  see also heterosexual sex cultures; straight men
Mendelsohn, Daniel
  "When Did Gays Get So Straight?" 57–8, 59, 82
metrosexuality 109–10, 131
Meyers, Daniel J. 111
Michael, Robert T. 131, 132
Michaels, Stuart 131
Michelson, Noah 82
Middle Eastern countries
  attitudes to homosexuality 174, 175
military service and gays
  discrimination against 63
  Don't Ask, Don't Tell policy 103–4, 154
  language used in determining public attitudes to 153–4

216

Index

Mills, C. Wright 13, 148
Money, John 105
Montreal Gay Village 24
Moon, Dawne 59, 124
Moral Majority 99
Morgan, Diane 52
MSM (men who have sex with men) 151–2
Muslim countries
 attitudes to homosexuality 174
 mystique of heterosexuality 93–4

NARTH (National Association for Research and Therapy of Homosexuality) 168
National Gay and Lesbian Task Force 73
National Post
 on gayborhoods 22
National Survey of Family Growth
 on GLB-identified adults 142
Nazi Germany and homosexuality 105
New Left activists 67–8
New Republic
 on gays in the military 103–4
New York
 AIDS Coalition to Unleash Power (ACT UP) 69
 early twentieth-century 89
 Stonewall riots 33, 34, 37–9, 39
 urban sex cultures 28–9, 31, 33
New York Times
 articles on gay issues 22, 103, 107–8
 on metrosexuals 109
Newsom, Gavin 74
Newsweek magazine
 on heterosexual anxieties 103
 on the origins of homosexuality 105, 106
 on sexual conversion 167–8
Nicolson, Rebecca 87

North American Bisexual Network 69
Norway
 survey on GLB-identified adults 142, 143, 144, 146
Nussbaum, Martha 117

Obama, Barack 42, 76, 77, 79
The Observer (newspaper)
 on heterosexual sex cultures 108–9
ONE 63
O'Sullivan, Feargus 24
Owles, Jim 66

Pal Joey (musical) 95
parenthood
 and marriage equality 78
 same-sex parents 75, 78
Park, Robert E. 25
people of color
 and gay liberation 64–5, 66
 and marriage equality 77
 and same-sex behavior 121–2
 and studies of sexuality 164
Pew Research Centre
 global views on homosexuality 174–6, 177
place-based identities
 and urban sex cultures 28
pleasure
 Freud on sexual development and 6
 and the history of sexuality 92, 93, 94
 and sexual identity 9
Polari and gaydar 129, 131
police raids
 in gay neighborhoods 32–3, 63
political sex cultures 19, 61–2
 gay liberation 62, 63–7
 gayborhoods 37–40, 48–50, 53
 lesbian feminism 62, 65–7
 marriage equality 60, 62, 72–8
 and the meaning of victory 81–4

Index

political sex cultures (cont.)
  political dykes 113
  queer activism 60, 62, 67–72
  sameness/difference in 60–2, 75, 77, 79, 80, 82–4
  and "straight gays" 57–9, 83
population growth, urban 26
population size
  and gayborhoods 36–7
  see also GLB population studies
post-gay era 59
  and gayborhoods 40–50
  and gaydar 131
  legalization of same-sex marriage 41–2
post-structuralism 12
praxis
  and the cultural history of sexuality 181
prefigurative politics 65–6
pride parades 26, 35, 49, 53, 66, 68
  rainbow flag 68
  straight pride 125–6
privacy, sexual 5–6, 8
  and gays in the military 103–4
  and sodomy laws 101
  and transgender people 156
projective disgust 117
Proposition 8 (Prop 8) 75
psychoanalytic feminism 12
public opinion
  on AIDS 98–9
  and culture wars 182–5
  on homosexuality 41–2, 44, 171–4
  and LGBT activism 80
  on marriage equality 76, 137, 138, 174
  see also Gallup public opinion polls
Putin, Vladimir 84

queer activism 60, 62, 67–72, 79
  and marriage equality 73

queer cultures
  and gayborhoods 24
Queer Eye for the Straight Eye (TV programme) 109, 110
Queer Nation 69, 71, 72, 80
queer theory 12, 70

race
  and gender 122–3
  and GLB-identified adults 147–8, 149
  and same-sex behavior 120, 121–2
  and sexual identity 160
  see also people of color
rainbow flag 68
Reagan, Ronald 98, 99
Rebellow, Anthony 125–6
Reiss, Samuel 109
religious right
  and AIDS 98
  anti-gay attitudes 83, 99
  and culture wars 184
  and LGBT activism 72–3, 74
  "Special Rights" campaign 104, 105
reparative therapy 167–9
reproductive rights
  US Supreme Court rulings on 6, 8
resurgent gentrification 47–8
Rich, Adrienne 89, 96, 114
  "Compulsory Heterosexuality and Lesbian Existence" 113
Rivers, Ian 116
Robertson, Eileen A.
  Ordinary Families 95
Robertson, Pat 99, 184
Romesburg, Don 23
Rosenfeld, Michael 46
Rubin, Gayle 3, 6, 9–10, 16–17
Rubin, Jerry 67
Russia
  attitudes to homosexuality 84, 174

218

Index

same-sex couples
　in cities 22–3
　and culture wars 182–3
　gender and sexual identity
　　131–2
　and the Internet 47
　US privacy rights for 6
same-sex households
　economic inequalities 54
　and the Gay Index 48
　in gayborhoods 36, 40
　lesbians 52
same-sex kissing 86–8, 87, 115–17
same-sex marriage *see* marriage
　equality
San Francisco
　Castro district 22, 23, 26, 38, 39
　Daughters of Bilitis 63
　Gay Freedom Day parades 68,
　　71
　marriage equality activism 74–5
Saner, Emine 58–9
Saperstein, Aliya 158–9
sapiosexuality 185
Sapir–Whorf Hypothesis 154
Savin-Williams, Ritch C. 139, 140,
　141, 142, 149
science of sexuality 19
screenwriters
　portrayal of homosexual
　　characters 129
Seidman, Steve 11, 19, 59, 182
Seinfeld, Jerry 128
separatism
　and gay politics 61
　lesbian feminists 65, 67, 148
sex
　biological 8–9, 16
　culture and sexuality 8–12, 17,
　　18–21, 44, 133, 177–82
　having sex/sex acts 9, 16
sex and love
　and gayborhoods 35, 46–7

sex cultures
　as a historical construct 26–7
　learning about 15–17
sexology 5
sexual attraction
　GLB-identified adults 147
　and MSM studies 152
　and sex cultures 149
　and sexuality studies 137, 139,
　　140, 141–2, 147, 162–3
sexual behavior 88
　GLB-identified adults 147, 150
　homosexual behavior in straight
　　men 109, 117–22, 132
　public opinion on 171–4
　and sex cultures 149
　and studies of sexuality 137, 139,
　　140, 141–2, 161–2
　see also sodomy
Sexual Behavior in the Human Male
　(Kinsey) 5
sexual fluidity 113–14, 131, 132,
　133, 147, 164, 169, 183
sexual identity
　and culture 17, 121, 133
　and definitions of
　　homosexuality 132
　and degrees of
　　heterosexuality 86–7, 88
　fixity of 6–8
　gender and sexual
　　experiences 131–2
　and GLB-identified adults
　　150
　and heterosexual sex
　　cultures 107–23
　and pleasure 9
　self-identification in surveys 137,
　　139, 140, 141–2, 160–1
　and sex cultures 149
sexual intimacy
　US Supreme Court rulings on 6,
　　8

Index

sexual orientation
　essentialist view of 4
　research into gaydar 130
　studies of 134–54, 159, 165–6
　and transgender people 156, 157–8
　see also heterosexuality; homosexuality
sexuality
　cultural construction of 180–2
　and the cultural imagination 12–15
　cultural transition from sex to 27
　and LGBT activism 60
　and queer theory 70
　science of 19
　sex and culture 8–12, 17, 18–21, 44, 133, 177–82
　and sexual essentialism 4
sexuality studies 128–70
　best practices 159–64
　transgender population 155–9
　see also GLB population studies
Shelton, Blake 87, 110
Shilts, Randy 97–8, 98–9
silence
　and sex cultures 102
Silver, Nate 44
Simpson, Mark 109
The Social Construction of Reality (Berger and Luckmann) 11
social constructionism and
　sexuality 11, 17, 180–2
　heterosexuality 88, 89, 90
　homosexuality 88–9
social movements
　and cycles of contention 61
　and gayborhoods 32, 53
　and queer activism 69
social networks
　in the post-gay era 43
social problems
　and sexuality studies 164–5
society and sex
　and LGBT activism 60

sex cultures 15–17
sexual essentialism 3–5
sociological imagination 13, 148
sodomy
　laws 91, 92, 100–2, 104
　redefined as a disposition 70, 178
　Supreme Court criminalization of 69
Speakes, Larry 98
Sport Allies 125
Spring, Amy 40
Stein, Arlene 3
stereotypes
　and gaydar 130
Stewart, Jon
　on Toemaggedon 2, 10
Stewart-Winter, Timothy 83
Stonewall riots 33, 34, 37–9, 39, 63, 66
straight allies 111–13, 124
straight gays 57–9
straight men
　and gay vague 107–8
　homosexual behavior in 109, 117–22, 132, 148–9, 151–2
　and homosocial intimacy 86, 110, 114–15
　kissing 86–8, 87–8, 115–17
　naked rowers 124–5
straight people
　in gay neighborhoods 22, 23–4, 25, 183
straight pride 125–6
straight women
　allies 113
　kissing 87–8, 115–17
　political dykes/heterodykes 113
street festivals 26, 35
Sueyoshi, Amy 23
Sullivan, Andrew 81–2
Summers, Lawrence H. 4
Supreme Court (US federal)

Index

Bowers v. Hardwick 69, 100–2, 104
and marriage equality 76–7, 82, 137
United States v. Windsor 76
surveys *see* sexuality studies
symbols
  and the cultural imagination 14, 15
  of gender and sexuality 10
  of urban sex cultures 26

Tatchell, Peter 58, 59
Tavern Guild 32–4, 39
Taylor, Verta 77
Thomas Theorem 181
Toemaggedon case study (J. Crew ad) 1–2, 3, 5, 7, 10, 14–15
Toronto Gay Village 23
Torrick, Keith 100
Toub, Micah 23, 108
Transgender Nation 69
transgender people
  and culture 9
  and gender 155, 156–8
  incorporating gender into surveys 158–9
  and lesbian feminists 66
  and marriage equality 9
  and political sex cultures 79, 83
  studying the transgender population 155–9, 164
  and trans* people 155
truth
  and early Victorian true love 91

Uganda
  anti-gay laws 84
United Kingdom
  age and sexual identity 86–7
  gaydar and Polari 129, 131
  survey on GLB-identified adults 142, 143, 144, 146
  urban sex cultures 24, 37

United States
  culture wars 183–5
  Defense of Marriage Act (DOMA) 73–4, 76, 106–7
  Gay Index 48
  gaydar 128–9
  great gay migration 33–4, 36
  history of heterosexuality 93
  Lavender Scare 63, 79
  legislation of same-sex marriage 41–2, 76–7, 81
  LGBT activism 62
    in the post-gay era 40–3
  public estimates of the non-heterosexual population 134–7
  public opinion on homosexuality 171–4
  survey on GLB-identified adults 142, 143, 144, 146
  urban sex cultures 22–3, 24–5, 32–4, 52
  see also New York; religious right; San Francisco; Supreme Court (US federal)
urban planning 19
urban sex cultures 22–56
  closet era 27–31, 50
  coming out era 27, 31–40, 50, 51
  economics of 36–7, 47–8, 52, 54–5
  and lesbians 29–30, 51–3
  post-gay era 27, 40–50
  see also gay neighborhoods (gayborhoods)
US Supreme Court rulings
  on reproductive rights and sexual intimacy 6, 8
  on same-sex marriage 41–2

Vaid, Urvashi 59
Valocchi, Steve 7
Vancouver
  Davie Village 24

221

Index

Vermont Supreme Court
 ruling on marriage equality 74
Victorian era
 early Victorian true love 90, 91, 148
 late Victorian sex-love 90, 91–2
visibility
 lesbian feminists 66–7
 LGBT people 59

wage labor
 and urban sex cultures 27–8
Waidzunas, Tom 169
Ward, Jane 59, 119–21, 151
Warner, Michael 60
Warwick Rowers 124–5
Waters, John 81
"We Are Everywhere" slogan 67–8
Weeks, Jeffrey 20
Westbrook, Laurel 158–9
Whitman, Walt
 Leaves of Grass 92
Williams Institute
 on best practices in sexuality surveys 160, 161, 163, 165–6
Wittman, Carl
 A Gay Manifesto 38–9

women
 and economic inequality 52
 and Katz's history of heterosexuality 91, 94, 95
 and men who have sex with men 152
 romantic friendships between 29
 self-identification as bisexual 146–7
 sexual experiences and sexual identity 131–2
 sexual fluidity in 113–14, 147, 183
 straight women in gayborhoods 48
 support for same-sex marriage 137
 women of color and lesbian feminists 66
 see also feminism; lesbian feminism; lesbians; straight women
workplace discrimination 82
World War II
 and Katz's history of heterosexuality 94, 95
 and urban sex cultures 31–2, 34, 39

young people
 sexual identities of 86–7

222